THICK FACE, BLACK HEART
CONVINCED THE CRITICS.
NOW LET IT CONVINCE YOU.

"Chin-Ning Chu has written inspiring lessons on building inner strength. Gripping stories and principles reach from the mists of Chinese history to present-day entrepreneurial America. At once mystical and practical, this book will rearrange your brain and recharge your spirit."

—DUNCAN ANDERSON, editor, *Success* magazine

"This is a fabulous book, full of practical tips on turning adversity into victory. You've *got* to read this one!"

—GEORGE "SPARKY" ANDERSON, baseball legend

"This is for the housewife and the CEO, the fallen boxer and the victorious commander-in-chief. It is rapacious and tender, physical, mental, and above all, full of timeless spirit. If you have ever searched for the seeds that sprout passion, compassion, and success in any day and age, you want to read this book."

—THOM CALANDRA, *San Francisco Examiner*

"A provocative book that can affect everything from business decisions to romance. It stimulates considerable thought while providing specific examples."

—*Seattle Times*

"There needs to be a sympathetic, realistic, very practical approach [to business and life] and I think Chin-Ning Chu's latest book is going to help many people on this side of the Pacific, including many who didn't think they needed the lesson."

—JOHN CHARLTON, manag
Chase Manhattan Bank

"This challenging volume highlights principles worth any thinking manager's attentions."
—GEORGE VON PETERFFY,
president of North American Holdings,
former deputy assistant secretary of state

"The essence of universal wisdom which serves as the key to success as well as the salvation to the future. It is clearly and methodically written, a brilliant piece of work to be read and reread."
—C. Y. LEE, author of *Flower Drum Song,*
China Saga, and *Lover's Point*

"An astonishing revelation of balance. Poignant, revealing, and moving—a report card for those willing to change."
—TED R. WINNOWSKI, chairman and CEO,
Key Bank of Oregon

"A remarkable book from which all of us can learn the winning secrets of Asian philosophies."
—JOE CAPPO, publishing director,
Advertising Age

"Brings the timeless wisdom of the East to a level of practical and useful clarity for the Western business mind. Truly a 'how to' guide for the business person worldwide."
—DUANE L. BOWANS, managing director,
American Pacific Operations, Tektronix

"THICK FACE, BLACK HEART gave me much to think about, new directions to explore, new understanding of the power of potential. It's a remarkable achievement."
—MARCH FONG EU,
California secretary of state

"Provides the wisdom to build the inner strength necessary to sustain one's self and obtain victory on the battlefields of life. If life had an owner's manual it would be THICK FACE, BLACK HEART."

> —MICHAEL C. SEKORA,
> past director of Project SOCRATES,
> Defense Intelligence Agency

"It's a winner."

> —JAN ARNET, senior vice president,
> The Asia Society

"Hits the top of the self-help list. Author Chin-Ning Chu is on the road to fame with this challenging and unique motivational essay."

> —*Minneapolis Star Tribune*

"Puts a fresh face on efforts to remove barriers to success."

> —*Orange County Register*

"Really quite astounding. Chu delved into this black heart and emerged with universal lessons and applications for the rest of the world."

> —*Shambhala Star*

"Should be used by all students in college regardless of subject to aid them in their development of their careers and their lives."

> —MILO SHEPARD, executor, Jack London Estate

"It is of great fortune to our time that we are presented with such a remarkable work...will inspire readers to excel in their performance and enjoy the great satisfaction that accompanies success."

> —WUN-YU CHEN,
> innovator of the seedless watermelon

CHIN-NING CHU is president of Asian Marketing Consultants, Inc., and is an international lecturer, corporate trainer, consultant, and author of *The Chinese Mind Game* and *The Asian Mind Game*. She is considered the foremost expert in the world on the subject of understanding the Asian business psyche. She is also the premier best-selling business author in Asia.

Ms. Chu was born in China and raised in Taiwan after the fall of mainland China to the Communists. At age sixteen, she entered a Catholic convent in preparation for a life of asceticism. Her father later removed her from the convent and thrust her into the world of higher education.

Although she studied Catholicism from a very early age, she later expanded her spiritual horizons to include traditional Chinese philosophies, Zen Buddhism, and the ancient Hindu scriptures. Ms. Chu has traveled extensively and has studied the teachings of sages in India, China, and Europe. Her study of philosophies and spirituality has given her powerful tools with which to examine the complexities of today's business world.

Ms. Chu's work is highly praised by influential media worldwide, including the *Financial Times of London, USA Today,* Gannett News Service, *SUCCESS* magazine, *Orange County Register, San Francisco Chronicle, Seattle Times,* and many Asian publications. She is also a frequent guest on CNN programs, such as "Larry King Live," "CNN and Company," and the "International Hour," as well as other network television and radio stations nationwide.

THICK FACE, BLACK HEART

The Asian Path to Thriving,
Winning, & Succeeding

CHIN–NING CHU

NICHOLAS BREALEY
PUBLISHING
LONDON

First published in Great Britain in 1995 by
Nicholas Brealey Publishing Limited
21 Bloomsbury Way
London WC1A 2TH

© Chin-Ning Chu 1992, 1995
The rights of Chin-Ning Chu to be identified as the author of this work have
been asserted in accordance with the Copyright, Designs and Patents Act
1988.

This edition published by arrangement with Warner Books, Inc., New York.

ISBN. 1-85788-125-7

British Library Cataloguing in Publication Data
A catalogue record for this book is available from the British Library.

Printed and bound in Finland by Werner Söderström Oy

To the Supreme Father, to whom I owe everything.

To the eternal warriors,
the entrepreneurs of the world.
They are our hope and our future.

To Curt, my best friend.

Contents

Acknowledgments

My gratitude to all those who have passed through my life, whether in a positive or negative manner. All have contributed in some way to the substance of this book.

My gratitude to:

Karen M. Dibblee, without whose input this book would not have been the same

Gayle Vrla, my friend, who is always there for me

Dottie Walters, for her unfailing spirit and support

J. J. Liu Tsai, my former classmate, for her love and friendship

I give special thanks to the reference departments of the Marin County Library in California and the Multnomah County Library in Oregon.

To all I am indebted. Without their teamwork this book would not have been possible.

TO THE READER:

Throughout the book the generic *businessman* and the pronoun *he* have been used for the sake of brevity. In all instances, it is the author's intention to imply both the male and female gender.

Introduction

In 1949, at the age of three, holding tight onto my mother's skirt, I ran with my parents and two younger brothers across a Shanghai airport runway. Amid the sound of bombs blasting, we boarded the last commercial flight out of China.

From a life of affluence and privilege, my family was reduced to the condition of faceless immigrants among millions in Taiwan who had fled the conquering Communists. All the possessions we were able to salvage from the devastation of our lives fit into the suitcases my parents carried.

In 1969, when I was twenty-two, I left Taiwan to begin a new life in America. Once more a faceless immigrant, I arrived in Los Angeles with two suitcases containing the few possessions I was able to bring to my new home: clothes I had made for myself, a few personal effects, and two books.

By this time, I had already read hundreds of books, and I owned many; but I brought only two to the United States: Sun Tzu's *Art of War* and a slim, black-bound volume written by Lee Zhong Wu called *Thick Black Theory*.

The Art of War, an ancient book of strategy and wisdom, is fairly well known in the West. *Thick Black Theory*, however, is a relatively modern work and is still virtually unknown outside of China.

Although I cannot say exactly why I brought *Thick Black Theory* with me, at the time I had a strong, intuitive sense that it would prove to be very important. In its original form, it is an erratic, difficult book. Lee's writing is obscure. His arguments include great intuitive leaps that often left me behind. But after my first reading of *Thick Black Theory,* I knew that there was something very profound in it. For the past twenty years I have returned to this book time and time again, not quite knowing why, except for a powerful and disturbing sense that it held the key to a puzzle I was trying to solve. It has colored the way I now think about all my life experiences. I left many precious possessions behind in Taiwan, but was able to bring Lee's invaluable book with me to America.

Lee first published his ideas in 1911, a year of chaos and profound change in China. It was the year of the overthrow of the Ching dynasty, the last in a succession of imperial dynasties that stretched back to the beginning of human civilization.

Thick Black Theory has never been translated or published outside of China. Even within China, Lee's frank discussion of the uses of ruthlessness and hypocrisy was so disturbing to the ruthless and hypocritical that *Thick Black Theory* has been banned almost since the day of its publication.

Even if *Thick Black Theory* were to be faithfully translated, it would still be incomprehensible to most non-Chinese. The Chinese language is highly context-oriented. The basic building blocks of the language are short three-and four-character phrases that have an extended meaning far beyond the literal meaning of the characters that make up the phrase—somewhat like idiomatic expressions in English. This extended meaning is derived from history, ancient literature, folk-tales, and a myriad of other sources. Thus, in a few charac-ters, a Chinese writer can express a very complex idea by skillfully combining these associations. Foreigners who are considered fluent in Chinese but do not have an intimate knowledge of the Chinese culture often understand the words, but are unaware of the levels of meaning that are sub-tly implied.

With Lee's work, this difficulty is even more extreme. His chaotic style makes Lee difficult to understand even for learned Chinese. He writes in brief, disconnected epigrams that are meaningless to anyone not deeply immersed in Chinese literature. In its original form, Lee's *Thick Black Theory* is of little use to Westerners. But I have always felt that his profound yet bluntly honest vision of the world, which is the essence of Lee's philosophy, would be of great importance to anyone who desires to exert a measure of con-trol over his own life. It is this vision, this attitude, this essence, that I refer to simply as Thick Face, Black Heart.

Lee estimated that it would take three years of studious endeavor to master the practice of his ideas. Lee's ideas ignit-ed the sparks within me that led me to explore in great depth for the past twenty years the uncharted reality of our daily lives in relation to Thick Face, Black Heart.

In my inquiry, I discovered that there are two distinct lev-els of understanding. There is the superficial aspect: learning the methods and practices by which you can get what you want by imposing your will on others. And there is the deep-er, spiritual understanding of Thick Face, Black Heart as the natural and proper state of your soul.

Having been raised in China, I was already immersed in Buddhism, Taoism, and Confucianism, despite the fact that I was Catholic. The principles of these religions are so deeply ingrained in Chinese culture that it is not necessary to formally profess any of them to be influenced by them. My continuing search for understanding took me to all parts of the world. I studied the Hindu scriptures and Christian mystics. At one point in my life, I gave up my successful business career in Los Angeles and moved to a remote mountain in the Oregon Cascades for a long period of meditation and soul-searching.

As my horizons broadened, I came back to my Chinese roots with a new perspective. I looked at Buddhism, Taoism, Confucianism, and their Japanese extraction, Zen Buddhism. It became clearer and clearer to me that these diverse religions and philosophies shared the same central principle and that if I could understand and extract this principle, it would give me the power and control over my own life that I sought. In my struggle to articulate this principle, I kept coming back to Lee Zhong Wu and the phrase "Thick Face, Black Heart."

I do not believe that at the time he wrote *Thick Black Theory,* Lee himself clearly realized the full breadth and depth of his subject. Although I understand now that the value of Lee's work was in his putting a secular face on a principle that had previously always been discussed in abstract, religious, or philosophical terms.

For years I tried, without success, to write about *Thick Black Theory.* Finally, I turned away from it and wrote my first two books, *The Chinese Mind Game* and *The Asian Mind Game.* Now, at last, I can write *Thick Face, Black Heart.* The ideas I express are my own, but I wish to acknowledge my debt to Lee. However, my book is not an interpretation of Lee's work. To me, his book was not so much a source of knowledge as a way of looking at things, a starting point for the development of my own thoughts and a touchstone for the examination of new ideas and experiences.

The result of my inquiry is that from this book you can receive the instant benefit of the knowledge of Thick Face,

Black Heart as a concentrated, potent capsule. The knowledge revealed in this book will mirror your own life experiences that are familiar to you and that you are not able to verbalize. Because of the novel ideas in this book, a revelation in your understanding can occur in an instant.

Give up virtue, renounce wisdom;
people will benefit a thousand times.

Give up kindness, renounce morality,
people will embrace love and filial
piety.

Give up cleverness, renounce greed,
bandits and thieves will vanish.

—*Lao Tzu*, Tao Te Ching

1

The Essence of Thick Face, Black Heart

When you conceal your will from others, that is Thick.
When you impose your will on others, that is Black.

—*Lee Zhong Wu*

Thick Face, Black Heart describes the secret law of nature that governs successful behavior in every aspect of life. The American pioneers had it. Asian businessmen use it. From ancient times to the present, all successful people utilize the secret. Thick Face, Black Heart is the wisdom of the soul, and it knows no division of nationality, race, or religion. The implementation of this law benefits people in their business practices as well as in their personal lives. Being true to the law of nature in our daily encounters fulfills the highest potential within and around us, thus leading us to the proper unfolding of our destiny. Through the utilization of the power of Thick Face, Black Heart, each one of us will discover the destiny to which we must be true.

Americans are constantly bombarded through the media with images of success and happiness. Success is often judged by our possessions: the make of car we drive, the designer watch we sport, or the latest fashions we have wrapped around our bodies. Yet, a successful life is one that is lived through understanding and pursuing one's own path, not chasing after the dreams or fulfilling the expectations of others.

Many people are so completely obsessed with the pursuit of false euphoria that they attempt to deny the existence of life's difficulties. A positive attitude is important, but it is only part of the story. Understanding how to surmount pain, doubt, and failure is a vital component in winning the game of life. So often we are so concerned with what makes us feel good that we forget what makes us great.

Character is not made out of sunshine and roses. Like steel, it is forged in fire, between the hammer and the anvil. By getting in touch with the power of Thick Face, Black Heart, you will realize a new consciousness. One of the results of reading this book will be the shattering of your traditional concepts of ruthlessness. Thick Face, Black Heart is and is not about ruthlessness. You will learn that by adapting and adopting a form of nondestructive ruthlessness, you will gain the freedom necessary to achieve effective execution of your life's tasks.

Thick Face, Black Heart is not about mastering a specific skill, nor is it something I can give to you. The power of Thick Face, Black Heart is already within you. It is your inner strength and the natural state of your true self, where perfect joy, clarity, courage, and compassion are an inseparable part of you.

By tapping into this power, to whatever degree you can, you cannot fail to benefit. The power of Thick Face, Black Heart will guide you to be effective in your actions and lead you to your desired results. Most of all, by getting in touch with this power within you, you will gain unshakable clarity and focus to help you discover and achieve your intended destiny.

THE INWARD STATE

Thick Face, Black Heart is not a doctrine in itself. Rather, it concerns an element that is common to many doctrines. On its practical, less philosophical level, Thick Face, Black Heart is simply about action and its effectiveness.

To take an example from modern America: Dozens of books are published each year that attempt to teach you how to make yourself a more effective executive, a better salesperson, and generally a happier, more dynamic individual. In these books, the author prescribes a course of action that will lead to the desired result. Typically, it is a plan that has worked for the author and for some of his students. But it doesn't necessarily work well for many readers, even though they carefully follow the author's instructions. For example, two people can read the same book on lion-taming. They can enter the lion's cage dressed identically. They can use identical gestures and words to command the lion. But the results will not be the same. One of them will get the lion to jump through the hoop, and the other will end up as a gruesome mess on the floor of the lion's cage.

These authors do not seem to be aware that there is an inward state that must be achieved in order for words and actions to be effective. The experts who write these books are good at what they do because they have had the luck to achieve that state intuitively or unconsciously. They do not seem to comprehend the problems of those who have not been so fortunate.

Thick Face, Black Heart is a theory of great practical use. It can be applied to any endeavor, and utilized for either good or evil purposes. The first superficial exposure to Thick Face, Black Heart is often shocking and repellent because it can serve the criminal as easily as the saint. It seems to be a self-ish, ruthless, and completely amoral concept. However, I contend that these do not necessarily have to be destructive attributes.

As the name implies, there are two elements to this inward state: the Thick Face and the Black Heart.

Thick Face—The Shield

Consider the Asian concept of face. It refers to how other people think about you and treat you. Most Asians are tremendously concerned that others think well of them and especially that others display respect for their personal digni-ty. Juxtapose this idea with the Western notion that having a thick skin and being insensitive to criticism and the negative opinions of others is best. Fused together, these two ideas approximate the concept of Thick Face: a shield to protect our self-esteem from the bad opinions of others. A person adept at Thick Face creates his own positive self-image despite the criticism of others.

In attempting any goal, there is always room for doubt about our ability to achieve, our motives for achieving, or our worthiness to receive the benefits of achievement. Often we feel a need to first improve ourselves, believing that only after we have become more worthy will we be able to achieve the fulfillment of our dreams.

The thick-faced person has the ability to put self-doubt aside. He refuses to accept the limitations that others have tried to impose on him and, more importantly, he does not accept any of the limitations that we commonly impose on ourselves. He does not question his ability or worthiness. In his own eyes, he is perfect.

The world has a tendency to accept our own judgment of ourselves. By his absolute self-confidence, the thick-faced person instills confidence in others. They see him as successful and allow him the latitude to succeed.

Former president Ronald Reagan represents a good example of a Thick Face. He had very limited skills as an administrator. His aides' most important job was to prevent him from making off-the-cuff remarks about complex issues. Whenever he did, he invariably betrayed an appalling ignorance of the subject. But Mr. Reagan had such an unshakable image of himself as a great statesman that he acted decisively even when totally ignorant of the issues involved. His simple answers made America feel confident. After years of social turmoil at home and humiliation abroad, Americans began to feel good again, to feel that things were under control once more. The American people shared Ronald Reagan's opinion of himself, and he finished his term of office as the most popular president in recent history.

On the other hand, another former president, Jimmy Carter, better understood the awesome responsibilities of his office, but was completely overwhelmed by them. He was too keenly aware of his own limitations. Consequently, he agonized over important issues. The American people interpreted his agony as incompetence and turned him out of office by a wide majority. By truly appreciating the difficulties facing the nation and allowing the public to share in his insecurities, Carter projected a sense of powerless despair.

If Colonel Oliver North had felt one shred of guilt about the crimes in the Iran-Contra Affair to which he admitted involvement, he would be in jail today. Instead, he is a free man, a symbol of patriotism to millions and a speaker who commands huge fees. He expressed no remorse for his criminal actions. Oliver North believed so strongly that he was a patriot that he communicated a heroic image to millions of people. A man less convinced of his own righteousness would have been severely punished for his crimes and ostracized by the public.

A Thick Face need not be assertive or aggressive. He may be humble and submissive. Thick Face is the ability to adopt whatever manner the situation calls for without regard for what other people think of you.

There is an ancient Chinese story about a young man named Han Xin who had a reputation as a skilled Kung Fu fighter. One day when Han was walking through the streets of his city, he was stopped by two men who had heard of his skill. The pair challenged him to a fight to the death. Han tried to decline the challenge, but the men would not let him walk away. They insisted he must either fight or crawl like a dog through the leader's outspread legs. Although to the Chinese this is an unspeakable humiliation, Han Xin chose to crawl rather than fight.

Word of his humiliation and his cowardice spread quickly through the city. He was laughed at openly, yet he never once offered any excuse or explanation for his seemingly spineless action. Later in his life, he revealed himself to be one of the most formidable and fearless warriors in the history of China. To him, the pair of unschooled ruffians had posed no threat. It was simply that they were unworthy adversaries. In his heart he knew himself to be a fearless warrior. He did not care what anyone else thought. Han's Thick Face was a meek and cowardly facade, adopted to save himself the trouble of killing two such inconsequential hoodlums.

In contrast to Han Xin's inner sense of worth, there is the case of a friend of mine who is currently involved in helping a doctor develop and patent a prototype piece of medical equipment. In the beginning, there was a vague and inconclusive discussion about a partnership in exchange for my friend's technical expertise in building the apparatus. Since then, my friend has worked tirelessly, but nothing more has been said about the partnership or any other form of compensation. My friend is reluctant to bring it up because he does not have the prototype working properly, and he does not feel worthy of compensation. He has not asked for my advice, so I have not given it. I think he would do well to adopt the thick face of a man with a strong sense of his own worth. He would get his partnership for precisely the reason he is using as an excuse not to confront the doctor: the device is not yet working right. He is still needed.

When he has it working and feels confident enough to go to the doctor to discuss compensation, who knows what he will get? At that point, he will be at a severe disadvantage. The doctor will have already achieved his objective and may have no further use for him.

Black Heart—The Spear

Black Heart is the ability to take action without regard to how the consequences will affect others. A Black Heart is ruthless, but it is not necessarily evil.

Before the advent of modern medicine, a surgeon operated without being able to anesthetize the patient. He had to be able to cut swiftly and decisively without any regard for his patient's screams and entreaties. In order to be effective, he had to be extremely callous and emotionally detached from the pain he caused.

Conversely, a general who is so full of human compassion that he is reluctant to order soldiers to their death is of no use to his country. He will be defeated and his people conquered; whereas a black-hearted general can put the carnage of battle out of his mind and fully concentrate on the required result: victory.

An entrepreneur must be able to make hard decisions regarding unprofitable operations. If he cannot, his company will fail. The end result of shortsighted compassion for some employers will be the closure of their entire operation and all of their employees out of work.

The black-hearted person is above shortsighted compassion. He focuses his attention on his goals and ignores the cost.

A black-hearted person has the courage to fail. Attempting effective action always implies the risk of failure. A surgeon who has an accident victim in need of a potentially dangerous operation knows that the safest course is not to operate. Although the patient is likely to die, the surgeon risks little censure. If he operates and the patient dies, he knows that he risks being blamed for the death.

Two Sides of the Same Coin

Thick Face and Black Heart are two sides of the same coin. When one possesses the strength of Thick Face, one can ignore the criticism and disapproval of the masses. This same strength is also the source of the Black Heart; it allows one to effectively use the spear to cut through the ignorant and preconceived ideas of the masses.

It is not possible to practice Thick Face without Black Heart, just as it is not possible to practice Black Heart without Thick Face. The Thick Face, Black Heart practitioner must exercise his ability to ignore criticism, ridicule, and vilification from others, while simultaneously carrying out his

duties as he sees fit. At any given time, he may freely draw
upon more power of Thick Face and less power of Black
Heart, or vice versa, as the situation dictates.

THREE PHASES OF THICK FACE, BLACK HEART

Phase One: Winning At All Costs

Thick Face, Black Heart at its crudest level has no moral
overtones. It purely addresses how to get what you want: in
other words, winning at all costs. Thick Face at this level is
total lack of conscience; Black Heart is absolute ruthlessness.

In its crudest, most superficial form, Thick Face, Black
Heart is not about ethics; it is about effective action. A brief
glance at the newspaper provides an example: Employees of
a major airline have been caught falsifying maintenance
reports and safety checks in order to reduce operating costs.
The executives who ordered these falsifications clearly
understood that they were placing the lives of their passengers, pilots, and crews in great jeopardy—which was totally
disproportionate to the money they were saving.

A spear is a useful tool for peacekeeping as well as a
weapon of death. Thick Face, Black Heart, like the spear,
does not in itself contain evil; yet, one can apply Thick Face,
Black Heart purely for the pursuit of selfish gains at any
costs. Some people are intuitively skillful at utilizing Thick
Face, Black Heart as a tool to fulfill their selfish motives. For
these people, no price is too high to pay for victory, so long
as it is achieved at someone else's expense.

From ancient times to the present, from East to West,
there are many instances of people who have gained through

the utilization of Phase One Thick Face, Black Heart. Observe the failure of the American savings and loan institutions and the illegal dealings of the Bank of Credit and Commerce International. All of the "prestigious" individuals behind the scenes of these institutions are masters of Thick Face, Black Heart at its crudest level.

Their face is impenetrably thick; shielding them from all possible criticism from others and from their own conscience. Their heart is so black that when they used their spears on the unsuspecting, trusting public, these innocent depositors were fated to slow death from financial bleeding. For these individuals, selfish gain is the aim, and Thick Face, Black Heart is the means.

Phase One Thick Face, Black Heart leads us to winning, yet our victory often has no sweetness. More often than not, life, through its mysterious forces, will cause our ill deeds to catch up with us. To conquer others through ruthless means is not difficult: all you must do is agree to sell your soul to the devil.

There are three stages of the phase one level:

The first stage: thick as a castle wall, black as charcoal. This is the level of the cheap hustler, crook, and con man. Although the face is as thick as a castle wall, it is penetrable. Their blackness is apparent to all who see them. They are distasteful and repulsive in everyone's eyes.

The second stage: thick and hard, black and shimmering. These are the more advanced practitioners. They have strengthened their face by hardening it; they have polished their Black Heart to make it more appealing. They are no longer the cheap hustler. Their outward appearance is respectable. They are the kind of people you think you can trust, only to discover later that you have been taken.

The third stage: so thick it is formless, so black it is colorless—the highest level. This is the level of seemingly virtuous men who can ruthlessly pursue their own ends while being extolled by their victims for their virtue. Some of our politicians, from the past to the present, have achieved such a state.

Phase Two: Self-Inquiry

Conquering others requires force.
Conquering oneself requires strength.

—LAO TZU, TAO TE CHING

Beneath Phase One lie deeper essences of Thick Face, Black Heart. When some people practice Phase One Thick Face, Black Heart, they find it to be repellent, even to themselves. Consequently, they begin a process of self-inquiry.

Self-inquiry is a spiritual process. We cannot honestly or completely address Thick Face, Black Heart without mentioning the spiritual side of life, as this aspect colors the realities of all of our business practices and personal conduct. People bring who they are to business, and they usually behave in business as they behave everywhere else.

In the eyes of the Oriental, there are no divisions between business, the art of war, philosophy, and spirituality. The wisdom of spirituality is the root of mundane living. While the wisdom is one, the applications are infinite. Conversely, the Western world generally segments the knowledge of living into pieces and then files them away in separate compartments. Those who practice Phase One of Thick Face, Black Heart without the cultivation of Phase Two can become dangerous people.

At the stage of self-inquiry, the individual is often

vulnerable because he has rejected the powerful, wicked behaviors of Phase One and is in search of the realm of the unknown. His spirit is also demanding greater satisfaction from his conduct. He is in a state of uncertainty, confusion, and sometimes pain and anger.

He is overwhelmed by his own new discovery of a multitude of enemies within himself in the form of his own character defects: greed, anger, self-doubt, self-limitation, jealousy, envy, fear, shame, worry, small-mindedness, hatred, delusion, desire, selfishness, laziness, hypocrisy, and pretension. He has discovered that his own mind is the root of high and low, honor and insult, joy and sorrow, while at the same time his foes are many and his capacity to overcome these obstacles is meager.

At this stage, even though he may look disheveled and be considered disjointed by others, within himself he is going through a powerful transformation.

Phase Three: The Warrior

This final phase is the combination of both previous phases. Here you will be able to create a meeting ground for the sublime and the ruthless. The following are the qualities of a warrior.

DISPASSION AND DETACHMENT

After Phase Two, the practitioner becomes indifferent and courageous. He adopts the warrior's attitude—dispassion and detachment. He sees life as a battle that must be fought. There is no way out. Victory is the only aim.

He dispassionately does battle with the wicked outer elements while courageously facing his inner enemies. He is then able to detach from them, so that their presence does not thwart him. It is this power of detachment and dispassion that enables the warrior to face life's challenges with calm and grace.

The thirteenth-century Hindu philosopher Shankaracharya mentioned that even the greatest warrior, when standing in the midst of the battlefield, sweats with fear. However, while his body is fearful and his mind is fearful, his spirit is fearless. He is able to detach himself from the fear of the body and the mind, clinging instead to the fearlessness of his spirit.

Recently, I watched an old movie, a story about the courage and love of the early American pioneer settlers. It was evident that they understood the sublime state of calm detachment. They were indifferent to suffering, taking action in spite of their fear, enduring the loneliness, quietly accepting and overcoming the adversity while never losing sight of their objectives. Witnessing their warrior-like courage and self-determination moved me many times to tears during the film.

It is not that you are not affected by the challenges and become inert in this state of detachment. Rather, you are not controlled by your emotions, so you may press on with greater courage and renewed energy.

FIT FOR GREATNESS

I have seen many people grow old, but not graciously. Their eyes reflect pain and disillusionment. They have been beaten by life; they have so many broken dreams. The hope and expectations of youth have vanished—only death awaits.

The mistake they made was in not preparing themselves for the harsh lessons their Creator set for them on life's path—necessary lessons to strengthen their spirit and make them fit for greatness. Unlike the warrior who accepts harsh discipline as a privilege and honor, these people are like pieces of grain caught in the millstone, ground down by the wheel of life, in agony and in pain.

As most do, I used to pray for good times and good fortune. The prayer "Let thy will be done" used to scare me to death. In reality, though, this world in which we live is fragile and ever-changing, and our existence and survival are delicately connected to the invisible thread of God's grace. Gain and loss are the constant human condition.

As I watched the fire in the Oakland and Berkeley hills in the San Francisco Bay Area that burned seven hundred luxury homes, it confirmed again that it does not matter how much we wish to ignore the possibility of any negative and unpleasant aspects of our lives, our Creator writes His own script for life. Now when I pray, I pray for the unshakable inner strength and the strength of the warrior to accept these harsh lessons and learn from them, not to be destroyed by them.

THE UNION OF THE SPIRITUAL AND MATERIAL WORLDS

In this book, we will be dealing mostly with Phase Three. We will learn how to live in this world and not be a victim of it; nor will we impose pain and loss unjustly on those who do not deserve it. Our objective in practicing Thick Face, Black Heart is to be able to defend ourselves against others' aggression.

In this way we become warriors, but not in the traditional Western sense of "killing machines." The outer ability of the warrior to effectively execute his objective is guided by inner wisdom, which is cultivated through the acceptance of life's challenges and the quest for spiritual balance.

The sixteenth-century Japanese sword master Miyomoto Musashi said, "The warrior is one who uses the pen and sword with equal skill." The message here is that to be a truly great warrior, you must be skilled with more than your weapon. The great soldier is a balanced being, who through his understanding of life is able to master the virtue of his weapons. How the samurai handles his sword is metaphorically equivalent to how we handle our daily tasks, especially the task of surviving. Musashi also said, "The way of warrior skill is the way of nature. When you are in line with the power of nature, knowing the rhythm of all situations, you will be able to cut and strike the enemy naturally."

As you practice Phase Three Thick Face, Black Heart, gradually you will see no division or conflict between the spiritual world and the mundane world. Your spiritual strength will become an essential tool to conquer the day-to-day realities. As we incorporate the sublime spiritual insights into the ruthless business world, we will gain the best of both worlds.

A TRUE THICK FACE, BLACK HEART PRACTITIONER

When the great Tao is forgotten,
virtue and morality arise.

When knowledge and intelligence are born,
the great pretense begins.

When there is no harmony within the family,
filial piety and devotion arise.

When the country is confused and in chaos,
loyal officials appear.

—*LAO TZU,* TAO TE CHING

In every action there are two aspects—the inner and the outer. The inner is the force that motivates one's actions. It is unseen by anyone. The outer is the expression of the inner state. It is visible to all.

Contrary to common understanding, a good man's actions are not always gentle. They may be ruthless, cold, and dispassionate. A friend of mind once made a very profound statement when he said, "When people act overly nice, I always wonder about their motives."

There was once a master who had charge over many disciples. All entertained great intentions to gain enlightenment, yet each waged battle with his uncontrolled desires. The master would appear to ignore their misbehavior and allow them to indulge in their minor mischief, then, suddenly, like a thunderbolt, he would strike. He punished the offenders severely, sometimes even with a whip across the body, so the disciple would never forget the lesson. A witness may have believed this action by the master to be violent and cruel. Yet the disciples only experienced the love of the master and were grateful for the master's teaching.

In the Christian Holy Bible, St. Mark tells the story of the money changers, in which Jesus Christ goes into the temple in Jerusalem and angrily overturns all their tables and chairs, saying that God's temple was for prayer, not for use as "a den of thieves." Even though Jesus' outward expression was one of anger, this did not affect his peaceful inner state.

Conversely, some people wear permanent, plastic smiles on their face in their eagerness to be considered by others as nice people. It is very obvious to most that the smile is merely skin deep, yet these people spend all of their constructive energies putting up this sweet facade, which leaves them empty and powerless within.

A good man's outward appearance and actions sometimes may appear to be cruel and violent and his expression egotistical, yet he possesses a pure heart within. On the other hand, a false prophet may express an apparent high degree of outward humility and gentleness, but inwardly his sole objective is self-gain. A false prophet, in order to thrive, is dependent on the approval of the public, whereas a good man lives in harmony with himself—he neither seeks nor needs external approval.

The natural way of Thick Face, Black Heart is beyond human manipulation, beyond the petty standards of human judgment. When one acts in harmony with the Universal Will, one's actions are aligned with the good of all and the benefit of all. You are neither self-righteous nor too eager to please; nor are you seeking approval. In action, you are swift, competent, and dispassionate. In yielding, you are unabashed and have no concern for others' judgments. In conquering, you are effective and can be ruthless. In action and nonaction, you are changeless. You are a true Thick Face, Black Heart practitioner.

SUMMARY OF KEY POINTS

- Thick Face, Black Heart is the secret law of nature that governs successful behavior in every aspect of one's life.

- Often we are so concerned with what makes us feel good that we forget what makes us great. Understanding how to surmount pain, doubt, and failure is an important aspect of the game of winning at life.

• Character is not made of sunshine and roses. Like steel, it is forged in fire, between the hammer and the anvil.

• A successful life is one that is lived through understanding and pursuing one's own path, not chasing after the dreams of others.

• Thick Face, Black Heart is and is not about ruthlessness, yet you will learn that by adapting and adopting nondestructive ruthlessness, you will gain the freedom in actions necessary to achieve effectiveness in the execution of your life's task.

• By getting in touch with this power within you, you will gain unshakable clarity and focus to help you discover and achieve your intended destiny.

• Thick Face—the shield: to protect yourself from the criticism and the negative opinions of others.

• The thick-faced person has the ability to put self-doubt aside. He refuses to accept the limitations that others have tried to impose on him; more importantly, he does not accept any of the limitations that we commonly impose on ourselves. In his eyes, he is perfect.

• Black Heart—the spear: to do battle with others and yourself.

• A Black Heart is ruthless, but not necessarily evil.

• The black-hearted person is above shortsighted compassion. He focuses his attention on his goals and ignores the cost. A black-hearted person has the courage to fail.

- The Thick Face, Black Heart practitioner must exercise his ability to ignore criticism, ridicule, and vilification from others, and at the same time carry out his duties as he sees fit.

- Thick Face, Black Heart at its crudest level has no moral overtones. It is purely addressing how to get what you want. Thick Face at this level is totally unconscionable; Black Heart is absolutely ruthless.

- The wisdom of spirituality is the root of mundane living. The ability to judge good from evil is essential to the practitioners of Thick Face, Black Heart. There is no one out there you have to conquer. When you have successfully conquered yourself, the world will be at your feet.

- The ultimate courage of a Thick Face, Black Heart warrior is dispassion. This means having the courage to fight in spite of fear; to be able to detach from the emotions associated with defeat so that its presence does not thwart you.

- The union of the spiritual and material worlds: You will be able to create a meeting ground for the sublime spiritual world and the ruthless business world. Ultimately, you will see no division or conflict between the spiritual world and the ruthless world. Your sublime spiritual insight will become an essential tool to conquer the day-to-day realities.

- When one acts in harmony with the Universal Will, one's actions are aligned with the good of all and the benefit of all. You are neither self-righteous nor too eager to please, nor are you seeking approval. In conquering, you are ruthless. In action and nonaction, you are changeless. You are a true Thick Face, Black Heart practitioner.

*The proper function of man
is to live,
not to exist.*

—JACK LONDON

2

Preparation for Thick Face, Black Heart: Eleven Principles of Unlearning

The flower which is single
Need not envy the thorns
That are numerous.

—*RABINDRANATH TAGORE*

Thick Face, Black Heart is not simply a clever way to manipulate the world for your personal advantage. It is the natural state of our being. This state has been lost to us because of well-meaning people who drilled into us all the rules of how we ought to behave and feel. It is lost to us because of an inner image we have created of ourselves out of other people's expectations and beliefs. Achieving Thick Face, Black Heart means first reclaiming the natural state of our true self.

27

I. BREAK THE CONSTRAINTS OF INNER IMAGES AND EXTERNAL STANDARDS

A friend of mine in his late forties had been one hundred pounds overweight most of his adult life. Although he had lost all the weight at least seven times, he would always gain it back. During a psychological consultation, he discovered the root cause of his problem. He realized that whenever he was skinny he would act much more aggressive and not be so "jolly and nice" to others. Since childhood, his family had taught him that the most valued virtue is to be "nice" to people. Consequently, he ate to suppress his more expressive energy.

Beginning with childhood, most of us have been taught that the highest prize in the world is the approval of others. Perhaps it is not stated in so many words, but it is implied in everything we are told is right and good. We are obedient in order to please our parents. We are studious and well-behaved in order to please our teachers. We share our toys so our playmates will like us. When we try to get our own way, we are told we are being selfish and bad. Somehow, ideas of good and bad get tangled up in our young minds with the need to gain the approval of others. In fact, the people who teach us right and wrong are themselves victims of this same confusion.

As we grow older, it becomes apparent that to defer constantly to others and seek their approval is not the most efficient way to get ahead. Yet, most of us continue with this ineffective behavior. Sometimes we experiment with selfishness but usually discover that it produces bad feelings within us as a result of our early conditioning. "Nice" people aren't supposed to be selfish too often. Even though we know that success in our endeavors requires a certain measure of self-centeredness, we continue to be nice. The only reward for this is our self-righteousness about our great "virtue."

So it is with many of the other "selfless" virtues. But this is, in fact, pretentious and covert behavior. Often we disguise our concern for ourselves as concern for others, and we continue to purchase the approval of others by giving up our right to get our own way.

We often allow others to treat us unfairly because we do not want to confront or challenge them, nor do we wish to disturb our deeply ingrained notions of right and wrong. Instead, we comfort ourselves with feelings of moral superiority. We tell ourselves that we are above engaging in conflict over unimportant trifles. But despite what we think, we turn the other cheek. Not because it is right, but because it is easy.

A Thirty-Three Thousand Dollar Lesson

I learned the lesson that "trying to be nice" may not be the right thing to do by paying a thirty-three thousand dollar tuition fee.

Jim is a successful Washington, D.C.–based businessman. He is one of the most respected people in the world of political forums. He books speakers for political meetings and conferences, and publishes a weekly political newsletter. The day we met, we liked each other instantly. He is a warm-hearted individual with a passion for Asian culture.

At one point, Jim came to Portland, Oregon, where I was living at the time. He was accompanying a political candidate on the campaign trail. Later, we met for dinner. While we were chatting, I asked how his newly published book was doing. He told me that he had employed a publicity firm on a retainer for the past ten months, and although it cost several thousand dollars per month, he had received many requests to appear on television and radio as a result of the publicists' work.

Jim proudly pulled out five or six typewritten pages to show to me. The pages contained a list of the television and radio shows on which he had appeared. Impressed, I took a closer look. Except for one appearance on KABC-TV, the rest were only minor radio stations! I couldn't believe my eyes. Why hadn't they booked him on some of the more popular radio and TV talk shows, I wondered. What were these publicists doing for their money?

After I left Jim, I thought to myself that perhaps he'd like me to give him some help. Because I had been doing my own publicity for the past three years, I had learned quite a bit about the business. I knew, for example, that to be booked on one popular show is a hundred times better than being booked on innumerable insignificant shows. I also knew that some press agents try to justify their retainers by filling their client's calendar with a clutter of small bookings, often on radio shows that have very few listeners. It is truly no trouble for me to help him out, I thought. I have many good contacts who would take my recommendation seriously.

The next day I called Jim. I said I wanted to help him by giving him some of my contacts and that he could use my name as a referral. He was very happy. He thanked me profusely, then added, "I would like to review your new book, *The Asian Mind Game,* in my next newsletter."

The next morning my phone rang. It was Jim's cheerful voice. "I wanted to thank you again for giving me those names yesterday," he said.

"You are most welcome," I replied. "No problem at all."

He continued, "My company publishes a booklet listing every organization that employs political speakers."

"I know. I have one," I replied.

He added, "And this is updated monthly. It now contains over three hundred listings."

I was not sure where he was leading with this conversation. Maybe he wanted to thank me for my help by giving me an updated list as a gift.

But he continued, "My secretary tells me you have let your subscription run out."

"Yes, because I was moving, many things fell through the cracks." I was trying to be nice by lying. The truth was I had six months' worth of the newsletter still sitting in my filing cabinet waiting to be read, and I certainly didn't want to continue my subscription.

Disregarding me entirely, Jim came in for the kill: "How would you like to pay for it—credit card or check?"

"Can you bill me? I'm in the middle of something and I don't want to stop," I said vaguely. I was feeling very uncomfortable about his pressure to renew a subscription I really didn't want. I tried to be as polite as I could. I wanted to brush him off and get rid of him quickly.

But Jim pushed even more. "We do not review books for people who are not our subscribers." He wanted his money, and he wanted it now.

Still wishing to be nice, I said reluctantly, "Okay, I will go and get my credit card." Consequently, I paid him three hundred dollars.

I had spent thousands of dollars to generate those contacts. Telephone calls, faxes, promotion, travel—it all came to quite an investment. And I gave the names to him as a favor. Surely he realized that? He then asked me to pay for a three hundred dollar subscription by way of thanks!

Of course, I was facing a master Thick Face, Black Heart practitioner. He was a Thick Face practitioner because he had no consideration of what I would think of him. His eyes were on his objective. Although I had not openly said I did not care to continue the subscription, I had sent many subtle messages. He either didn't hear these messages or didn't care.

He was a Black Heart master because he was willing for me to dig into my pocket to support his newsletter, even after I had already given him thousands of dollars' worth of information.

Jim was doing everything right according to Thick Face, Black Heart. My mistake was that I did not even have a business objective beyond wanting to be nice to him. Worse yet, I had not set a value on my press booking recommendations. I gave them away as if they had no value at all. I gave Jim the contacts in the belief that "nice" people do nice things for each other.

He was merely being true to *his* objective: to get ahead. On the other hand, if I had truly given with no strings attached, then what he had done would not have been offensive to me. The truth was my niceness was a false gesture used to try to gain approval from Jim.

We can easily fall into this kind of trap. Idealistically we are taught to give, expecting nothing in return, but realistically most of us are conditioned to give with expectations. In this encounter with Jim, at the back of my mind I had been doing my bookkeeping.

Our conversation should have gone more like this: "Jim, would you like me to introduce you to some of the great shows I was on? They made a really significant impact on the promotion and sales of my books." Jim would, of course, have said yes.

I then would have continued: "For the past three years, I have very actively promoted my books among television and radio stations. I have gained a great deal of insight. You can sell more books by going on one good show than you can with a hundred small stations or unpopular shows. I would personally like to call these shows for you to recommend you and your book. How much would this be worth to you?"

Since I would be putting Jim on the spot, he probably would say something like he hadn't intended to pay me, or he might ask me how much I wanted for my service.

I then would have said: "Jim, I don't want you to pay me in cash. I'm suggesting we set up an agreement to barter each other's services. Let me propose something. These booking connections represent an investment of three years of promotional effort. The talk show hosts and I have very good relationships. The time investment alone is worth thousands of dollars. I sold my first self-published book, *The Chinese Mind Game,* solely through media exposure, with no distribution setup. As a result, I earned six figures in one year. I think placing a barter value of about ten thousand dollars would be fair. Don't you think so?"

If he didn't like the ten thousand dollars, I would have negotiated. Once the price was established, we would talk about the proposed barter method. The service I wanted that Jim had to offer was to book me on speaking engagements. Since he charges a 30 per cent commission per booking, in order to earn his ten thousand dollars, he would have to generate thirty-three thousand dollars worth of bookings for me.

Jim taught me a valuable lesson. Being nice for the sake of gaining the approval of others can be very costly.

A genuine friendship in personal or business life can be a tangible commodity, yet it also demands unconditional giving and support of each other. A false niceness with a secret agenda can turn good friends into the worst enemies by thwarting expectations of each other.

II. SEARCH FOR YOUR OWN
INNER CONVICTION

When his duty is to face danger
and he flees, it is cowardice.

—MAHATMA GANDHI

Many of us were taught that when someone slaps you, you should turn the other cheek. This is not always the best course of action. There is a time to submit to being slapped, and there is a time to hit back twice so you will not be slapped again. If someone slaps your face, you might turn the other cheek for one of several reasons. Perhaps you have chosen the path of submission with a full understanding of what that means. It might be that even though you feel the impulse to strike back, you suppress your anger because you have been taught that violence is wrong. Or it might be that you are afraid to further provoke your antagonist.

If you turn the other cheek out of an inner conviction, as Han Xin did in the previous chapter, so be it. If you have to suppress an impulse to strike back, it means that you have not truly accepted the truth of turning the other cheek, but have allowed your actions to be constrained by the standards of others. This in turn perpetuates the role of the victim for yourself. If you turn the other cheek because you are afraid to hit back, it does not mean you are morally superior. It simply means you are a coward.

The Thick Face, Black Heart practitioner understands that hitting back does not necessarily make you a bad person. It might well be that in punishing violent behavior, you are acting as a peacemaker. The truth is that most of the commonly accepted standards of behavior are arbitrary, and the arbitrators themselves are often flawed individuals who, under the guise of virtue, have perpetuated their own weakness and fear.

III. DISCOVER THE MYSTERY WITHIN THE STAUNCHNESS OF THE OAK AND THE YIELDING OF THE GRASS

The world consists of a delicate balance of two great opposing forces. Asian philosophy refers to them as Yin and Yang. All things are composed of these two forces. Things that are thought to be opposite are more intimately related than is commonly believed. Opposites are not two entities that balance each other. They are, in reality, two aspects of the same thing. Darkness cannot exist without light, nor good without evil. Violence and nonviolence arise out of the same place in the human soul.

Just as there are two aspects to all things, there are two aspects to human actions: the inward motivation and the outward appearance. Without considering the inward motivation, it is impossible for us to judge our own actions or the actions of others. The sage and the criminal might commit the same crime against the state out of entirely different motives. Christ was crucified between two thieves because those who stood in judgment of him saw no great difference between his actions and those of two petty criminals.

You need to understand that you possess creative and destructive forces in equal measure. Both complement each other and cannot be judged by common standards of good and evil. Each has its proper time. It is part of understanding yourself and your destiny to know when to exercise your destructive force and when to submit to the destructive force of others. The grass bends easily in the wind. The great oak stands unmoved. A strong wind can uproot the oak, but no wind, however strong, can uproot the grass that bends flat before it.

The ideal practitioner of Thick Face, Black Heart is the one who has Thick Face, Black Heart inwardly, yet whose outward appearance can be dominating or submissive as the situation calls for. He does not have a public or private image of himself to live up to or one that dictates how he must behave.

In the ancient Chinese classic *The 36 Strategies,* Strategy 27 states: "Pretend to be a Pig in Order to Eat the Tiger." According to this concept, when the Asian hunter is ready to hunt the tiger, he will sit and contemplate the easiest way to bag a tiger. The conclusion he reaches is that he will make himself the bait for the tiger. He dresses in a pig's skin and waits in the woods. The tiger will come close, thinking this pig will make a delicious lunch. When the tiger is so close that the hunter cannot miss, he will shoot the tiger.

In Asia, heroes are not judged for their prowess in hunting and shooting tigers, but rather for their strength and ability to endure the humiliation of being pigs.

When you have no evidence that you are greater than your circumstances, you must never let go of your vision of victory. Einstein noted that a great person knows of his or her greatness long before anyone else does. If you are willing to do whatever is needed to overcome the strongest opposition—even including yielding and being able, when necessary, to look like a pig—you will win.

Furthermore, you must be able to endure the humiliation that others so willingly impose on you for your apparent failures. A person who can do this is destined to be great.

IV. UNDERSTAND YOURSELF

To achieve the state of Thick Face, Black Heart, examine the role you are currently playing in this world. In order to

free yourself from the domination of arbitrary ideals and discover the true standards by which you should behave, you
need to find the courage to do what must be done without
regard to what others may think.

Extraordinary people don't care what others think of
them. Thick Face, Black Heart seems to come naturally to
them. They do well in getting what they want because they
are unencumbered by others' opinions. However, most people have been conditioned to be affected by the opinions of
others.

I am not advising you to become an amoral, self-centered
person, but to recognize the difficulties that are involved for
a naturally caring, sensitive person such as yourself to pursue
your own legitimate self-interest. There is something valuable for you to learn from these more detached people: their
disregard for others' opinions enables them to focus on the
accomplishment of their objectives. This can only be done by
achieving a clear understanding of yourself and your actions.

Self-observation is essential to self-growth. You must first
understand the motives for your own actions in order to
understand others. It is especially important to look within
yourself in times of great distress and misfortune. If you can
succeed in detaching yourself from the misery of your experience, you will see, with complete clarity, the real nature of
the situation. The proper course of action will then shine
forth.

The world is not so simple that we can just make and follow rules about what is wrong and right. We seek an understanding of ourselves so that we will know what we ought to
do in any given situation. You will gradually replace the
beliefs you were taught with the truths you discover. It is not
whether you turn the other cheek that is important. *Why* you
do or do not is most significant.

Self-knowledge is a more reliable guide to behavior than

adherence to arbitrarily imposed standards, though both are susceptible to error. You will make mistakes no matter which path you follow, but mistakes made on the path to self-discovery will correct themselves, while those made through blind adherence to subjective standards simply perpetuate the folly.

In this sifting process, you will discover that many of the concepts you were taught were, in fact, correct after all; but your self-examination will not have been in vain. Your beliefs will become your convictions. More importantly, you will have freed yourself from the need for others' approval.

But don't take my word. Carefully observe your thoughts and actions. You will see for yourself the false and arbitrary nature of many of the standards under which you are laboring.

Within each one of us there is a silent voice that wants to cry out and shout: "I exist! I exist! I have needs, wants, and desires which are noble and good. My ideas and rules may be different from yours, but they are mine and deserve to be expressed. Unless I am nourished, satisfied, and fulfilled, how can I be of use to anyone else?"

Coco Chanel, the famous French fashion designer, started her career not as a designer but as a well-to-do society lady. She always dressed in the manner she liked, regardless of current trends. Her unique style, particularly her bobbed hair and raised hemline, went against all fashion standards of the time. Even though at first she was heavily criticized for her eccentricities, she ended up providing a basis for the radical changes in fashions of the 1920s. Now, nearly a century later, her name, Coco Chanel, epitomizes the very best in the world of haute couture.

Recently, I was at my athletic club pedaling a stationary bicycle and casually flipping through a magazine for young women. One tip given for gaining "acceptance" was to leave home with wet hair while carrying a large bag, then run the last half block to the office. The idea was to create the "health club before work" look. The magazine also encouraged readers to leave a few cassettes by hot new musical groups lying around the house to create a hip image, even if they are never played.

I fail to see how these image-creating devices can possibly help young women gain the success they are seeking. They are merely receiving advice on how to get others' approval by spending a great deal of energy creating lies, rather than spending their energy in the pursuit of genuine interests.

V. BREAK THE BONDAGE OF FEAR OF SUCCESS AND FEAR OF FAILURE

The fear of success is much more powerful than the fear of failure. That is why there are so many more people prone to become failures than successes.

Each one of us is driven to a certain extent by fear—fear to rise, fear to fall, fear that we will remain in the same place. So many of us think that we want to be rich, that we want to be famous, that we want to accomplish great deeds, but often these feelings are just idle ruminations. Most of the things we think we want come at the price of leaving behind our familiar life and venturing into the unknown. Every time we accomplish something and move ahead, we have to exchange the known conditions of our life for uncertainty and unfamiliarity. Even though most people think they are trying to succeed, they are simply going through the motions. The last thing in the world that they want is to get off the familiar treadmill and actually get somewhere.

Before we can succeed, we must clearly understand that success means change and the risk of failure. The failure of those who do not try anything great is commonplace and comfortably private. The failure of those who attempt extraordinary accomplishments is much more public and generally accompanied by sighs of satisfaction from ordinary failures. When we don't pay our bills, a computer somewhere writes us a nasty letter. When Donald Trump doesn't pay his bills, it makes the six o'clock news.

Success also requires the courage to risk disapproval. Most independent thought, new ideas, or endeavors beyond the common measure are greeted with disapproval, ranging from skepticism and ridicule to violent outrage. To persevere in anything exceptional requires inner strength and the unshakable conviction that you are right.

VI. UNDERSTAND THE NATURE OF ILLUSION AND REALITY

This is perfect.
This is perfect.
From the perfect springs the perfect.
If the perfect is taken from the perfect,
only the perfect remains.

—ANCIENT HINDU SCRIPTURE

In ancient India, a group of young monks were watching their master prepare chappatis (pancakes). He would pour out a ladle full of batter and watch it spread across the surface of the hot griddle, forming an odd round shape. As the pancake assumed its final form, he would smile and say, "Perfect."

The students were puzzled. Each of the pancakes was a different shape, some of them were burned around the edges, and none were perfectly round. Finally, one of the students asked the master, "Master, how can these pancakes be perfect? Pancakes are supposed to be round, and they are not supposed to be burned."

The master lifted the last pancake off the griddle and put it on his young disciple's plate. It was shaped somewhat like a gourd. "Perfect," he repeated.

Once a great teacher told me, "If you don't like the world you see, change the prescription of your glasses."

Recently, I spoke to an old friend on the telephone. We had not met for over ten years. As we recalled some of our past encounters, I remarked, "Everything that has happened is perfect." My friend said, "I don't understand what you mean, and I am not sure you do either."

The truth is as simple as "change your prescription." There is nothing wrong with the world but your view of it. How do I know this? Maybe you are thinking the same thing as my friend: "These are just words. How does she know what she is talking about?" The way I know this to be true is through direct experience.

Years ago, I spent a great deal of time in deep spiritual contemplation and meditation. One day, after I finished my daily meditation, I was in an ecstatic state. My heart was bursting with love and joy. I experienced that the only substance existing in the universe was love and nothing but love. God had truly created this universe out of His own love.

While I was in this state, I got into my car and drove to my appointment across town. On this hot and smoggy summer afternoon, I was driving along the San Diego Freeway in the midst of chaotic traffic. Normally I would have seen Los Angeles and the freeway as an irritating bunch of people displaying their vicious manners and driving senselessly trying to get to wherever they were going. I had always thought drivers in Los Angeles should drive tanks instead of cars. But this time, my experience was transformed: I felt there was only love. I felt that the whole of Los Angeles was an extension of myself. In fact, I experienced that oneness with the whole universe. At that moment, I saw only perfection. Even a chaotic freeway was part of the expression of God's perfection.

For me, this state did not last. It faded away eventually. But a glimpse of this perfect vision was enough. I knew then through my intuitive mind that the reality of the world is always perfect, even when we do not perceive it to be so. While I was privileged to have a glimpse of this reality, I also then knew that the very wise ones from the ancient to the modern are always living in this state of understanding.

In our everyday lives, we constantly attempt to fix our reality. We want it to fit into our concept of "perfection."

A couple of years ago, I conducted a radio interview with Joseph Barbera, the founder of Hanna-Barbera Studios and creator of the animated cartoon classics "Yogi Bear," "Tom and Jerry," plus many more. During our conversation, he spoke of how perfectly his life had turned out. He said that sometimes when you are in the midst of it, it may not seem to be going well, but when you look back, then the perfection is apparent.

Joseph Barbera was once a struggling cartoonist, making a living by selling his cartoon pieces to New York magazines. He selected some of his better cartoons and sent them to Walt Disney to request a job. For a struggling cartoonist, working for the Disney Studio was the ultimate dream come true. Disney replied, writing that he would interview Mr. Barbera on his next trip to New York. But Disney never called on him. Obviously, at that time it was a great disappointment for Barbera. Now, as he looks back, he is delighted that Walt Disney didn't come to see him. Barbera said, "I probably would have become a devoted member of his staff and still would be with Disney studios today."

The concept of seeing everything as perfect is not only a

comforting thought when you are experiencing life's major disappointments. It is also a powerful tool for the Thick Face, Black Heart practitioner when applied to insignificant day-to-day annoyances.

As I was writing this chapter, I took a break to run some errands. On the way to each destination, even though they were places I had been to before, I kept getting hopelessly lost. It was a hot summer day, and I was driving a half-ton 4x4 pickup truck. I thought to myself, "I really fail to see any purpose for repeatedly getting lost." In the midst of this, the thought of seeing every manifestation as perfection entered my mind. I knew that in the mystery of life, there is perfection beyond my understanding. If our Divine Maker does not will it, not even a single leaf will dare to fall.

I calmly accepted this irritating experience. Although I continued to get lost, my state of mind had transformed from potentially explosive to relaxed and calm. I realized that there were benefits to be reaped even by this seemingly pointless and frustrating experience. At that moment, I was able to master my thoughts and direct them positively.

Through that experience, I was reminded of countless other similar events. By having the incident happen to me at this time, it became important for me to share it with you. In this way, we can all look back and examine similar incidents in our past. Consequently, in the future, we can place them in the proper perspective of seeing the imperfect manifestation of reality as perfect.

I remember a time when, unexpectedly stuck in heavy traffic, I had consciously decided to enjoy the view of the San Francisco Bay while waiting for the blockage to clear. I noticed directly behind me, in another car, an attractive and professionally dressed woman who was alone. She was screaming at the traffic and beating her fists on the steering wheel, while her face was flushing to ever deeper shades of crimson. Her irritation and frustration served only to exacerbate her agitation and had no impact on the traffic at all.

Like the monks, you may have an idealized vision of how things are supposed to be. But the world unfolds to its own rhythm and purpose. It is important for you to strive beyond common human understanding, beyond preconceptions of what should be and what shouldn't be. In time, you will see the perfection in the seemingly imperfect manifestations of the world.

VII. MASTER THE DISTINCTIONS BETWEEN VIRTUE AND VANITY

While God waits for His church
to be built of love,
men bring stones.

— *RABINDRANATH TAGORE*

A Holy Man's Sacred Vow

A holy man was meditating beneath a tree at the crossing of two roads. His meditation was interrupted by a young man running frantically down the road toward him.

"Help me," the young man pleaded. "A man has wrongly accused me of stealing. He is pursuing me with a great crowd of people. If they catch me, they will chop off my hands."

The young man climbed the tree beneath which the sage had been meditating and hid himself in the branches. "Please don't tell them where I am hiding," he begged.

The holy man saw with the clear vision of a saint that the young man was telling him the truth. The lad was not a thief.

A few moments later, the crowd of villagers approached, and the leader asked, "Have you seen a young man run by here?"

Many years earlier, the holy man had taken a vow to always speak the truth, so he said that he had.

"Where did he go?" the leader asked.

The holy man did not want to betray the innocent young man, but his vow was sacred to him. He pointed up into the tree. The villagers dragged the young man out of the tree and chopped off his hands.

When the holy man died and stood before Judgment, he was condemned for his behavior in regard to the unfortunate young man.

"But," he protested, "I had made a holy vow to speak only the truth. I was bound to act as I did."

"On that day," came the reply, "you loved vanity more than virtue. It was not for virtue's sake that you delivered the innocent man over to his persecutors, but to preserve a vain image of yourself as a virtuous person."

The limited human wisdom that guides our concept of virtue often becomes our compelling force for evil. Our false concept of virtue often is nothing but vanity and an attempt to gain praise or to be self-righteous about how "virtuous" we are, so we may feel superior to others. So many times, because this false virtue is accompanied by a dose of human ignorance, virtue becomes an effective weapon in making humanity a victim.

The Crimes against Humanity

When it comes to the victimization of humanity under the banner of "virtue," there are no divisions of East or West, past or present.

In China, near the end of the Ming Dynasty (early 1600s

A.D.), bandits and peasant forces rose against the Ming Court. The rebellious horde rode through villages robbing the villagers and raping young girls. Female virtue was sacred in China at that time. When a young girl was raped, the only option available to her parents was to serve her a strong poison, thus cleansing the family name. So, when a young girl experienced the horrible fate of being raped, she then had to face the even worse fate of being poisoned by her family.

When Galileo made his findings known to the world— namely, that the sun does not circle the earth but vice versa— all the "most virtuous" members of the Catholic Church condemned him by burning his books and imprisoning him for most of his remaining life.

Such ignorance-guided virtue is not the sole property of the past. Not so long ago, in the 1950s, the United States as a nation went through its own witch-hunt, led by Senator Joseph McCarthy.

Today, "virtuous" citizens with sincere intentions attempt to impose their standards and moral codes regarding many social issues onto others in the name of "goodness and decency." The question we have to ask ourselves is, can we be so sure that our concept of virtue has not become a compelling force for hatred, intolerance, and hypocrisy? Are we not, once more, victimizing humanity?

Virtue, contrary to what most people think, is not something you wear outside of yourself for public display, as the following story demonstrates.

The Whore and the Priest

A Hindu priest lived across the street from a prostitute. Each day as he was going in to do his prayers and meditation, he would see men coming and going from the prostitute's room. He would see the woman herself greeting them or bidding them farewell. Each day the priest would imagine and ponder the shameful acts that were committed in the whore's room, and his heart would fill with strong disapproval of the woman's immorality.

· Each day the prostitute would see the priest at his spiritual practices. She would think how beautiful it must be to be so pure, to spend one's time in prayer and meditation. "But," she would sigh, "it is my lot to be a whore. My mother was a whore, and my daughter will be one too. Such are the ways of this land."

The priest and the whore died on the same day and stood before Judgment together. Much to his astonishment, the priest was condemned for his wickedness.

"But," he protested, "my life has been one of purity. I have spent my days in prayer and meditation."

"Yes," said Judgment, "but while your body was engaged in those holy actions, your heart was consumed with vicious judgments and your soul was ravaged by your lustful imagination."

The whore was commended for her purity.

"I do not understand," she said. "For all my life, I have sold my body to every man who has had the price."

"Your life's circumstances placed you in a whorehouse. You were born there, and it was beyond your strength to do otherwise. But while your body was performing unworthy acts, your heart was always pure and forever fixed in contemplation on the purity of the holy man's prayers and meditation."

The Mourning

Mourning can be a vain competition among the survivors to demonstrate a deeper attachment to the departed and a greater bereavement. This is especially true in Asian society.

While I was attending college in Taipei, I rented a room in the house of a wealthy widow, where she lived with her three sons and their families. During the time I stayed there, the widow, in her eighties, fell ill and was hospitalized. A month later, she was brought home and died.

The sons arranged for an elaborate mourning ritual and burial. The body was laid out in the main room of the house. For the next week, every afternoon at three, a Tao priest would arrive in his huge colorful robe to perform a ritual for the dead, and the family would gather for an hour of mourning. As soon as the priest began chanting, fifteen people would simultaneously break out in loud, forlorn wailing. They would alternate inarticulate sobs and cries with articulate expressions of grief. "How could you leave us here without your wisdom and guidance?" one would wail. "You suffered so much because we failed in our familial duties!" another would lament. Each lamentation grew louder and more disconsolate than the last, until the bellowing was quite unbelievable. Then, precisely at four o'clock, it ceased and everyone went about his business until the following day at the same time.

As the week wore on, the eyes grew drier, even though the wailing remained just as loud. It was not only important to demonstrate the depth of bereavement to the other members of the family, but the sound of grief had to carry all the way to the neighbors' houses. My room was directly above the room where the body was laid out. I was completely exhausted just listening to the daily mourning. The participants were also absolutely drained. It was with unmistakable relief that they finally buried the old woman.

It was not a tragic or unexpected death. The woman had lived a long and very comfortable life. Her death had come peacefully after a brief illness. There was no cause to feel sorry for her at all. In a land where one does not have to walk far to encounter truly tragic and pathetic lives, her life was a cause for celebration. The mourning was entirely for the benefit of the survivors and the neighbors.

Virtue is a delicate substance. No one can judge or measure your virtue, not even yourself. When you are truly aligned with virtue, there is no sense of arrogance, righteousness, or superiority. When you are truly aligned with virtue, a harmony pervades.

VIII. OVERCOME FEAR

Fear is the most destructive of emotions. Fear is to a man's soul as a drop of poison is to a well of springwater. Fear wears so many different masks and comes in so many forms. Deep down in our subconscious, we are wise enough to recognize the fragility of how this universe was put together; that our existence and survival hang on the invisible threads of God's grace. In our conscious awareness, fear is a vague but constantly nagging uneasiness. Most people do not even know that they are afraid most of the time.

Once there was a reporter who during an interview asked a well-known national news anchorman, "What are you afraid of?" The anchorman was taken by surprise and placed in a potentially vulnerable position. He would have to truly expose himself if he were to deal with it honestly. He quickly addressed the question by giving superficial answers: "I am afraid of natural events such as earthquakes and floods."

The reporter asked him if there was anything else, and he said no. The anchorman could not tell the truth for fear of what his audience would think. He was in the public eye and was protecting his public image. It was obvious that one of his biggest fears was to answer this question. But it was not his fault that he felt the need to lie by omission. In general, it is unacceptable in our society to admit your fears in a formal or business environment.

Wherever we turn, we are face to face with different aspects of fear. It is the biggest barrier for us to overcome in order to experience and fulfill our true potential. If you intend to practice Thick Face, Black Heart, it is vitally important that you take a good look at how and when fear manifests itself in your life. Although the experience of fear is universal, it assumes different forms for each individual.

I grew up in a family in which fear was the regular staple served during breakfast, lunch, and dinner. My parents grew up under the domination of the Japanese Imperial Army in Manchuria. Fear was the main element that the Japanese utilized to control the Chinese citizens. After the Japanese defeat at the end of World War II, my family had to live through the devastating experience of the collapse of the Chinese government and monetary system. In addition, as large landholders, they had to cope with the threat of the new Communist policy to eradicate "evil" landlords from the face of the earth. Forced to leave China, my parents had their fears worsened by the hopelessness of living as refugees in Taiwan with three young children to care for.

Fear was a permanent resident in our household. The air was so thick with fear that even when we were not afraid, we were afraid. I remember a couple of years ago, while I was lying in bed, out of nowhere a tremendous feeling of fear hit me. I had never before experienced such potency of feeling. Though I could think of no reason to be fearful, I was so afraid that I got sick to my stomach.

Suddenly, I realized, that the fear I felt was the fear from my parents—fear of the unpredictability of the fragile material world in which they had lived. I had swallowed their fear just by being in their environment and, in that moment, I had recreated it in its full intensity. All my life, I have watched how fear works. I contemplate the mystery within the fear.

Not long ago I was in a shopping mall at closing time. I saw a young store clerk looking terribly frustrated. She was kneeling near a rolldown steel door, with sweat showing through her thin blouse. I asked her what was wrong and if she needed any help.

She told me she had been trying to lock the door for the past half hour, but she couldn't. She said that until the door was locked, she couldn't go home. After I looked at the steel door, it was clear that the position of the lever at the bottom had moved past the slot on the side of the door frame. However, she would not allow me to lift the steel door even slightly, for fear the alarm would go off. She told me that once the door was down, if it was lifted, the alarm would be triggered.

This young woman's attention was focused solely on the fear of the alarm going off. I finally convinced her to lift the door just a bit higher to find the slot. Out of desperation, she gave up her position, and we locked the door. Instead of controlling her fear, the salesgirl had allowed it to dominate her actions to the point where she was completely inert and helpless.

Fear does not have to be a negative entity. Through my life experience practicing Thick Face, Black Heart, I have discovered that there are six elements involved in handling fear.

1. The Usefulness of Fear

There is a popular Chinese maxim: "The hat is good, the shoes are good. However, if you put the hat on your feet, and the shoes on your head, then both become useless."

The emotion of fear is not bad, as everything under heaven has its purpose. If we understand the purpose of fear, we may use the emotion of fear to benefit our life rather than empower fear to hasten our self-destruction.

Fear does not have to be destructive. If we learn to respect fear and channel the emotion of fear for a higher purpose, it will benefit us. Just think: if you never experience any fear, it is probably because you are living your life too safely, beneath your capacity and avoiding challenges. Such a life can be summed up in one word—nothing. An ancient wise man once said, "I would rather have fear and worry than nothing."

Due to the grace of fear, we learn to respect the laws of nature. We do not foolishly jump into a blazing fire or drown ourselves in the depths of the ocean. We do not jump out of an airplane without proper training and equipment. Due to the grace of fear, a mother will tenderly watch and protect her child from harm.

During the course of my work, an FBI agent contacted me to ask for my assistance. He wanted me to watch for Chinese spies who were pretending to be members of visiting delegations. He told me these people came to the United States and secretly contacted their people here. I told him that all the people I had come across were who they said they were. Even during my visits to China, they were still working at the same posts. Furthermore, what he was asking might give the Chinese government cause to imprison me, and I had no desire to spend my retirement in a Chinese jail. I was not afraid to be honest about this, nor was I ashamed of my great fear of Chinese jails, where human rights are given no consideration at all.

As a matter of fact, he was rather relieved at my unwillingness to cooperate. I think one of his objectives in speaking with me was to find out whether or not I was sympathetic to the People's Republic of China, above and beyond my allegiance to the United States of America.

Do not be afraid of fear. Employ Thick Face, Black Heart to shield and protect you from your illusion of harm. Our Creator did not place fear in our hearts in order to destroy us, but rather to guide and protect us. Understand your fear, befriend your fear. Talk to your fear, and ask how you can utilize it for your benefit rather than your destruction. To the grace of fear, I pay respect and bow deeply.

2. The Eyes of Fear

The content of fear may be intense and gripping,
so much so that it overwhelms us completely.
But when we look beyond that content at the fear itself,
what do we find?
Pure energy, energy which, if we focus on it directly,
will begin to reveal its real nature.
Then, instead of filling us with agitation,
the energy of fear can actually lead us
to a state of exhilaration, or intense concentration,
or love.

—ANCIENT HINDU SCRIPTURE

To overcome fear, first you have to find the courage and will to confront fear. Fear is never so terrifying once you look into its eyes. A Thick Face, Black Heart practitioner will use his spear to pierce the eye of fear.

For no apparent reason, I had always been afraid of deep water. Whenever I was swimming in the deeper part of a pool, I felt panic and fear. Whenever I took a dive, from the moment my body touched the bottom until I came up, I felt that the time seemed unbearably long.

Fifteen years ago I took a cruise to the Caribbean. While the ship was anchored in the U.S. Virgin Islands, I took a deep-sea diving class. I decided to take a look at what it would really be like if I went down to the bottom of the sea.

After a half hour of brief instruction, with a group of ten people and an instructor, I walked into the sea with my oxygen tank. While in the water, whenever my mind thought about being at the bottom of the sea, I felt fearful. I would then say to myself, "I am one with the ocean. I am one with all the creatures in the ocean. I am God's child. Wherever I am, I belong. I have the same right as the fish to make this ocean my own." These were not just words, they were direction and guidance for my mind. The words became thoughts and experiences. I then felt at ease with the idea of swimming at the bottom of the sea.

My diving experience was the highlight of my whole trip. In fact, it was one of the highlights of my life. I knew then that I could master my fear at will: I just had to look into its eyes.

Years ago, I decided to organize and conduct a full-day seminar about how to do business with Asians. The morning of the seminar, while I was dressing, I was overcome by fear. Suddenly it hit me: I had never spoken in front of any large groups. What if I opened my mouth and nothing came out? What would this do for my professional reputation? How would I get through this day? In that instant, I had envisioned the entire day and was convinced I would fail and be devastated.

As I was driving toward the hotel, I thought to myself, "I

either shape up or admit defeat." I decided the only way I could get rid of my fear was to stop wanting to avoid the feeling of being fearful. To stop resisting it. The more I did not want to feel fearful, the more intense the fear got. I mentally took my fear from my heart, placed it in front of me on my dashboard, and started to stare into this fear with great intensity. I said to myself, "Let me be more fierce than fear itself." Suddenly the fear I had been feeling was replaced by the intense courage that I had created to stare at the fear. By the time I arrived at the hotel, I was charged with power and enthusiasm.

My first seminar was a great success. After I had finished at 4:00 p.m., no one wanted to leave—they wanted to hear more!

My experience was not extraordinary. Often the bravest warriors were originally the greatest cowards. The more fear you confront and conquer, the greater courage you will possess.

3. Diversity Is Fear

The most profound knowledge is often only available through direct perception and experience. Words alone are never sufficient to explain such mysteries. Understanding the nature of fear and how to take control of it is of great importance in our daily life. Knowing the source of fear is the essential element; without it, your understanding of fear will not be complete.

The profound and simple truth is that the universe was created by our Divine Maker. He created the whole universe out of Himself and no other substance. In reality, all things and creatures are one with our Maker. Just as in the material world, all elements consist of atomic particles, yet they are manifested as infinitely different forms. Whenever we experience ourselves as separate from that power of Oneness, fear enters.

When I was afraid of deep water, the source of my fear was that I experienced myself as being separate from the water. When I focused my mind and heart and concentrated on becoming one with the water and all the creations within, then I expanded to include the water and the One who created the water. I also was included within it.

A friend of mine shared with me that normally she is extremely afraid about the judgments and opinions of others. For her, this was a source of constant anxiety. Once, after completing a spiritual retreat, for a few days she experienced a state of complete serenity. She was without fear.

In this state of fearlessness, there was no effort needed not to be afraid. There was simply a sense of pure peace, serenity, harmony, and great clarity. A feeling of well-being in which she saw that although she was different from others, in essence she was the same. There was no diversity. She experienced that all of creation was one with the Creator. Yet she was not consciously experiencing the thought. In that oneness, you are part of the whole in each pulsating moment. Thought does not exist.

This harmonious state is experienced by those who dedicate their lives to vigilance in practicing the highest form of Thick Face, Black Heart. To obtain this state is within human reach, but make no mistake about it, it is only through rigorous vigilance and practice that it will manifest.

The experience of diversity manifests in a way that affects our daily lives. For example, in the business world, whenever a salesman sees that his own interest is the opposite of his potential customer's, he is fearful. He sees that in order for him to make a dollar, the potential customer will have to dish out ten dollars. Deep down, he knows he is a noble human being. He does not wish to have a total stranger "lose" ten dollars so that he may gain one dollar. Consequently, he is afraid to approach the customer.

If the salesman took a different perspective and sought unity among his customer's interests, then his fear would not exist. Would you be afraid if you knew for certain that by communicating information concerning your service or product to the potential buyer, he would benefit tremendously? In our daily lives, whenever you can find unity among diversity, you will experience no fear.

4. Master Detachment

Performing your duty without attachment or aversion is a great antidote to the poison of fear.

—BHAGAVAD GITA

If you are not concerned about the outcome of a circumstance, you will experience no fear. When you attach yourself to expectations, anxiety and fear will overcome you. The outcome will be what it will be, regardless of your expectations and fears.

5. Ignore the Fear

I am an old man and have a great many troubles, but most of them never happened.

—MARK TWAIN

For most of us, fear is not grounded in any real possibility of catastrophe; rather, it is a state of emotional uneasiness. Mark Twain clearly understood this well when he said that most of our worries and fears never come true. Don't give your fear too much importance. An ignored guest often departs unannounced.

6. In Spite of Your Fear, Do What You Have to Do

Faith is the bird that feels the light
and sings when the dawn is still dark.

—*RABINDRANATH TAGORE*

This is the essence of the message of fear. During your daily encounters, in spite of your fear, do what you have to do. As the Thick Face, Black Heart practitioner, you will press ahead and walk through the clouds of fear that may arise on your path to success.

IX. VOYAGE BEYOND THE AVOIDANCE OF PAIN AND THE PURSUIT OF PLEASURE

The man who is not troubled by pain and pleasure,
who remains the same,
he is wise and makes himself fit for eternal life.

—BHAGAVAD GITA

Beneath the fear of success and failure is the fear of pain. The most motivating factor in human actions is the desire to avoid pain and do what promises us pleasure.

There may be religious individuals who would argue that this is not so with them. The aim of devotion, however, is the possible deliverance out of eternal pain into eternal pleasure—the bliss of God.

If an individual can convince others that doing things his way will increase the pleasure of living and lessen the pain of life, that individual will certainly be a popular man. Just look at political speeches given during the past hundred years. They have changed very little: "If you vote for me, your life is going to be better, you will have more money to spend, your children will have a higher standard of education to ensure their prosperous future, you will have luxurious low-cost housing, you will have a strong defense, you will have cultural programs to enrich your lives, and I promise you that there will be no increase in taxes." Whoever can paint the most convincing mental picture gets elected.

Hitler understood this principle. When he came to power in 1933, Germany was in a deep economic slump. The German people were still carrying the heavy disgrace of their defeat in World War I. They were suffering both physically and emotionally.

Hitler's quasi-socialist Nazi Party promised a better economic life and the possibility of a reglorified Germany. The promise of a better life was more attractive than the harsh and hopeless reality. The German people opened their arms and embraced him.

Hitler delivered on his promise. He brought Germany out of economic depression and went on to unite the German-speaking world. In 1938, he was at the top. According to some historians, if Hitler had died in 1938, he would now be known as the greatest statesman in the history of Germany.

Eva Duarte Peron of Argentina, popularly known as Evita, seemed to have acquired something akin to sainthood by the time of her death in 1952. She used only one weapon to secure the dictatorial position of her husband. She convinced the poor masses of Argentina that she and her husband were their only hope for a better life. She used herself as an example, having been raised in the slums of Buenos Aires.

"Follow me. You too can rise to the top." Argentina believed her.

Hitler delivered something tangible. Eva Peron delivered hope. Both convinced the masses that they had the means to lessen the pain and increase the pleasures of life.

Half a century later, people have not grown wiser. We are still eager to embrace anyone who promises to increase our pleasure and lessen our pain. We operate our whole lives out of a desire for pleasure and the avoidance of pain. We are like laboratory rats who have found out which door hides the cheese.

Former president Ronald Reagan is a master at manipulating this simple human emotion. In order to fulfill his promise of making the American people "feel good," he had to create a false prosperity. He borrowed against America's future, turning the United States from the largest creditor nation to the largest debtor nation in eight short years.

History has proven that the blind pursuit of pleasure and avoidance of pain cause the human race to sabotage itself. We blindly pursue individual pleasure at any cost and rob ourselves of our possibility to be great. The remedy to cure this current national character defect is Thick Face, Black Heart. Abraham Lincoln understood that the price of greatness lay beyond the pursuit of pleasure and avoidance of pain. He fought for the very existence of the principle of democratic government and was willing to risk the devastating destruction of his beloved nation.

X. ACQUIRE THE COURAGE TO BELIEVE IN YOURSELF

Many of the things that you have been taught were at one time the radical ideas of individuals who had the courage to believe what their own hearts and minds told them was true, rather than accept the common beliefs of their day. In the world of science, Galileo and Darwin come immediately to mind. Their ideas questioned the cherished belief of man's preeminent place in God's universe. They threw the dogmatic religious establishment into paroxysms of rage.

I spent the first part of my life in provincial China and the subsequent years in modern America. Time and time again, I have noticed how customs that seem of such fundamental and unquestioned importance in one culture reveal themselves to be trivial and arbitrary when viewed from the perspective of a different culture.

I remember an old woman who lived on our street when I was a child. We children called her Auntie Wong. Though elderly, she was a lively and energetic person. Like other women her age, she dressed in the old style and pulled her hair back in a neat bun, ornamenting it with a jade and silver stickpin. But unlike the other old women, Auntie Wong moved purposefully when she walked. She did not hobble slowly on tiny, broken, and disfigured feet.

In Auntie Wong's youth, it had been the custom to break the bones of young girls' feet and then bind them tightly with the toes bent under so they would heal into tiny, deformed feet. It was ingrained into people's thinking that these misshapen feet were a necessary component of female beauty. Besides being thought of as beautiful in and of themselves, bound feet caused a woman's hips to sway in what was considered a most irresistible manner. But sensuality really had nothing to do with it. A woman's hips swayed because she could not walk straight.

But Auntie Wong's mother had been a woman of enormous courage. She forbade anyone to bind her child's feet. She physically restrained the members of her outraged family from performing the ritual. For the remainder of her life, she stood as a shield between her daughter and those who would cripple her. When Auntie Wong's mother died, Auntie Wong was thirteen years old and her feet were already much too large to bind.

From the vantage point of twentieth-century America, it is easy to minimize the enormity of Auntie Wong's mother's courage. Foot binding is to us such an obviously barbaric and pointless practice that it seems common sense would prohibit it. However, in Auntie Wong's world, only servants and peasant women had unbound feet. It brought great shame on her family to have a daughter whose very feet proclaimed her to be coarse and without breeding.

But many old customs changed in China during the early years of this century. Foot binding fell out of favor. Auntie Wong's generation was the last to be subjected to it. Rather than spending her life as a social pariah, Auntie Wong was one of the few women of her generation to be in tune with the prevailing standards of the new China. The women who had been crippled by foot binding grew old as relics of a bygone era. The invisible chains of customs and cultural practices are more binding than shackles of iron. Your life will be very difficult if you violate accepted standards of conduct without important reasons.

Nonetheless, as a Thick Face, Black Heart practitioner, you must break free from the bondage and have the courage to be true to your convictions.

XI. REALIZE THE THICK FACE, BLACK HEART NATURE OF THE CREATOR

To every thing there is a season,
and a time to every purpose under heaven.

—ECCLESIASTES

Most of the religions of the world recognize a Creator or Creative Force. They may differ regarding His specific identity and many of His attributes, but there is surprising agreement on the idea that all things happen through the will of the Creator. One of the great mysteries of religion is why a benign and omnipotent Creator would allow suffering to come into the world. God may mark the sparrow's fall, but He nevertheless lets him fall. The Creator's destructive force is so violent and causes so much human misery, through both the blind forces of nature and the actions of the wicked, that He seems callous and unjust.

But the created universe is huge, spanning unthinkable ranges of time and distance. Galaxies coalesce out of clouds of dust drifting in the vast icy blackness of interstellar space. Stars ignite, planets form, and life begins. Eventually it is all consumed in its own fire and returns to dust, ready for the cycle to begin again. The Creator does not modify His plan for the convenience of an infinitesimal fragment of creation, nor does He explain Himself. The universe is run according to immutable principles that are far, far greater than our small concerns.

Creation and destruction are not opposites, as they seem. They are two aspects of a single force. The universe is a constant cycle of creation and destruction. Both are equally necessary.

As I write this, there is a huge forest fire raging out of control in the mountains nearby. Despite the fact that scientists clearly understand the need for periodic fires to maintain a healthy forest, hundreds of men using millions of dollars' worth of equipment are frantically trying to extinguish the flames. The local timber industry cannot see beyond its need for the standing timber being lost. Animal lovers lament the loss of animal life without considering that this cataclysm is a necessary and natural part of preparing the way for the generations of wild beasts to come. Only the Creator has a face thick enough and a heart black enough to allow His grand design to unfold without concern for these matters.

Often when we categorize something as wrong or bad, it is because we do not possess the breadth of vision to see its necessity in the overall scheme of things.

SUMMARY OF KEY POINTS

• Break the Constraints of the Inner Images and External Standards. From childhood, most of us have been taught that the highest prize in the world is the approval of others. Perhaps it is not stated in so many words, but it is implied in everything that we are told is right and good. Thick Face, Black Heart is the natural state of your being. This state has been lost to you because of well-meaning people who drilled into you all the rules about how you ought to behave and feel. It is also lost to you because of an inner image you have created of yourself out of other people's expectations and beliefs. You must reclaim the natural state of your true self.

• Search for Your Own Inner Conviction. There is time to submit to being slapped, and there is a time to hit back twice. It is not whether or not you turn the other cheek that is important. It is why you do, or do not, that counts the most.

- Discover the Mystery within the Staunchness of the Oak and the Yielding of the Grass. The grass bends easily in the wind; the great oak stands unmoved. A strong wind can uproot the oak, but no wind, however strong, can uproot the grass that bends flat before it. The ideal practitioner of Thick Face, Black Heart is one who possesses Thick Face, Black Heart inwardly, yet whose outward appearance can be dominating or submissive as the situation demands. He does not have a public or private image of himself to live up to or one that dictates how he must behave.

- Understand Yourself. In order to free yourself from the domination of arbitrary standards and discover the true standards by which you should behave, you need to find the courage to do what you must without regard to what others may think.

- Self-observation is Essential to Self-growth. You must first understand the motives for your own actions in order to understand others.

- Self-knowledge is a more reliable guide to behavior than adherence to arbitrarily imposed standards.

- Break the Bondage of Fear of Success and Fear of Failure. Success means change and risk of failure. The failure of those who attempt extraordinary accomplishments is much more public than ordinary failures and is generally accompanied by sighs of satisfaction. Success also requires the courage to risk disapproval. All independent thought, new ideas, or endeavors beyond the common measure are greeted with disapproval, ranging from skepticism and ridicule to violent outrage. To persevere in anything exceptional requires inner strength and the unshakable conviction that you are right.

• Understand the Nature of Illusion and Reality. In our everyday lives, we constantly attempt to fix our reality. We want it to fit into our concept of "perfection." Seeing everything as perfect is not only a comforting thought when you are experiencing life's major disappointments, it is also a powerful tool to the Thick Face, Black Heart practitioner when applied to insignificant, day-to-day annoyances.

• Master the Distinctions between Virtue and Vanity. The limited human wisdom that guides our concept of virtue often becomes the compelling force for evil. Our false concept of virtue often is nothing but vanity and an attempt to gain praise or to be self-righteous about how "virtuous" we are, so we may feel superior to others. Often, because this false virtue is accompanied by a dose of human ignorance, virtue becomes an effective weapon in making humanity a victim.

• Overcome Fear. Fear is to man's soul as a drop of poison is to a well of springwater.

• Everything under heaven has its purpose: if we understand the purpose of fear, we may use the emotion of fear to benefit our life rather than empower fear to hasten our self-destruction.

• Fear is never so fearful once you look it in the eyes.

• In reality, all things and creatures are one with our Maker—just as in the material world, all elements consist of atomic particles, yet they manifest themselves in infinitely different forms. Whenever we experience ourselves as separate from that power of Oneness, fear enters. When a salesman sees that his own interest is the opposite of his potential customer's, he is fearful. When a salesman seeks unity with his customer's interests, then his fear does not exist.

- If you are not concerned about the outcome of a circumstance, you will experience no fear. Whatever the outcome will be, will be, whether you fear it or not.

- Don't give your fear too much importance. An ignored guest often departs unannounced.

- In spite of your fear, do what you have to do.

- Voyage beyond the Avoidance of Pain and the Pursuit of Pleasure. We operate our whole lives on the desire for pleasure and the avoidance of pain. We are like laboratory rats who have found out which door hides the cheese. History has proven that the blind pursuit of pleasure and avoidance of pain cause the human race to sabotage itself. The price of greatness lies beyond the pursuit of pleasure and avoidance of pain.

- Acquire the Courage to Believe in Yourself. Many of the things that you have been taught were at one time the radical ideas of individuals who had the courage to believe what their own hearts and minds told them was true, rather than accept the common beliefs of their day.

- Realize the Thick Face, Black Heart Nature of the Creator. Destruction is an essential part of Creation. Only the Creator has a face thick enough and a heart black enough to allow His grand design to ruthlessly unfold. The Creator does not modify His plan for the convenience of an infinitesimal fragment of Creation, nor does He explain Himself. The universe is run according to immutable principles that are far greater than our small concerns

According to your life,
your duties have been prescribed for you;

follow them and your
desires will be naturally fulfilled.

—BHAGAVAD GITA

3

Dharma:
The Wish-Fulfilling
Tree

Dharma is the foundation that supports life.

—*Mahabharata*

THE CONCEPT OF DHARMA

The word *Dharma* comes from Sanskrit, the oldest language in the world, which originated in ancient India. It has been confirmed by leading Western linguists that Sanskrit is the root of virtually all known languages. According to Hindu mythology, it is the language spoken by the gods. Dharma came from the root word *dhar,* which means "to support, uphold, and nourish." So Dharma is often defined as that which supports life. It is the sustaining force of the world, the divine coherence of the universe.

Dharma is the understanding of appropriate action for any given circumstance. It means "to act in accordance with one's duty." Each person, depending on his station in life,

69

will have a different Dharma. For example, a warrior's Dharma is to slay the enemies of his nation. A physician's Dharma is to save lives, even the lives of his enemies. These two actions, although completely different, are both correct. If Dharma is followed, the world will be in harmony with the natural law.

Dharma is the foundation of Thick Face, Black Heart. In order for one to successfully become a righteous Thick Face, Black Heart practitioner, the awareness of Dharma must be constantly in one's consciousness. Otherwise, as mentioned in chapter 1, you will become an unconscionable Thick Face, Black Heart practitioner who is willing to win at all costs but without any regard for the consequences to other people. Only by maintaining this awareness of Dharma will we begin to gain insight into what is required for proper discrimination in thought and in action.

DHARMA—YOUR PROTECTOR AND LIBERATOR

People who practice Dharma accept life as it comes and perform their duty accordingly. Dharma is a natural law that guides us to recognize at any given moment the role each one of us is playing in life. Being true to the duty of that particular role at any given time and the very act of accepting and performing that action to the best of our ability—that is following Dharma. That act will become our protector and savior. The following Hindu story demonstrates the practicality of this concept.

Two frogs, a father and his son, accidentally fell into a bucket of milk. They started swimming for their lives. They swam for a long time, but there seemed no hope of their getting out. The father said to the son, "I am getting tired. I am going to drown." The son tried to encourage his father: "No, keep swimming, keep swimming. Something will happen. Have faith." So the father kept swimming. But half an hour later, the father gave up and sank to the bottom. The son went on swimming. During this time, the churning milk, whipped by his unceasing efforts to save his life, had begun to form a ball of butter that soon became solid beneath his feet. Using this island of butter as a platform, he managed to hop out of the bucket. He mourned, "If my father had just held on a little longer, he'd be with me now."

Dharma works for humans just as it does for frogs. Seventeen years ago, Leslie was a teenager who used to help me clean my house in exchange for piano lessons. Five years ago, I talked with her mother and asked how Leslie was doing, as I had not seen her for many years. It was then that I learned the following fantastic story.

The Miracle Power of Dharma

After Leslie graduated from high school, she began working as a bookkeeper for a small manufacturer. The company produced a certain unique component, and produced it better and more cheaply than anyone else. Not only did they sell the component all over the United States, they also exported it to other countries.

After working there for about eight years, Leslie began to discover evidence that indicated that the company managers, the owner's two sons, were stealing company money from the sole owner: their mother. Knowing full well that it might mean losing her job—after all, it is not uncommon to "shoot the messenger"—she nevertheless decided she was duty-bound to inform her employer of her sons' theft.

As the owner never actually came to the factory, Leslie

made an appointment to meet with her at her home. At this meeting, Leslie carefully showed the woman the books and other details that clearly laid out the extent and magnitude of the sons' theft. Instead of shooting the messenger as Leslie had feared, the woman turned to her and said, "I want to sell this company, and I would like you to buy it."

"I have no money," Leslie said.

To which the owner replied, "This is what we will do. I will set a value for the purchase of the company. You will pay me a certain amount of money from the company's receivables each month, over a five-year period, after which time you will own the company free and clear." She then promptly fired her sons and had the paperwork drawn up for the sale. Leslie has now owned the company for years and employs her own mother as the office manager.

In this story, Leslie and the company owner had both demonstrated impeccable commitment to their Dharma. The company owner, who was also a mother, followed her Dharma and dedicated herself to restoring the integrity of her company and, at the same time, taught an unforgettable lesson to her own sons.

Leslie was willing to risk her livelihood in performing the job she was paid to do. Her dedication and courage as an employee was rewarded by gaining the sole ownership of a company without actively pursuing it and without any capital of her own. This outcome was beyond her wildest dreams.

Thick Face, Black Heart practitioners are vigorous in pursuing the rightness of their actions. They question themselves in each and every situation: "What is my Dharma at this moment?" As mentioned before, the Dharma of a warrior is the opposite of a physician's, yet they are both correct. On the other hand, if a warrior refuses to kill and a physician refuses to save, then both actions would be insupportable. By being true to their Dharma, their actions will be guided by the rhythm of natural law, which will protect and support all their efforts.

The Grace of Dharma

The grace of Dharma works in subtle and mysterious ways throughout our life. John is in commercial real estate sales. He is hardworking and always performs his duties diligently, but as sometimes happens in this business, he went through a dry period. He spent an entire month carrying out his normal activities: lots of cold calls to prospects and visits to potential customers in an attempt to generate new business. All he got were rejections.

John was so depressed that he decided he could use a little vacation and took a trip to Hawaii. Once there, he quickly relaxed at the beach and started to enjoy himself. Within a couple of days, he ran into a fellow traveler who turned out to be a wealthy real estate investor. After all his hard work, and when and where he least expected it, he set up a very profitable deal.

John was puzzled: "All the hard work I did produced no results, yet here I am out playing, with work the furthest thing from my mind, and what do I get? A great client. Maybe working so hard is not healthy for business." What John did not know was that, due to his hard work, the power of Dharma shone its grace upon him as reward for his commitment to duty. Dharma became his protector and liberator.

Dharma of a Debtor and a Creditor

Financial misfortune happens all too often in today's uncertain economic arena. Previously stable individuals suddenly are unable to fulfill their obligations or repay their debts. If you should ever find yourself in this situation, after the shock of feeling helpless, ask yourself, "What is my Dharma?"

The Dharma of a debtor in this case is to do the best he can to show goodwill and intent to repay the debt. He must make the necessary sacrifices and adjust his lifestyle accordingly, without paying out so much that he destroys any possibility of recovery. He must not deprive himself or his family of essential needs.

On the other hand, a creditor's Dharma is to allow the debtor to restructure the debt so that he may continue with his basic living and have a chance to recover financially. He will therefore have the means to repay the original debt. I am not telling you something you don't already know. I merely relate this to you to illustrate the framework of Dharma.

A Warrior's Dharma

George is an important officer at the Pentagon. He participated in the strategic designs for the Grenada invasion, the takeover in Panama, and the speedy victory of Operation Desert Storm in the Gulf. From his outward appearance, he is a military man. Yet privately he is a very spiritually minded individual. His whole life is centered around his spiritual commitment. Those who know about his devotion to the spiritual life have asked him, "How can you be in the military? How can you design the ways and means to kill people and still be such a spiritual man?" He answers, "It is my Dharma

to be a military man, just like Arjuna in the *Bhagavad Gita.*
I too am a warrior."

The *Bhagavad Gita* or "Song of God" is the most sacred
of Hindu scriptures. Written in approximately 2000 B.C., it is
an epic poem that chronicles the battle between two branches of a ruling family over the succession to the throne. The
old King, Dhritarashtra, scion of the Kaurava clan, decrees
that his own son, Duryodhana, is less worthy to succeed him
than Yudhishthira, the pure-hearted leader of the Pandava
clan. Duryodhana rebels against his father's will and gathers
the forces of the Kaurava clan to claim the throne by force.

The *Bhagavad Gita* is a conversation between a great warrior of the Pandava clan, Arjuna, the brother of Yudhishthira,
and the Lord Krishna, a divine embodiment of God, who is
serving as Arjuna's charioteer for the coming battle. We pick
up the story after the armies have been arrayed against each
other, and just before battle is to commence. Arjuna requests
that Krishna drive his chariot between the two armies for his
last observations.

Arjuna is the greatest warrior in the world. He has slain
men, serpents, and demons. He has even conquered the God
of death. Yet when he sees relatives and friends lined up to
do battle with each other, he is overcome with doubts. He
cries out to Lord Krishna:

"I see my kinsmen. They are all standing arrayed for battle. How can this be right for me? I do not long for victory,
nor kingdoms, nor pleasures, because in order to gain these I
must kill my own relatives, elders, and benefactors. I would
not kill them even if it gained me the universe and beyond;
how much less for the sake of the earth?

"O Lord, if the righteousness within me is destroyed, Thy
love for me would vanish, and Thou wouldst abandon me.
Without Thee, my heart would be shattered with grief."

Arjuna throws away his mighty bow and sinks down into

the seat of his chariot, disconsolate. He is ready to renounce his family's claim to the throne.

In his divine wisdom, Lord Krishna understands the dual nature of Arjuna's agony: it is as difficult for Arjuna to detach himself from the familiar feelings of compassion and familial loyalty as it is to make war on his cousins. Krishna counsels him to rid himself of his false compassion. He advises him to fight the battle without anger or passion, but in fulfillment of his duty to himself and his country. The fight is not about the throne and the kingdom, it is about fighting to sustain the Dharma, the natural order of the world.

The Battle Must Be Fought

Each one of us is a warrior in our own right. We are the warriors of life, and life is an eternal battle. We choose to enter the battlefield from the day we are born. We are committed to win the battle of life—just as for a warrior in the midst of a fierce fight, there is no way out. He can choose to fight courageously to ensure his survival and victory, or he can choose to get killed. We do not have to like the fight. We simply have to fight to the best of our abilities. To survive in life, we have to confront the inner negativities and the outer realities.

I have a friend who is always complaining how hard her life is, and how hard her job is. She is always hoping for a new profession that will be easy. She's a dreamer who is unwilling to make any effort in life. One time, during one of our chats, I mentioned that a literary agent has to read reams of unsolicited proposals and manuscripts. He has to decide whom he will take on as new clients. He has to contact publishers and announce the new works he is representing. He must then follow up with the publishers and negotiate contracts with them. In addition, he has to try to convince the authors that the deals he is presenting are good ones and to convince the publishers they should pay more for their interest. He has to try to sell foreign rights, movie rights, and recording rights, and must simultaneously handle masses of problems between the authors and publishers. All this takes place from the time a book is sold to the time the book goes out of print, and includes the complex management of his administrative staff and the multitude of menial tasks involved. An agent has to juggle all the balls in the air, often with many clients. My friend got the point and remarked, "I thought *my* job was hard."

In fact, nothing is hard or easy. Competition for survival is the condition of life. It is our Dharma to fight the battle of life courageously and righteously.

A Soldier's Dharma

During Operation Desert Storm, some soldiers refused to fight. They said that killing others was against their personal and religious beliefs. I thought this was nonsensical, considering they had signed up voluntarily as members of the armed forces, whose main duty is to defend the nation when we are at war. There is a popular Chinese maxim: "A nation may support its troops for thousands of years to prepare for the few moments when they will be needed."

When you sign up as a member of the armed forces, you give up your personal rights. It does not matter if you approve of the cause or the war. You do not have to like killing other fellow beings. Your Dharma is to obey and perform your duty as you have been trained to do.

The soldier's Dharma is not to receive a monthly salary and hang around collecting GI educational benefits or to enjoy the glamour of traveling around the world—although these are side benefits. For thousands of years, the soldier's Dharma has always been to kill and be killed in the name of defending the nation he serves.

The Guiding Force

Where there is Dharma, there is victory.

—*MAHABHARATA*

Neil works for a structural engineering company. One day I received a call from him. He said, "My employer asked me to go to Spain to oversee a project that we have been working on for nearly two years. I don't really want to go, as I may have to be there for three to six months, or even longer. I don't want to leave my girlfriend for such a lengthy period."

I asked, "Can they send someone else?"

"Not really," he said. "This project is my responsibility."

I replied, "Then the decision is easy. As an employee of a small, newly established company, it is your Dharma to support and serve your employer and make sure of the total success of the company. If I were you, I would tell your employer, 'It is my intention to serve you in any way I can. I will gladly go to Spain for as long as I am needed, as you see fit.'" And I added, "As for your girlfriend, you will just have to invite her to Spain to spend some time with you."

A Salesman's Dharma

I myself had a profound experience while traveling in Taiwan on business. One of my objectives there was to represent a U.S. firm on a visit to the firm's Taiwan representative. The Taiwan company had been doing a very poor job of selling the U.S. company's product.

I spent a long time rehearsing in my mind how I should approach the Taiwan company. Should I be casual and friendly or take a more official stand to find out why their sales performance had been so poor? I went through many ways to open the conversation, but none felt right. The problem was that the Taiwan company's owner was a dear friend of mine. Being heavy-handed or coming to him with a very light touch seemed equally inappropriate. During my self-inquiry, I was undecided.

I asked myself, what is the Dharma in this situation? I then realized the only proper way to approach the Taiwan company was to be open and direct and to find out how I (representing the U.S. company's interest) could better serve them. I should find out what their difficulties were and how I could help. If I supported them in doing their job better, they would in turn do a better job for my U.S. client.

As soon as I realized what my Dharma was in this circumstance, I felt totally open and positive toward these people. I no longer had to rehearse how to speak to them. Since I now had a proper attitude toward the situation, the words that came out of my mouth could only be right.

THE ADHARMA OF BENAZIR BHUTTO AND CORAZON AQUINO

The opposite of Dharma is Adharma, which is defined as going against one's proper duty in life. During my recent trip to Asia, I had an extensive discussion with a U.S. news agency Asian bureau chief regarding the former Philippine president, Corazon Aquino, and the former Pakistani prime minister, Benazir Bhutto. I asked him about his impressions

of both women, since he had met them several times and followed their political careers closely. Among the many points
we discussed, one interesting observation he made was that
Bhutto and Aquino both inherited their political image from
others: Bhutto from her father, Aquino from her husband.

Bhutto is strong-willed, combative in nature, and often
provokes confrontations with the opposition. She inherited
her father's political popularity along with his political enemies. She made no attempt to soften the opposition's tension.
Bhutto was removed from office in August 1990.

Aquino inherited her husband's image as the guardian of
democracy for the Philippine people. During her presidency,
Aquino weathered a total of seven coup attempts. She dealt
with the rebels initially in the style of a democratic goddess;
with a gentle slap on the hands, she told them not to do it
again. Although she survived the coup attempts, her administrative and political credibility was damaged. She did not
produce the promised better life for her people.

Bhutto and Aquino had seemingly opposite styles: one
hard and one soft. Logically, if the soft line did not work,
then the hard one should. What went wrong?

Outwardly the two leaders were doing opposite things. In
essence, however, they did exactly the same.

Bhutto, in order to be Bhutto, had to be confrontational.
That was the style of her father, which she had adopted and
her supporters expected. Aquino, in order to be Aquino,
needed to be kind and benevolent. Such was the image of her
husband, which she had adopted as her own.

The images that brought Bhutto and Aquino to power are
no longer beneficial to them as rulers. Popularity does not
feed starving people, nor does it secure a party's political
position.

Bhutto should have made peace with the oppositional
forces. She should have gotten them to join her in working

for the good of the land. Aquino should have been severe in her punishment of those who participated in the first coup attempt. She should have set an example for military discipline that would have established clear standards of reward for the loyal and punishment for the rebellious.

Nature's law, unlike Aquino's, is that you must choose before you act. After an action is delivered, absolute consequences follow. A friend of mine who is a fervent Christian mentioned to me after he read this passage, "Unlike the Eastern concept, the Christian God is compassionate." My answer to him was, "Try jumping off the thirteenth floor and see if you fly. Will God change his law for you?"

Aquino should have given up her benevolent, motherlike image and concentrated on the business of reconstructing the devastated Philippine national economy. That was more important than laboring over the fundamental elements of governing, the internal stability of her government, and her own life.

Both Bhutto and Aquino are women who labored under the burden of someone else's destiny. In Aquino's case, it was the destiny of her martyred husband; in Bhutto's, that of her executed father. Both of their failures came about because they did not exercise the powers of their office according to the requirements of their own destiny—their actions were adharmic.

Both betrayed their Dharma—as the protector of the land and their people. The people of these nations who had supported them lost, once again.

KNOW THY DHARMA

I am totally convinced that whatever your occupation, you will do well if you can properly identify your Dharma for that job. A chair, to be useful, must understand its Dharma and be willing to let people sit on it. A pencil is only useful when it carries out the Dharma of a pencil. If the chair refuses to let people sit on it or the pencil refuses to perform its writing function, they are useless.

When a manufacturing engineer is hired to create new products but insists on sharing his "wisdom" in accounting with the company controller, he is not going to last long in that company.

The American Pioneer's Dharma

The Salomon Brothers' illegal cornering of the American bond market was all over the financial newspapers. Whatever the cause of this incident and whoever was responsible for it, the answer is simple. These people were motivated by greed and driven by the intense desire for instant gratification. Perhaps the fault does not lie solely with those individuals who have committed the crimes. Rather, it lies deeply in the present American social culture.

America as a nation has recently become obsessed with the idea of instant gratification. There is a popular saying, "There is no free lunch." Ever so many people, especially during the past decade, have dedicated their entire energy in the pursuit of instant gratification. When a nation begins to disproportionately place value on individuals who can generate the largest sum of money within the shortest time as a measure of success, the nation's character has to suffer.

Two hundred years ago, America was founded by people of character who were true to the spirit of Thick Face, Black Heart. They understood the simple Dharma of how to make a nation strong for generations to come. They understood the fundamental value of hard work and endurance. I often ask myself, "What would America be today if, two hundred years ago, our founding fathers and early settlers had been driven solely by the desire for instant gratification?"

Mrs. Chen's Miscalculation

Mrs. Chen was Japanese. During World War II, she married a young Taiwanese physician who was studying in Japan. She accompanied her husband to Taiwan. As the Japanese were not regarded as benevolent rulers by some Taiwanese subjects, she was not well received by Mr. Chen's family.

A couple of years later, she had a child, who unfortunately (by her cultural standards) was a girl. After the delivery, she was told she could not have another child. Mrs. Chen was an intelligent and practical woman. Long-term planning was the pride of the Japanese and their trademark. Mrs. Chen definitely had inherited this Japanese characteristic. She thought to herself that in order to secure her position in this family she must have a son, for only a son could take care of her in her old age. While she was raising her daughter, in her heart she was planning how she could gain a son. She talked over her concerns with some close Japanese women friends nearby. One of the women in the group was pregnant and already had four sons, who were becoming financial burdens on the family. An agreement was reached. A son was born, and Mrs. Chen adopted him. She had found the solution to her fear.

Forty-five years later, times have changed. Mrs. Chen's daughter turned out to be an extremely capable young physician and inherited her father's medical practice. Mrs. Chen is now living with her daughter and son-in-law and has done so for the past twenty years, since her husband's death. Her adopted son, who originally was supposed to be the solution to her fear, instead turned out to be the source of her fear and anxieties. He failed in school and became a compulsive gambler. He went through a great deal of the family fortune and borrowed money from unsuspecting family friends and relatives.

TRIAL AND ERROR

To discover the right action at any given moment in your life is not an easy task. Even the best of people do not always know their Dharma in accordance with destiny. Often we discover our Dharma through trial and error.

St. Francis of Assisi, in his younger years, had a strong desire to be a martyr, so he traveled to Morocco, a Moslem nation that strongly opposed Christianity and killed many of its followers. Convinced that he would be killed, St. Francis instructed his followers to continue his teaching and live austere lives. After he undertook the long and difficult journey, he could not even get himself arrested. Although disappointed, he was wise enough to realize that a silent power was calling him to a different path. Obviously, the Dharma of St. Francis was not to get himself needlessly killed, but rather to fulfill his destiny as a great teacher and spiritual aspirant.

As we pursue a better understanding of our Dharma through trial and error, we begin to fine-tune ourselves to recognize the silent voice of the universal will.

CONCLUSION

Dharma, the natural law that guides the rightness of our actions, is the foundation of Thick Face, Black Heart. By pursuing Dharma, our life will unfold naturally and thus produce the proper fruit at each given stage of our life. By living under the grace and guidance of Dharma, life itself becomes the eternal wish-fulfilling tree.

SUMMARY OF KEY POINTS

- Dharma is the understanding of proper actions in any given circumstance. It means "to act in accordance with one's duty."

- Dharma is a natural law that guides us to recognize at any given moment the role each one of us is playing in life. Being true to the duty of that particular role at any time and the very act of accepting and performing that action to the highest of our ability—that is following Dharma. That act will become our protector and liberator.

- Dharma is the foundation of Thick Face, Black Heart. Thick Face, Black Heart practitioners are vigorous in pursuing the rightness of their actions. They ask themselves in each and every situation, "What is my Dharma at this moment?"

- The grace of Dharma works in subtle and mysterious ways throughout our lives.

- Where there is Dharma, there is victory.

- Whatever your occupation, you will do well if you can properly identify your Dharma for that job. A chair, to be useful, must understand its Dharma and be willing to let people sit on it. A pencil is only useful when it carries out the Dharma of a pencil. If the chair refuses to let people sit on it or the pencil refuses to perform its writing function, they are useless.

• For a truly spiritual individual, the path of spirituality is like walking on a razor's edge; it is a diligent pursuit of one's perfection. However, for others, the pursuit of spirituality is merely a vague notion; it actually is a pretext, an excuse to practice inertia and avoidance of life's challenges.

• Nature's law, unlike man's, is that you must choose before you act. After an action is delivered, absolute consequences follow.

*The lotus
offers its beauty to the heaven,
the grass
its service to the earth.*

—RABINDRANATH TAGORE

4

Dharma and Destiny

M any teachers preach that you must do what you love, then you will be very good at your job. That is only part of the story. Most people have not reached a clear state of realizing exactly what they love to do and what they are good at. These people need to go through a period of discovery. The familiar question, "What do you want to do when you grow up?" is not an easy one to answer, even for adults of any age.

A DESTINY WAITS TO UNFOLD

If you feel you are stuck in your work right now, whatever it is, keep on doing it with dedication and devotion. You were not placed in that position entirely by accident. There are lessons there for you to learn. Your total commitment to your present work and the experience you accumulate can serve as a springboard for the unfolding of your greater destiny.

Take me, for example. I had been a consultant for U.S. companies and individuals who were doing or wished to do business with Asians. I liked my work but always felt there was something missing. Yet I performed my work faithfully. Only by doing so was I able to discover what was missing in my work: the satisfaction I could gain from my ability to reach large numbers of people and inspire their thinking.

By continuing to perform my work, and through my experience of doing business with Asians, I realized that there was a need for Americans, in their business dealings, to understand the Asian mind in depth. It was then I saw that the way to reach and inspire large numbers of people would be through writing a book about this very issue. Accordingly, I wrote about the Asian mind-set in business dealings with Westerners.

The success of the book led to great personal satisfaction. I went on to write more books, expanding the topic. Years later, I realized I did not have to write only about Asian business strategies. There was an abundance of rich wisdom from the Orient that I could communicate to Western readers. It was due to this realization that you are now reading *Thick Face, Black Heart*.

The most amazing thing about this is that I had totally forgotten that I had always been passionate about writing. I had written many short stories when I was in seventh grade, many of which appeared in student publications. By eighth grade, I felt ready to write a long Chinese novel. I spent every moment I could writing and finished the novel in one semester. I have no idea what was taught during that time. My grades suffered severely as a result of my obsession, but I didn't care. My reality existed only in the characters I created for my book. The rest of the world seemed to be covered by a haze of unreality.

When I finished, having no idea how to get a novel published, I sent my only manuscript to the top newspaper editor in Taiwan. The editor returned my manuscript with a very kind letter. I felt so embarrassed at having been rejected that I threw it into the school trash dump and never wrote again. Finally, twenty-five years later, I am back to writing again. The circle has come full course.

By simply being aware that there is a Divine plan for your life that waits to unfold in the course of life itself, you will begin to be consciously in tune with every incident that comes into your professional and personal life. Treat each incident with the eye of a good detective and try to unveil the mystery of your fate. This is the first and the most essential Dharma in discovering your destiny and your life path.

OCCUPATION IN DHARMA

The most frequently asked question is, How can I find out what kind of occupation is best suited for me? To begin to answer it, examine the following list:

1. While performing your present duties, utilize Thick Face, Black Heart to seek in your mind and in your soul the vocation that will satisfy you both spiritually and materially. The key here is "while performing your present duties," because most of us do not have the luxury to quit our work and go out searching for ourselves for an indefinite period. Furthermore, your very station in life is often the best place to provide answers to your unanswered questions.

2. Give everything you've got to the job that you are doing. By doing so you will feel good about yourself. Maybe your job is unimportant, but your effort and dedication will

uplift you and give you greater daily satisfaction. In turn, that satisfaction will work as your anchor for greater accomplishments.

3. By diligently performing your duty, you may shorten the time it will take to learn whatever lessons await you from working in that position. Life may then more quickly reveal your next stage of progress. This could be a promotion to a position that is more suited to the grand design of your life's objectives. Or perhaps you will perform your job so well that you become a threat to your immediate superior, and get fired. If the latter happens, then you know for sure the universe is saying, "You have stayed too long on this job, and something better awaits you now." You may gain so much self-esteem and self-confidence that you see you have no need of that job, and you will quickly take a better one. A better offer might come to you out of nowhere. In any case, the result is that you will create movement in your life that will lead you to the next level.

4. Do not get discouraged. Know that everything you ever learn from life is not wasted, even simple tasks such as learning how to index or file documents. One day when you discover your intended occupation, you will realize why you were put into those meaningless jobs. There is a reason for everything, even if it is not clear at the time.

5. Follow the above Dharma. Life cannot withhold from you what is rightfully yours.

6. Patience is the greatest virtue. Give life time.

DHARMA OF ACCEPTANCE
AND SURRENDER

The opportunity for victory is provided by the enemy.

—*SUN TZU'S* ART OF WAR

Once a good commander has fully utilized all his facilities to win the battle, then he awaits the opportunity for victory to be provided by his enemy.

In life's battle, once you have done everything within your power to realize your life's vision, all that remains to be done is graciously to accept the outcome and proceed.

A good friend of mine has often said, "I'd rather be lucky than smart." However, luck is not something you can always depend upon; it is smart to understand the Dharma of acceptance and benefit from it.

I learned this through firsthand experience. All my life I have been a champion of self-effort. Sometimes my self-effort paid off and other times the result was meager, but nothing has affected me so fundamentally as the experience of a recent event.

When I was writing my last book, I had done everything right. I worked overtime to get my finished work to the publisher on time. I had successfully obtained an endorsement from the Texas oilman, T. Boone Pickens, Jr., in addition to one from an editor of *USA Today*. The book was scheduled to be published on February 15, 1991. Then came Desert Storm in January. All the media's attention turned toward the war, and my book missed its opportunity for its grand entrance. Nevertheless, I learned an invaluable lesson. If I had not pushed myself and my editor to the limit in order to get the work done, if I had been late in turning in my manuscript, things might have worked out better.

There are wise words from the Chinese tradition, "Human

beings' efforts to mold the outcome of a given situation are nothing compared to what Heaven can do." These are no longer just words. Because of the book incident, they have become ingrained in my soul. When things don't turn out as expected, it may be a blessing in disguise. Now, after I have done my best, I relax and watch to see the outcome. Deep down at an unseen level, I know I will never be the same again. To others, I may not look any different, but I know I have gained a unique insight into the Dharma of acceptance and surrender.

Shortly after this realization, I attended a convention. I was scheduled at one in the afternoon as the opening speaker. However, when I got there, I discovered that the convention was in total disarray. While I was standing in the hallway for over forty-five minutes, waiting for the convention staff to clear up the confusion, a distinguished gentleman passed by me. I recognized him as the president of a large national retail outlet. I had recently been attempting to convince that particular company's buyer to purchase a new patented invention that my partner and I had developed. The buyer had been interested but noncommittal. The delay created by the poorly organized convention caused me to be standing in the hallway that led to my meeting with the chief decision maker of that company. That incident ultimately resulted in a very financially rewarding situation.

Learn the Dharma of acceptance and surrender because you never know what awaits you in its intricate and mysterious weavings.

PREDESTINY AND SELF-EFFORT

I explained to two people that I was writing a book entitled *Thick Face, Black Heart*. On these two separate occasions, immediately following my communications, both asked me, "Do you think life is predestined or the result of self-effort?" Initially, I did not think the question related to the topic of Thick Face, Black Heart. However, as it seemed that other people thought it should be part of the book, I have decided to include it.

Nature equips a bee with everything it needs to fulfill its intended destiny. In the same way, our Maker has provided us with everything we need to achieve our highest potential. It was no accident that you were born into your family, received a certain education, and were confronted with certain unique experiences in life. All these are part of the training necessary to prepare a person for a successful journey through life.

Let us take a look at two prime ministers of Great Britain, John Major and Margaret Thatcher. John Major did not fin ish high school, and Margaret Thatcher was a grocer's daughter. But these apparent disadvantages became important elements that molded their character and distinguished them from the traditional aristocratic politicians. Their humble backgrounds, rather than being a disadvantage, actually contributed to the success of their political popularity.

During my first ten years in the United States, I was caught between two cultures. I was no longer Chinese, but neither was I an American. I was like a fish out of water. As time progressed, I began to see that my knowledge and experience of both East and West had become a great asset rather than a liability. Every incident in life, big or small, joyful or painful, occurs not by accident. Our lives are carefully guided by unseen forces that govern and control every aspect of the universe. These mysterious workings are designed to facilitate our personal growth and fulfillment.

Each one of us is born into a certain environment in order to fulfill our intended destiny. It is possible that self-effort which incorporates human will, desire, and ability, is part of predestination. However, this predestiny cannot unfold on its own accord. Even if you know your destiny, it is only as good as the effort you make to bring it to reality. Therefore, pre-destiny and self-effort become two wheels of the same cart. Believe it or not, even in ancient China, there was a phrase, "Heaven helps those who help themselves."

There is a story of two sons who were born on the same day. One was born into a rich family, the other into poverty. Both mothers took their sons to the same fortune-teller in town. The fortune-teller told the rich lady that her son would be exalted and would assist the emperor of China. The poor lady was told that her son would be a beggar.

Because the rich lady thought her son was going to be important when he grew up, she spoiled him. This resulted in his wasting his life away, along with his family's wealth. In the end, his family's own residence was repossessed by the debtor, and they were forced out of their home and had to live on the street. On the other hand, the poor lady, terrified by the prophecy, diligently educated her son in an effort to assist him to avoid his ill-fated destiny. The son studied relentless-ly and excelled through the ancient examination system. He was consequently exalted and assisted the emperor of China.

However, while self-effort is vitally important, some of the undeniable evidence of my own life leaves me unable to totally discount the inexplicable mystery within the concept of predestiny or the existence of fate.

Years ago, I took an interest in studying Chinese antique jade artifacts. My teacher is also a renowned Chinese Tao scholar and well versed in the *I Ching*. He did a calculation of my past and future, recounting details that I found very coincidental. My personal chart indicated that I was born into a royal family who lost favor with the new ruler of the land and were sent into exile. These ancient texts were written thousands of years ago. Many concepts, such as royalty and the ruler of the land, have become outdated. However we still can find an equivalent of those terms in today's world. My family in the early twentieth century were the equivalent of royalty, and the Communists were the equivalent of the new ruler of the land. My family was exiled to Taiwan. Furthermore, my chart indicated that my younger brother would have some of his limbs damaged, and, as a consequence, his activities would be restricted. My younger brother in fact contracted polio when he was ten months old.

Although the knowledge of predestination may be an intriguing subject, it has very little use to us without our self-effort, especially as most of the sources that provide the information concerning predestination are questionable and often unreliable. Therefore, self-effort is the only thing that we can count on in our day-to-day lives.

THE DHARMA OF SELF-EFFORT

The following are important factors to the Dharma of self effort:

1. Quest for harmony: self-effort does not mean blind effort. The Dharma of self-effort also includes striving to know when to exercise the discrimination of acceptance and surrender to a disappointing outcome. However, this does not mean giving up, but rather finding harmony within oneself in order to regather the necessary strength and move on to the next level of life.

2. Tenacious determination: the American cartoonist and creator of "Pogo," Walt Kelly, often said, "We have seen the enemy, and he is us." In the battle of life, you are the enemy, and you are the warrior. In the battle of life, as long as you

are fighting, you are winning. Each day, if you fail a hundred times but win once, that single win will strengthen you and provide you the strength for the next win. Never let go of your fight.

Our Almighty Creator could have fashioned a more gentle, harmonious living environment, yet the world we ended up with obviously delights his heart. God seems to be content with his wholly imperfect world. As I often have said, God is a low achiever. Look what fun He has watching us, as we draw upon all our faculties in an effort to persevere and overcome the obstacles within and around us.

3. There is no quitting: life is a school. This school does not give out passing grades, but demands a perfect A from each student on every subject. You can never quit this school, and this school has no time limit for graduation. You will not graduate until you get it "right." If you are a Christian, your schooling might end when you draw your last breath. If you are Hindu or Buddhist, then you will never graduate until you realize your full Divinity, and that might take millions of incarnations. God is not democratic. He demands of His children the best they can be. He demands that they be like Him, and the cost for failing the courses is your liveliness and happiness. However, as long as you are fighting the battle tenaciously and courageously, the magical, unseen hand of the Divine is there to aid. This is not merely rhetoric, but a common experience that many people have found to be true.

4. All good things come to those who strive with patience: our sense of self-limitation did not form overnight. Thus, we require patience to readjust our course. A good phrase from the ancient Chinese elucidates this point: "Dripping water, in time, will cut a hole through the stone." When we were infants, like bees, we were in tune with our natural

instincts—we heard only the pure voice of our Divine Maker. As we learned the way of men, we adopted their "guidance" and tuned out the voice of our Maker. Whenever we are willing to listen to the criticism of others, there is never a shortage of volunteers.

If you have self-determination and self-effort, no one can keep you from manifesting your true destiny. The mystery of a towering fruit tree lies dormant within a tiny seed.

BE TRUE TO YOUR LIFE, TRUE TO YOUR DESIRES

Some people are not aware of the importance of searching for and discovering their proper and true role in life. A Thick Face, Black Heart practitioner knows the magnitude of this challenge. It is vital to discover what is right for you; and, to this end, in order to be able to put your plans into action, you must follow through with your plans and accept and endure whatever consequences occur. Furthermore, know when to make appropriate adjustments and have the courage to do so as each level of life unfolds and reveals itself.

Nita's Grief

Nita is a forty-one-year-old professional single woman working in insurance. Recently she told me about an experience of self-discovery. She had been born into a first-generation Japanese-American family. Her father, with his traditional Japanese attitudes about life, had placed much more importance on his two sons than his daughter. As a result of this, she had developed an unnaturally strong desire to please her father. Consequently, she unconsciously made a decision to gain her father's acceptance by doing highly respected work that was traditionally performed only by Japanese men.

She attended law school. She had no love for law; her real desire was to be a housewife and to have her husband take care of her while she did flower arranging and made ceramics. But she believed that becoming a lawyer was something that would please her father very much. She finished her three years in law school. She describes those years as being hell-like—the hardest thing she had ever done. After that, it took another year and a half, and three attempts, before she finally passed the bar exam. She said, "The whole thing almost killed me."

After all this, she found that she absolutely could not stand law. When she was being interviewed for her first legal position, the law firm gave her a personality analysis to help determine the field for which she was best suited. The test results showed that, for her, being a lawyer was about the worst possible choice she could have made. So she chose another "acceptable" Japanese male profession, this time in the world of insurance. This also served the purpose of pleasing her father, not herself. She said, "I spent twenty years of my life trying to please my father." When she finally began to come to terms with this, she cried uncontrollably. She deeply regretted that she had never lived with a man, had never been married, and consequently never had the opportunity to be a housewife.

Walking on a Razor's Edge

On the other hand, some spiritually minded people feel that they have no interest in participating in modern worldly affairs. They feel that their place is in the holy shrines and that making a living is beneath them. For a truly spiritual individual, the path of spirituality is like walking on a razor's edge; it is a diligent pursuit of one's perfection. However, for some others, the pursuit of spirituality is merely a vague notion; it actually is a pretext, an excuse to practice inertia and avoidance of life's challenges. It is impossible to attain true spiritual perfection if you have avoided discovering the path by which you can contribute to society as an individual.

GOD HAS SPOKEN, BUT YOU WEREN'T LISTENING

*Mankind is notoriously too dense to read the signs
that God sends them from time to time.
We require drums to be beaten into our ears,
before we would wake from our trance and
hear the warning....*

—*Mahatma Gandhi*

Individuals often come to consult with me about getting into the Asian business arena. Some of them are in their forties, with well-established career paths. They had begun their career some twenty years ago, guided by their elders' advice, in what was then considered to be an acceptable profession and one that would provide social status and financial security. All those years, they had never allowed themselves to discover their true destiny. In coming to me, these people were often simply looking for a way out of their present jobs.

Their situation felt more like prison than a promising career, and they thought that a drastic change such as moving into the Asian business world was probably the answer.

All these people had one thing in common: they didn't feel the work they were doing was meaningful. Some people say, "If God himself would just speak to me, let me know what he really wants me to do, I would be delighted to do that, no matter how meaningless and humble the work."

In fact, God has spoken many times, but they weren't listening. Sometimes people feel, no matter what work they do, that it could not be what God intended for them. They blame the work. The missing piece here is not what is wrong with the work they are doing, but rather understanding the work they are performing right now in the context of the bigger picture of their destiny.

AN EMPLOYEE'S DHARMA

An employee's Dharma is simple—support the employer wholeheartedly. Your employer may not be perfect, smart, or worthy of your service, but by your act of working at your particular company, you have entered into an unwritten contract of support.

I am a true believer that if you don't like the company you work for, quit your job. But if you choose to stay and draw a payroll check from that company, ethically, you don't have the freedom to sabotage the company's morale through your constant expressions of dissatisfaction. You are duty-bound to present any constructive suggestions that occur to you. If they are rejected and you feel that you no longer can serve the company without certain changes being made, then you have the choice to exercise your courage to resign your job.

If you wish to remain, then support the company and its management. The choice must always be yours.

I watched a client of mine fire one of his engineers, Hank. Hank is at the top of his field in terms of expertise and competence. However, he continually complained about the office and the owner. He even went so far as to make outrageous criticisms of the owner in front of customers. I personally witnessed the following incident.

I was at a New Year's party. The party host was the president of my client's customer's company. Hank attended the party as the representative of my client, his employer. Soon after the party began, Hank started his angry attack on his employer with great passion. This continued for three hours. Everyone at the party was embarrassed by his behavior, except Hank. The more he talked, the more emotional he became. After three hours of verbal assault, our hostess was very concerned that her husband might jeopardize his professional position by doing business with such a questionable company.

Hank's behavior was caused by his lack of inner harmony. Due to his unceasing criticism from within, he was in turn abusive to others. The one who finds fault in others is always first unconsciously finding fault in himself.

Hank's mind was out of control—like an undisciplined dog on a leash. Instead of following the owner, it leads the owner in all directions, yet it has no idea where it is going. It finally makes a victim of its owner. Hank had been fired by his previous employer for similar conduct.

Hank's behavior may be extreme, but by no means is he an isolated case. I have known so many companies in which the employees' favorite pastime is to gather together and criticize the company's management team. In such a situation, the employees victimize themselves as well as the company.

DHARMA OF SUPPORT

A Thick Face, Black Heart practitioner understands that the Dharma of success includes support. It is essential, if you wish to succeed in life, to find someone who is willing to support you unconditionally in fulfilling your dreams, or else realize that you and your mind must form your own support troops. Without support in the tough competitive world of survival, the task of achieving extraordinary success will be inordinately difficult. This is also true for business. Without the support of their employees, it would be difficult for businesses to compete in today's fierce market.

SUMMARY OF KEY POINTS

- According to your life, your duties have been prescribed for you; follow them and your desires will be naturally fulfilled.

- Many teachers preach that you must do what you love, then you will be very good at your job. This is only part of the story. Most people have not reached a clear state of realizing exactly what they love to do and what they are good at. These people need to go through a period of discovery.

- By simply being aware that there is a Divine plan for your life that waits to unfold in the course of life itself, you will begin to be consciously in tune with every incident that comes into your professional and personal life. Treat each incident with the eye of a good detective and try to unveil the mystery of your fate.

- It is impossible to attain true spiritual perfection if you have avoided discovering the path by which you can contribute to society as an individual.

- Human beings' efforts to mold the outcome of given situations is nothing compared to what Heaven can do. When things don't turn out as expected, it might be a blessing in disguise. Understand the wisdom of the Dharma of acceptance and surrender.

- It is possible that self-effort, which incorporates human will, desire, and ability, is part of predestination, and this predestiny cannot unfold of its own accord. Therefore, predestiny and self-effort become two wheels of the same cart.

- Be true to your life, true to your desires

- Some people say, "If God himself would just speak to me and let me know what He really wants me to do, I would be delighted to do that, no matter how meaningless and humble the work." In fact, God has spoken many times, but they weren't listening.

- Sometimes people feel that whatever the work they are doing, it could not be what God intended for them. They blame the work. The missing piece here is not what is wrong with the work they are doing, but rather understanding the work they are performing right now in the context of the bigger picture of their destiny.

- The Dharma of an employee is to support the employer wholeheartedly. If you cannot support the company you work for, quit your job. You don't have the freedom to sabotage the company's morale and reputation through your constant expression of dissatisfaction.

- By living under the grace and guidance of Dharma, life itself becomes the eternal wish-fulfilling tree.

All effort was sacred to Him.
Between the most negative, foolish,
and ignorant of people,
and the most positive, confident, self-assured,
there lies a space so small that our Maker
regards it with a smile.

—CHIN-NING CHU,
inspired by ELIZABETH WATERHOUSE

5

Winning through Negative Thinking

Thick Face, Black Heart practitioners do not accept the common rules of success. They need no assurance of their validity from others. They investigate uncharted ideas by observing the natural workings of the world.

In this chapter, you might find inconsistencies with other chapters. Thick Face, Black Heart reveals the workings of the universe the way it is and seeks no consistency, since inconsistency is an important element of the real world.

YOU CAN SUCCEED THE WAY YOU ARE

In past decades, the idea that we need to change our negative attitudes to positive ones before we can succeed has been pounded into us. If you learn only one thing from reading this book, it should be that you can succeed the way you are.

For once, those who have been annoyed by the concept of superficial positive thinking have a method they can live by and believe in.

A Death Sentence Awaits

If you do not consider yourself the most positive person you have ever known, don't worry. The secret is that most of the perky people lie about how positive they are. Even the best motivational teachers, speakers, or authors have their moments of private grief. No one in the world is purely positive or absolutely negative. However, those whose livelihood depends upon promoting the concept of positive thinking have been able to convince the rest of the world that if you are not absolutely positive about life at all times and under any circumstances, then you are an inferior being. The pressure of not being like "everyone else," so optimistic and cheerful, is worse than actually experiencing negativity. We all thought, somehow, that something must have been terribly wrong with us, making us unable to embrace positivity. All these ideas lead to the final logical conclusion: "I am just no good and a born loser."

In truth, each one of us since the moment of our birth has been given a death sentence—only the date is unknown. However, the fact of death is always present in the deepest part of our subconscious mind. Between the time of birth and the time of death, we do the best we know how. If you and I have acted to the best of our abilities, it will more than fulfill the bargain we made with our Creator at the moment of birth.

Success Has No Rules

Success comes in every shape and profile. Countless good books have been published on this subject. All this information can contribute to our effort toward success, but the truth remains—success has no rules. Success comes to some of the most negative people as well as the most positive ones. Success comes to those who try hard and even to those who make no visible effort. What promoters of positive thinking theories fail to realize is that success does not discriminate; it can come to those who project either negative or positive attitudes.

I am not deprecating the validity of positive thinking. However, if you are just not a naturally positive thinker, no matter how you try, then we have to take a moment to examine the negativity and find evidence that you can be successful even though you are negative by nature. For example, Mark Twain was labeled a pessimist and a sarcastic skeptic, and his stories were often about "the damned human race," yet these unique qualities made Mark Twain, Mark Twain. His negativity contributed to his literary genius.

Let us further examine some popular personalities with whom we are all familiar. Elizabeth Taylor, for example, is always in the news. Most of her news is inspired by her negative nature: her weight, her drinking, her drug addiction, her marriages and divorces. Furthermore, she is regarded by one of her ex-husbands as a champion when it comes to her ability to create her own sicknesses. Despite all of these "negative" qualities, she has enjoyed a life of unsurpassed success.

Spencer Tracy, according to Katharine Hepburn, was an extremely moody, guilt-driven individual. He thought the world would have been better if he hadn't been born. Despite his low "self-esteem," he was, and still is, a great screen presence.

Humphrey Bogart is one of the greatest film stars who ever lived. His personality was not generally considered "lighthearted and cheerful." He could never be like Ronald Reagan. Humphrey Bogart was successful because of his unique personality. People loved him for what he was.

Marilyn Monroe and Ernest Hemingway were considered emotional, unstable, highly erratic, classic cases of manic depression. Both ended their lives by their own hands; however, their "negativities" became essential elements in success during their lifetimes. These "negativities" were made up of who they were and didn't prevent them from manifesting career success beyond their dreams.

I am not an advocate of copying their suicidal personalities, but I use these examples to exaggerate a point. Your negativities will not stand in the way of success in your worldly pursuits. They are part of you. Learn to love them, accept them, and use them.

A friend of mine, a successful television sitcom star, was at the height of his career when I first met him in the late 1970s. His show was often rated No. 1 during the seven years it ran. Two years ago another show was created around him, and that show was also a hit. The character he portrayed in the story is very much like himself, a rather negative, pessimistic, but lovable fellow. While receiving a six-figure salary per episode, he still worried to death about whether or not he could make his mortgage payment. In fact, he worries from one television hit to another.

If You Have Chicken Manure, Sell Fertilizer

If you have chicken manure, you would do well to sell fertilizer. Even chicken manure has its value. As the Tibetans say, "If you are lying on the ground, you must use the ground to raise yourself." If you are negative, use those negativities to succeed.

Chris is a brilliant man. The main problem with his career development, however, is that he is too smart for his own good. Because he is a quick learner with an inquiring mind, he has learned just about everything he ever wanted to know during his forty years of life. During his college years, he was eighty credits over the graduation requirements, yet he received no degree. He was interested in the pursuit of knowledge, not in obtaining a diploma. Later, he found this hurt him in his search for employment.

Chris has tremendous ability to master knowledge, yet this is his biggest curse as well as his biggest blessing. He knows a little of everything. In short, to the general public, Chris appears to be a jack-of-all-trades and master of none.

Chris once told me he was tired of getting nowhere in his career. He knew so much, yet he could not put all he knew and had done on his résumé. If he did, it would make him look ridiculous. What he did choose to put on his résumé was not very impressive compared to the experience of other people who had led more focused lives.

Chris began to hate his life and his ability to quickly pick up knowledge, but I encouraged him to utilize his natural ability as a quick and deep learner to advance himself. The only minor adjustment he needed was 'to add a little practicality and focus in his life. Chris enrolled in a university MBA program, which accepted him and gave him credit for his work experiences. Chris finished the program effortlessly in his spare time while keeping his job. After he complet-

ed the program, his company promoted him to the position he
had always dreamed about.

LET NEGATIVITIES BE

We are all programmed to believe that certain behavior
and tendencies are considered positive, and others negative.
We commonly accept that a successful person is a positive
person, and if you are not positive, you are doomed to fail
unless you can change. Therefore, we spend enormous energy attempting to change, rather than focusing on being successful.

If you consider yourself a negative individual and your
inner voice often tells you that you "can't do it," don't fight
back. Yield to your voice by ignoring it. Don't focus your
energy in an attempt to change your opinion of yourself. By
ignoring your voice, you are able to free yourself from the
trap that says, "change comes before success."

You can be as negative as you want to be, moping and
cursing all the way, while doing what you are supposed to in
the course of achieving success. Bette Midler, a very popular
singer, film star, and comedienne, mentioned once during an
interview that her husband thought she was the most
pessimistic person he had ever known. Then she burst out
laughing. Obviously her pessimistic outlook didn't bother her.
She was able to talk about it in public and laugh openly.

The Power of Hating Life

If you think your life is a drag and you hate it, I will not attempt to talk you out of your opinion. However, I think you can benefit much more if you change the object of your hatred. Instead of hating life, hate God.

That was not a typo—you read correctly. Hate God. Ironically, so many people love God but hate everybody else. The man who hates his fellow man and loves only God is no lover of God.

If hatred exists within you, then the best thing you can do is rechannel the hate from man to God, since the essence of God is love. Other people's attitudes toward Him are inconsequential. Unlike humans, God cares not whether you hate Him or love Him. He is like a fire, which you may love or hate, but as long as you come close to fire, it will warm you. The emotions of hate and love come from the same source. Hate is the other side of love, and only due to love can hate exist. In the Bible, Revelation 3:16 says, "So then because thou art lukewarm and neither cold nor hot, I will spew thee out of my mouth." The only time God will ignore you and silently wait for you is when you totally ignore Him.

As long as you focus your attention toward God, He will purify you, support you, and rehabilitate you. You may then see your hatred transformed into divine love.

Your Negativity Does Not Have As Much Power As Your Imagination Thinks It Has

We all have been told at one time or another how powerful our thoughts are. This concept has exacerbated our fear of our uncontrolled, negative thoughts. What would happen if all our negative thoughts came true? However, the power of thinking is not that simple. You have no power to manifest your every thought. Not yet. I am telling you that your negativity does not have as much power as your imagination believes it to have.

Every time a commercial jet takes off with hundreds of passengers aboard, a large percentage of the passengers entertain the possibility of an airplane crash. If your power of negative thinking is as powerful as you have imagined, with the collective negative power among the passengers, we might never have a successful landing. Don't fear your negative thoughts. Devote yourself to your craft with tenacity and determination, and you will be much closer to success than by struggling to change yourself first.

The Standards of Negativity Are Not Carved in Stone

The standards of judging negativity are artificial human manipulations and are not carved in stone. The standards often change according to our time and culture. What was considered positive in a given era or place may be considered negative in another. For example, the aggressive, high-tone, pushy, go-getting manner is considered a great attribute in the American business world. However, when applied in certain parts of Asia, it is considered repulsive.

Being able to look directly into your counterpart's eyes is considered a very positive personal attribute in America. Yet in certain parts of Asia, it is considered offensive.

REALISM IS A POSITIVE ATTRIBUTE

Negativities do not have to be liabilities. I resent the term "negativity." It sounds so negative! Often, the so-called "negative" people are the most realistic. On the other hand, being overtly optimistic sometimes can be a liability in the real world. A CEO cannot afford the luxury of excessive optimism, because it will lead him to failure—just as an overly optimistic general who becomes careless will underestimate his battlefield foe and lead his troops to their demise. The results can be costly.

Similarly, the coach and the quarterback shouldn't adopt the cheerleader's ardent enthusiasm. If the coach and the quarterback fail to realistically size up the opposing team's strengths, their positive thinking alone will not assure them victory.

A realistic person tends to forecast potential problems and anticipate difficulties realistically. The Texas oil entrepreneur, T. Boone Pickens, Jr., explains that the shortcoming of most geologists is that they are too optimistic. As an independent oilman without the backing of huge conglomerates, he has had to be much more pragmatic about his drilling ventures.

When I was younger, I used to be obsessed with optimism. I could not tolerate any thought of a possible ill outcome. If anyone even suggested that I should weigh the worst-case scenarios with the best-case scenarios, I was offended. The truth is, I was too scared to examine "real life." Instead, I lived in the world of "make-believe."

It is good to have a positive attitude because it allows you to see everything as within your reach. The possibility of ill fate or bad luck becomes the sole property of those people who think negatively.

Now, I realize that being realistic is not being negative. It is positive. It is not because of negativity that a cruise ship captain educates his passengers on how to behave in an emergency. He doesn't plan on having the ship sink. He is merely realistic and prepared.

Gilbert, a vice president in charge of commercial loans at a major bank, told me he preferred working with the realistic borrower as opposed to the overly enthusiastic one. The realistic borrower understands the potential difficulties and is prepared to ride the waves of challenge, while an overly enthusiastic borrower tends to underestimate the actualities of starting or expanding a business.

USE NEGATIVITIES AS SPRINGBOARDS TO SUCCESS

If you are inclined to be jealous and envious of the success of others, do not try to eliminate these thoughts of negativity; rather, use them to fuel your life's engine. When you become jealous and envious of others' accomplishments, you must search within yourself to learn how you can surpass them and let them become jealous of you instead. Do not waste your energy attempting to overcome your jealousy.

If you are angry at others for the injustices they have done to you, the greatest revenge is to light your own fire of rage and rise above them to the top. The greatest revenge is to live well, prosper, and succeed.

If you are greedy, expand your greed. Be the best greedy person you know. Go beyond the greed for things. Trade the greed and desire of hoarding material items for that of hoarding success. Also, become greedy to know God, your Maker.

If you like to worry, then divert that energy from worry to action. Worry will not prevent destiny from unfolding. However, self-effort has the power to change destiny. Worry can be your motivational force for action. No matter what your shortcomings, learn to use them to enhance who you are.

Most people working in film or theater often are more willing to be honest and expose their personal "defects" than business people. Some of our greatest actors and actresses are uncomfortable being themselves. This very quality makes it easy for them to adapt to any character presented to them. While most people are obsessed with "finding themselves," these stars are uncomfortable doing so. Ironically, this same "defect" contributes to their professional success and financial prosperity.

Whatever your negativities are, contemplate them. Find how you can channel that energy and use it as a springboard for success.

Thriving on Others' Negativity

The only way to succeed is to make people hate you.

—JOSEF VON STERNBERG

"This is just another of your stupid dreams, just look at you... why can't you face who you really are?"

When others tell you that you can't do this, you can't do that, you're a lofty dreamer, a chronic loser, you feel hurt and angry. Use their negative energy plus the negativity that you feel for them to create an emotion explosive enough to support and realize your dreams. Again, success is the sweetest revenge.

Allow a Little Room to Fail

Most of us do much better with agreements that we make with others than with those we make with ourselves.

In the closing sentence of J. D. Salinger's novel *The Catcher in the Rye,* Holden says, "How do you know what you're going to do till you do it? The answer is, you don't."

If you are one of those perfect human beings who always knows what your agenda is and can always keep every resolution you make, more power to you. If you find you are having problems keeping those rules you made with yourself, such as "Starting tomorrow, I will lose weight" or "I am going to stop smoking tomorrow" or "I will never do that again," you are not alone.

Somehow, deep in ourselves we feel inadequate when we can't stick to our own resolutions. Ironically, we become the lawmaker, then the lawbreaker, then the judge and executioner. We are the source of our own misery.

Since you initiated the rules, you can also *un*initiate them or create others tomorrow. The evil is not so much in breaking the rules, but in the shame and guilt that make you judge yourself as "unworthy."

Thick Face, Black Heart practitioners accept and acknowledge truthfully their own inadequacies. They are free from guilt and shame. They will break their resolutions and create others at will. After all, failing in your resolutions and creating others is part of the game. While the intent is noble, the flesh is at times weak. Don't lose heart, give yourself a little room to fail, and empathize with others when they fail.

Moderate Versus Extreme Criticism

I have seen mediocre authors publishing best-sellers while brilliant, talented writers create no work at all. Randall is a graduate of English literature and is working as an assistant manager at a supermarket. He has great passion for literature and the talent to match it. When reading others' work, he is extremely critical and thinks their work isn't worth the paper it's written on. However, he will never write anything himself. If he does start a piece, he never finishes it. Halfway to completion he gives up because he finds it is just not good enough and doesn't deserve to be finished.

The real reason Randall doesn't finish his work is that he is so afraid that others will judge his work as harshly as he judges theirs. Moderate criticism is beneficial for maintaining high professional standards. However, when you overdo it to the point of paralyzing your own creativity, the self-criticism becomes detrimental. Use Thick Face to shield yourself from potential criticism and send your work into the world. You might be surprised at its reception.

MAKE FEWER AGREEMENTS

If you are the type of person who cannot keep your agreements with others, make a rule that you will not make an agreement simply because it is expected of you. Tell the truth to yourself about your deficiency. Then you will liberate yourself from the remorse of broken agreements and the damage they cause your personal and professional reputations.

A friend of mine always practices this. He never "volunteers" to agree to do anything because he may regret it or leave a promise unfulfilled. If he is cornered, he will consider everything carefully before he responds with a "yes." If you keep a few agreements that are vital, you will be known as a person who keeps his agreements and can be trusted.

THE POSITIVE ASPECT OF PROCRASTINATION

No human trait is absolutely bad or good, not even the greatest weakness of them all—procrastination. When it is applied properly, procrastination can be a great asset.

When we move too fast, we sometimes have to reverse the consequences of our previous actions just to arrive on neutral ground. Sometimes, by not taking action hastily, you can let your idea simmer and mature. Only act when you have clearly identified the proper course of action.

Recently, within a twenty-four-hour period, I received three or four phone messages from a client. He didn't call the second day. Somehow, intuitively, I didn't think I should call him back too soon. I waited another day. When I did speak with him, he told me it was a good thing that I hadn't called him back immediately or he would have given me a piece of his mind. He thought something had gone wrong at the time of his calls. Later, he discovered that his assumption was in error. If I had called him back the first day, he would have had to apologize later, and I would have had to listen to his rancor.

Sometimes problems do have a way of working themselves out. The more we try to fix them, the worse they get. That is the time to procrastinate a little and let time do its work.

THE VIRTUE OF INCONSISTENCIES

Only the mediocre are always at their best.

—*JEAN GIRAUDOUX*

Consistency is not always a virtue unless you are an accountant. Somehow, our world tends to consider consistency a positive trademark and inconsistency a negative one. In reality, consistency and inconsistency are equally valuable.

If you are one who thinks you are cursed by inconsistency, you have overlooked its virtues. In fact, not even God Himself is always consistent. He creates drought during the rainy seasons and floods during the dry seasons. Due to the power of his inconsistencies, we fear Him and offer our unceasing prayers to appease Him.

Just imagine what our world would be like if all the human beings on earth were always consistent. We would have the same music, the same paintings, the same architecture, the same fashions, the same movies, and the same books. There would be no poetry or romance. Inconsistency makes the world ever new. Furthermore, in business, your inconsistency will always keep your opponents on their toes. In marriage, inconsistency will keep your spouse fascinated and your marriage new.

In ancient Japan, the greatest honor for a warrior was to die on the battlefield. A fourteenth-century Japanese warrior was going to war to support the cause of the Emperor. He knew that the Emperor's cause for war was wrong and that the Emperor did not have the support of the people. He also knew that losing the war and suffering his own death were inevitable. Nevertheless, his loyalty compelled him to do his duty.

His thirteen-year-old son followed him to the battlefield, as the good son of a warrior should. But the warrior asked his son to leave and go back home. The son requested the honor to follow the ancient Samurai code and die with his father. The warrior had to choose between dishonoring the tradition of the Samurai code and causing the death of his only son — a waste of precious life for a lost and unjust cause.

The warrior told his son that he should live and grow up to watch the changes to come. This ancient warrior broke a sacred code by sparing his son's life and sending him home alone so he could grow up to celebrate life.

NEGATIVITY AND CREATIVITY

Certain personalities are like slow trains, always moving steadily. Others shoot out like a rocket, soar high, then die. The world needs both kinds.

Regular, stable people rarely have the capacity to achieve greatness. Unlike them, your negativities and manic depressive moods can be your greatest assets.

A high jumper must bend his knees and lower his body just before he makes that high leap. Like the high jumper, some people must have a period of inactivity before they can take the necessary leap into productivity. The bear and the snake hibernate before the season of activity resumes.

For some, the time of hibernating and resting is the essential process for generating highly creative energies. The important thing is to love your negativities and not judge them, and learn to use them to raise yourself up. Enjoy your nonproductivity; know that it is part of your productivity. When you are inspired, you will soar like a rocket and burn like a comet.

The famous American author Jack London once remarked, "I would rather be a superb meteor, every atom of me in magnificent glow, than a sleepy and permanent planet."

NEUROSIS AND INSECURITY

Today in our society, it is vital to exhibit your sense of self-confidence. It is a delight to watch people who are absolutely secure with themselves. However, if you are not among them, don't lose heart. The secret is to fake it until others are convinced that you are not faking.

I am going to reveal one of the greatest secrets: only fools and saints are totally and absolutely secure about themselves. The rest of the world is faking it to different degrees, and some are better fakers than others.

Only an absolute fool can be so ignorant of the way of the universe that he feels secure in his blissful ignorance. Within each one of us, we have this ever-present suspicion that we are much greater than our circumstances. The potential for who we are and what we could be is so vast that we have not begun to scratch the surface. We know we will not find security within us until we have touched all the Void with our mind and our soul. In the meantime, we are, to different degrees, faking our security.

NEGATIVITY IS NOT THE SOURCE OF YOUR PROBLEM

Often we blame our negativity as the cause of failure in our work. In fact, the source of our problem is not our negativities, but rather that we have chosen uninspiring tasks that bring forth our negativities.

Recently, I was with my partner doing a patent search for our new invention. As I was doing the work, I found that I was very negative toward the whole process of the search. I felt ashamed of my selfishness and unwillingness to help. I asked myself why I was behaving this way. Then I realized that it was not because I was negative and unwilling to do the work. I was willing to do the work, but I just didn't want to do *that* work. I couldn't stand being in that patent office doing repetitive, numerical, rule-following tasks, which I have always hated. My conclusion was that I am neither lazy nor selfish. When I perform work that is suited to my nature, the job will be effortless and even inspiring. I finally paid an attorney to do the search.

MAKE YOUR NEGATIVITY PAY FOR ITSELF

During a recent trip to Australia, I visited a petting zoo and fell madly in love with the Australian wombat. It's a slow-moving creature that looks like a large fur ball with two pairs of short legs. It has thick skin, dense fur, and a fat belly, and it spends most of the day eating and sleeping. It's a cuddly animal though, and I found it to be a lovable, pettable one that would roll on its back and allow you to scratch its fat stomach. The wombat would make a great pet, and I wondered how such a precious animal is able to defend itself from predators in the wild.

Upon my return to the United States, I did some research on the wombat. I discovered that the wombat doesn't know his own shortcomings, that nobody had told him he was supposed to be a "lean and mean fighting machine." Instead, he utilizes all of his "negative features" to defend himself. When a predator comes near, the wombat will crawl into his small cave. He will curl up like a fur ball and tighten up his bony, thick skin and thick fur back, so the predator is unable to sink its teeth into him. At the same time, when a predator's head is in the wombat's cave, attempting to eat him, the wombat will raise his large body and crush the predator's head against the top of the cave with his back.

Whatever your negativity is, make it pay for itself. If your negativity is that you love to sit and do nothing but read, find out how you can read all day and get paid for it; perhaps find a job at a publishing company or library, or be a book critic. If your negativity is a love of eating, find out how you can get a job centered around food. Maybe you can be a chef or write a food column. If your negativity is a love of watching movies, turn the world upside down and find out how you can make a living in the movie business. If you cannot find an occupation centered around your favorite "negativity," create a job that no one else has thought about.

During one of my radio interviews with the legendary baseball manager, George "Sparky" Anderson, he told me his shortcoming was that he knew baseball inside out, but he couldn't play it well. Because "Sparky" Anderson couldn't play the game well enough to be a valuable player to the team, he later became a legendary baseball manager and coach. Within your so-called negativities there is a hidden asset waiting to be unfolded. Your negativity will pay for itself if you let it. The mystery of living is hidden in every corner within the mystery of your nature. Contemplate the wisdom of the wombat.

THE GHOSTS OF NEGATIVITY

The Blind Justifications

There is nothing wrong with your negativities and shortcomings. We human beings are told by others that our negativities are our defeat. Thus we are blinded and cannot discover the possibilities existing within the realm of our "negativities."

The ghost of negativity is never your negativities. It is your convenient use of your "negativity" as an anchor to justify your failures. "God helps those..." If you give your negativities enough thought, you may discover that they, in fact, could be the strongest assets in your professional and personal development.

The Wickedness within the Judgment

When you start to label your feelings, emotions, and activities as being negative by others' standards, you are judging yourself according to others' standards. You are in trouble. The evil of all negativities is not within the negativity itself, but in the judgment of our negativities. These judgments come in the vicious form of guilt, shame, and self-blame.

In the United States, anyone who gets up at noon is generally considered a person who has a negative outlook on life. The truth is, a late riser is a late riser, nothing more. You might have to find an occupation that fits your natural sleeping rhythm. When you start to add another's judgment about what a lazy bum you are for being a late riser, in addition to your own judgment and feelings of guilt about your inability to get up early in the morning, suddenly you have a bundle of negativities that you need to overcome. Worse yet, you may come to the conclusion that you are simply a hopeless failure.

Salvador Dali, the great Spanish artist, worked for days without sleep, then he would sleep for days or even weeks. Sometimes he was productive, and other times he just hibernated and did nothing. Winston Churchill was also a night owl and often slept to the noon hour. Hugh Hefner, the founder of *Playboy* magazine, is famous for his nighttime work schedule.

The root of this evil and wickedness is not in the late rising itself, but rather within the judgment about the late rising. Protect yourself from others' judgment by shielding yourself with Thick Face. Protect yourself from your own criticism, blame, and shame with a Thick Face and a Black Heart, detached and indifferent.

POSITIVELY NEGATIVE

You have spent years obsessed with being positive and trying to overcome your negativities. If you had spent that energy focusing on manifesting your dreams instead of trying to be positive, you might be much further ahead.

Look at the great determination you've exhibited in being so negative for so long. Utilize this determination, which can easily be turned around to become a force that actually nurtures the seed of success.

Tap into the power of your determination and refocus your attention away from your negativity. Instead, focus on your dreams and never let go of the flame of hope.

Life is made up of the unrealistic and the irrational, and the Thick Face, Black Heart practitioner knows this well. Make your hopes and dreams your tugboat of life, pulling you along. The moment our Creator creates us, He makes sure we have unlimited supplies of regenerated, ever-new hopes.

Let your negativity be. Do your work, focus your energy on the flame of hope. Be a positively negative thinker.

SUMMARY OF KEY POINTS

- You can succeed the way you are.

- Success comes in every shape and profile. Success comes to some of the most negative people as well as the most positive ones. Success has more equal vision and less prejudice than the positive thinking theory promoted by some people.

- If you give your negativities enough thought, you may discover that they are in fact the strongest assets in your professional development.

- Don't attempt to change your opinion about yourself. By ignoring your inner voice of self-judgment, you are able to free yourself from the trap that says, "change comes before success."

- Your negativity does not have as much power as your imagination thinks it has.

- The standards of judging negativity are artificially manipulated by humans and are not carved in stone. The standards often change according to the times and culture. What was considered positive in a given time or space may be considered negative in another.

- It is not so bad to break the rules you made with yourself. Since you initiated the rules, you can also *un*initiate them or create others tomorrow.

- The evil is not in breaking the rules, but in the shame and guilt that make you judge yourself as unworthy.

- By making and keeping a few vital agreements, you will actually be known as a man who keeps his agreements and can be trusted.

- Nothing is absolutely bad or good, not even procrastination. When applied properly, procrastination can be a great asset.

- Consistency is not always a virtue unless you are an accountant.

- A high jumper needs to bend his knees and lower his body before he makes that high leap. Like the high jumper, some people need to bend low in order to jump high in the game of life.

- For some, the time of hibernating and resting is an essential process for generating highly creative energies.

- Often we blame our negativities as the cause of failure in our work. In fact, the source of our problem is not our negativities, but rather that we have chosen uninspiring tasks that bring forth our negativities.

- The important thing is to love your negativities, not to judge them, and to learn to use them to raise you up.

- The evil of all negativities is not in emotions and thoughts themselves, but in the judgments of these emotions and thoughts. Often judgments come in the vicious form of guilt, shame, and self-blame.

- Gather all of your negativities, without the intention to correct them and without judgment. While living and working with your negativities, know that these qualities are what make you unique. Be positively negative.

- Do not focus your attention on your negativities but on your dreams, and never let go the flame of hope. Your hope might be unrealistic and irrational, but keep on hoping. Make your hopes and dreams be your tugboat of life, pulling you along.

- Remember the wombat.

Weeping may endureth for a night,
but joy cometh in the morning.

—PSALMS 30

6

The Magical Power of Endurance

*True end is not in the reaching of the limit,
but in a completion which is limitless.*

— *RABINDRANATH TAGORE*

One morning, years ago, I woke up with an overwhelming feeling of aloneness overtaking my soul. I felt as if my spirit were covered by layers of dark clouds. I lived but made no difference to the world. I had given nothing significant to the Mother Earth; I took what the world allowed me to take. In the realm of thoughts, I had left no mark and claimed no victory. I stood alone in the pit of my soul.

I felt the world could do very well without me. I didn't see any hope, only despair. Then I picked up a book that I had purchased many years earlier and had never opened. The book is called *Nan Hua Jin* by Chuang Tzu. Chuang Tzu was a great teacher and philosopher who lived in China over 2,200 years ago. When I opened the book to the first chapter, entitled "Soaring," tears welled up from the depths of my being. In this short story by Chuang Tzu, the mystery of my state of mind at that moment was revealed.

SOARING—THE FABLE OF THE PUNG BIRD

"In the North Sea of China," the legend says, "there is a fish called Kun which is thousands of meters long. This great fish evolves into a bird called Pung. Pung also measures thousands of meters long. Swooping as he flies, his wings expand like the clouds covering the sky. Pung flies over the great sea southward to his destination: the Celestial Pool.

"The great Pung flies toward the South Sea, beating the water with his majestic wings for over three thousand kilometers, but first he spins the wind into a tornado that rises to a height of ninety thousand kilometers. It takes six months to reach such a height; only then is the Pung bird ready. Now, with the Pung's back against the pure blue sky and nothing blocking it, the Pung can set upon his course southward with no obstacles. How can one compare such magnitude with the morning mists, the dust, or insignificant creatures?

"If the water is not deep, it cannot support a large ship; but empty a cup of water on the shallow floor, and a straw can float like a boat. If you place a cup there, it will sink. In the same way, if the wind is not sufficient, it cannot support huge wings. Only at a height of ninety thousand kilometers is there enough space to support the Pung. So the Pung can finally begin his great journey.

"When a cicada heard this story, he said to a dove, 'When I fly, I rise quickly to the elm tree. Sometimes I don't reach it and I simply fall back to the ground, but I make forward progress. Why does the Pung have to struggle upward ninety thousand kilometers, without making any visible progress, before starting his journey south?'

"When a person takes a journey to the nearby woods, to return a few hours later, he doesn't have to prepare a supply of food. If he has to travel one hundred kilometers, he would need to prepare food for overnight. If he has to travel one thousand kilometers, he would need to prepare food for three months. What do the cicadas and doves understand about such matters? The mountain cicadas never know spring and autumn, because they are short-lived."

As I was contemplating the moral of this story, I realized that when one is destined for greater accomplishments in life, the preparation for such a journey can be extensive.

Just as the Pung struggled upward without making any visible progress toward his destination and despite the ridicule from other birds and insects, he continued to flap his wings straight upward until he arrived at a great height above the earth's atmosphere. With lesser birds still chattering about his foolishness, he spread his great wings and soared effortlessly southward and into the Celestial Pool.

You must develop your powers of endurance as the Pung did, even in the face of criticism and ridicule, in order to achieve your goals. Armed with Thick Face, Black Heart, you too are able to soar ninety thousand kilometers upward to begin your glorious journey to victory.

WINNING IS A MATTER OF HOW YOU KEEP SCORE

In general, we are accustomed to judging a winner in relation to time. A horse is a winner if he comes in faster than the others. A student gets a high mark if he finishes his test within a given time. No matter how much knowledge the student has, if he cannot put it all down on paper within a certain time limit, his knowledge will not be reflected in his grades.

We are all programmed to judge success and winning in relation to how fast we can produce visible results. Seldom are people generous enough to give us time to cultivate ourselves, even though that cultivation would bring greater fruit. Like the Pung bird, we have to endure criticism from the lesser birds for our apparent failures and foolishness. Chuang Tzu, more than two thousand years ago, saw the difficulties that an extraordinary man with an extraordinary vision would encounter in the world in which we live. Two thousand years later, technology has advanced tremendously, but the human heart remains the same.

Fortunately, the time to judge the ultimate success of each individual is at the moment of his death. In this case, time is working in our favor. As long as we have the necessary strength to endure the time of self-cultivation, like the Pung bird, the ultimate victory belongs to those who endure and persist to the end.

DEFEAT IS THE MOTHER OF SUCCESS

*One who is skilled in defeat
shall never see destruction.*

—*Tai Gong Wong*

"Defeat Is the Mother of Success" is a popular Chinese maxim taught to all Chinese elementary school children. I can still clearly recall the lyrics and the music of a nursery rhyme adopting this principle in my first-grade class. "There is a good saying, 'Try it again.' After you fail once or twice, try it again. It will increase your determination. It will strengthen your endurance. Don't be afraid, be courageous, try it again." The older I grow, the more I appreciate this simple and profound wisdom.

The following is a story of one man's life. He failed in business at the age of twenty-one. He was defeated in a legislative race at the age of twenty-two, and failed again in business at twenty-four. He was devastated by the death of a sweetheart when he was twenty-six, and subsequently had a nervous breakdown when he was twenty-seven. At thirty-four, he lost a congressional race, and lost it again two years later. He lost a senatorial race at the age of forty-five. After another two years, he failed in an effort to become vice president. He then went on to lose another senatorial race at the age of forty-nine. Finally, at the age of fifty-two, he became the sixteenth president of the United States. The man was Abraham Lincoln.

President Lincoln is, among all the people from the past to the present, the man I most admire and respect. When his fellow men rejected him at the polls, Lincoln could have been devastated, but every disappointment brought forth the courage to march on toward his ordained destiny. He often tried to joke about his political defeats. He would say, "Well, I feel just like the boy who stubbed his toe — too damned badly hurt to laugh and too damned proud to cry."

ENDURE BY ENDURING

> *Understanding the difficulties,*
> *enduring the hardships,*
> *predicting the risks,*
> *tolerating the abuse;*
> *for such a person,*
> *all ensure fame and success.*
>
> —CHINESE MAXIM

Once I was reading an Asian classic in which a young man asked his elder, "How do I endure?" The elder answered, "You endure by enduring." This simple statement stayed with me.

Many people have told me they think Asian people are very patient. In fact, it is not that patience is their greatest virtue, but rather that these people have an infinite ability to endure the unendurable.

ENDURANCE AND THICK FACE, BLACK HEART

Our civilization, our culture, our independence,
depend not upon multiplying our wants: self-indulgence,
but upon restricting our wants: self-denial.

—MAHATMA GANDHI

What makes a great one great? It is not that he possesses the image of the knight in shining armor like St. George slaying the dragon. Such an image has been held dear by the executives who are climbing the corporate ladders. What makes one truly great is knowing how to suffer the insufferable and how to endure the unendurable.

Everyone knows how to thrive in the good times. It is the trying times that separate the one who has substance from the one who merely possesses the image. Through trials and tribulations, one endures by enduring. Thus, the human spirit triumphs over itself.

Thick Face, Black Heart is the foundation that supports you in enduring the humiliation of defeat and criticism, to rise above it and dare to do what is right in fulfilling your destiny. Abraham Lincoln said, "Let us have faith that right makes might, and in that faith, let us to the end, dare to do our duty as we understand it."

The power that gives us strength and courage to endure the unendurable is the power of Thick Face, Black Heart. All great people possess it. Thick Face, Black Heart is a state of mind, not an outward behavior.

LINCOLN'S THICK FACE, BLACK HEART

Lincoln, perhaps the greatest president in the history of the United States, possessed a complete understanding of Thick Face, Black Heart. He was often described as insecure, shy, depressed, gloomy, melancholy, secretive, nonconfrontational, self-doubting, and preoccupied with the idea of premature death and even the possibility that he might go mad. He was uncomfortable in high-society gatherings, and his etiquette was often considered substandard.

If we put all these pieces of the picture together, what we have is a rather unsuccessful, gloomy person struggling for professional and personal survival. It seems that the authors of all the twentieth-century self-help books had people like Abraham Lincoln in mind. On the contrary, Lincoln is a master among Thick Face, Black Heart practitioners. Let us examine some of his Thick Face, Black Heart characteristics.

Detachment

Lincoln's whole life was about fighting his own feelings of inadequacy. If all men were meant to be created equal, God was certainly stingy with Lincoln's humble beginnings. From childhood, Lincoln learned to endure the humiliation that accompanied the obvious disadvantage of being poor. His existence until the age of twenty-one, when he left his father's world, was no better than that of a workhorse.

After Lincoln left home, he never returned again. Lincoln might not have known what he wanted out of life at that time, but it was clear that he did not want what he had for his first twenty-one years.

Lincoln did not invite his father, Thomas Lincoln, to his wedding, nor did he take his family to visit Thomas Lincoln. When his father died in a nearby Illinois county in 1851, Lincoln did not attend the funeral.

Some historians think Lincoln had great contempt for his father's intellectual limitations. I think Lincoln was a man of principle with an intuitive direction of his life objectives. His father's environment was not nurturing physically or spiritually. As a child, Lincoln was deprived of family security, living in the violent environment of the frontier. Even more violent than the frontier was the poverty he experienced.

Lincoln did his duty for twenty-one years. Any contribution that he could have made toward his father had been made. They were clear of each other's debt. Without guilt or malice, Lincoln never saw his father again after the age of twenty-one. While some may regard his actions as heartless, those who understand Thick Face, Black Heart know that Lincoln acted in this manner in order to be true to his destiny.

One can see that Lincoln embodied the power of detachment. He forsook the harmful environment of his father and safeguarded himself from the judgment of others about his relationship with his father. Lincoln possessed the power of Thick Face, Black Heart. He demonstrated this ability repeatedly throughout his lifetime. He always sacrificed the small for the larger, "just" objectives.

Guarding His Interests

As a lawyer, Lincoln's fee was fair and reasonable, but he did expect prompt remuneration for his services. If clients refused to pay up, Lincoln sued them to get his money. He was a scrupulous warrior who defended his self-interest.

Labeled As Unholy

Lincoln was deeply religious, yet he belonged to no church. He read free-thinking philosophers such as Voltaire and Thomas Paine. Lincoln had to endure the humiliation of being labeled "an unholy and irreligious man." In that era, outwardly expressed morals were valued above all else. Lincoln had the self-confidence to know in his heart that he was devoted in the eyes of God, and that others' judgments should not affect him. He was a true man of Thick Face, Black Heart.

Enduring the War Years

Once Lincoln mentioned to an old friend that all the trouble and anxieties of his life could not equal the opposition and criticism he received during the Civil War. They were so great, Lincoln said, that he did not think he could possibly survive them.

In the flames of the Civil War, Lincoln endured. It seems that Lincoln was born into a tough environment to be trained as a man of Thick Face, Black Heart in order to lead this nation out of its darkest time. Lincoln had to endure massive hate mail. From all over the country came cries that he was too stupid and unfit to be president or to reunite the country.

Yes, Lincoln was unsure of himself, inexperienced, and melancholy. But he also was more than that. He was a man of conviction—a man of Thick Face, Black Heart.

Ruthlessness

As the war grew blacker, Lincoln grew blacker. Lincoln argued, "Necessity knows no law." Lincoln resorted to one harsh war measure after another: embracing martial law and military arrest. Civilians were tried in military courts without juries. He imprisoned at least fourteen thousand people, including a congressman.

When Lincoln was criticized, he replied that the only regret he had was that he hadn't arrested General Robert E. Lee when he had had the chance.

A Man Made for His Time

A great man such as Abraham Lincoln is a gift of the Creator to his time. Lincoln's strength was not tainted by his melancholy moods; rather, he drew strength from his personal history of tragedies. He had endured the unendurable from childhood to adulthood.

The hard life he had endured made him capable of enduring the burden of the whole nation. Thus, anchored on his personal strength, he led this nation through its most trying period.

IN SEARCH OF A STRESS-FREE LIFE

Imagine if I could give you a miracle formula or a pill that would enable you instantly to eliminate all the negative experiences in your life. How wonderful would your life be? You would have no worries and would live stress-free. Right? Wouldn't this be the ultimate dream come true?

But the fact is that if such a pill or formula existed, it would not make you happy or even stress-free. Researchers at the University of California at Berkeley have backed this up with a study that shows how our society puts too much emphasis on eliminating negative experiences when trying to alleviate stress.

The absence of negative experiences in our life does not alone contribute to the quality of our life. As humans we need challenges in order to develop fully and bring forth all the positive aspects within ourselves. The only way to feel truly happy is by confronting these challenges and overcoming them. As children of the Divine, we want to touch life's every fiber—even the negative ones—and feel alive by riding high on life itself.

ENDURANCE, CRISIS, AND OPPORTUNITY

God is the toughest taskmaster I have known.
He tries you through and through.
When you find your faith or your body is failing you,
and you are sinking,
He comes to your assistance.
He proves to you that you must not lose your faith....
I cannot recall a single instance when,
at the eleventh hour, He has forsaken me.

—MAHATMA GANDHI

The Chinese word for crisis is made by combining two characters: crisis and opportunity. By observing life, the ancient Chinese wise men realized that the true nature of crisis is an opportunity in disguise. This is similar to the Western concept of "When God closes a door, He opens a window."

Without the strength to endure the crisis, we will not see the opportunity within. It is within the process of endurance that opportunity reveals itself. Opportunity always exists within a crisis situation, but when we lose heart in a devastating crisis, we are blinded by our own emotion. When we can calmly endure the unendurable, the opportunity for a better alternative surfaces and reveals itself.

CRISIS—A RENOVATION OF YOUR LIFE

The divine guidance often comes
when the horizon is the blackest.

—*MAHATMA GANDHI*

We all welcome changes for the better. However, changing for the better sometimes becomes disguised. As with an old house, in order to renovate and redecorate the place, you first have to tear it up. Then you put it back together. The house does not panic. But when it comes to the reconstruction of our life, we panic and struggle.

Whenever there are crises, that is the time to test our ability for endurance. Without ability to endure emotional turmoil and the chaos that come with changes, there would be no hope for reconstruction. Endurance is never an easy task; however, it is an essential element in overcoming crises.

The following practical points are beneficial during a crisis situation. These remedies contain the elements of endurance that will propel you through the journey of your dark night.

1. Give Up Struggling

After we have done everything we can think of to fix a crisis, one of the following is likely to happen. One, we admit defeat and feel victimized by our circumstances. The other is that we finally get smart enough to give up struggling and stop trying to correct the situation according to our concept of "rightness." We gather our courage and face up to our fear. By doing so, we begin to detect new possibilities.

A drowning swimmer struggles with all his might, yet the

power of the waves is mightier than his meager human effort. He screams for help. Help arrives, yet no one can get ahold of him to rescue him because he will not stop struggling. Not until the swimmer is willing to give up struggling is he manageable and able to be rescued.

2. Allow a Solution to Make Itself Clear

When in crisis, we, like the drowning swimmer, render the Divine's helping hand unable to reach us by our panicky efforts and struggles. During each crisis, the helping hands of the Divine are always present in the form of new opportunities. The key to recognition of these opportunities is to stop panicking and go with the flow, allowing a solution to present itself.

3. Work through Your Agony and Grief

Whenever tragedy strikes, there is no point in me telling you not to grieve and instead to live life as if it were a dream. Life may be a dream and a play in the eyes of our Maker, but we are stuck with the nightmares.

During times of stress, work out your grief, because until you are able to thoroughly experience your pain, it will be harder to deal with any new possibilities. However, do not indulge in excess misery. Keep your misfortune private and only share it with those who can truly support you.

Walter received his layoff notice in December 1991, just before Christmas. He felt devastated and hurt when he walked out of his office, but when he got home he tried to tell his wife about his ill fate with dignity and courage. He wanted to act like a "man," to suppress his emotions. However, his wife, Karen, knew he hurt deeply, so she tried to get him to talk about the incident. At first she had tremendous difficulty getting him to open up, but finally he wept out loud and continued uncontrollably. As he wept, he poured out his worries—the guilt he felt over losing his job and other problems that he had carried hidden in him for a long time. He cried for three days.

The second day, after a sleepless night, he went out at 6:00 a.m. to the corner liquor store. The shop clerk, an intelligent-looking middle-aged man, asked him if he was celebrating Christmas early. Walter told him no, but that he had just lost his job.

"I understand," the clerk said. "I was in marketing and sales at a large corporation. But after I lost my job, my wife and kids left me, and I ended up working here."

Instantly the tears welled up in both of their eyes. At that instant, they both felt the depth of their wounds.

Walter normally didn't drink much, but after finishing off his beer that afternoon he wished to return to the liquor store, replenish his supply, and continue his conversation with the clerk. Karen told him not to commiserate with the liquor store clerk because it would only exacerbate Walter's own feelings of failure. She felt that Walter might develop the idea that he shared the same fate and would end up like the clerk. "Misery loves company," she said. "Visiting the clerk will only compound the pain for both of you."

After three days of weeping and drinking, Walter was emotionally and physically depleted, but he picked himself up and started talking with Karen about what he should do next. They scoured the newspaper ads, took inventory of their assets, borrowed books from the library on how to change careers, and read up on ways to write a dynamic résumé. Walter made finding a job his full-time work. Within three weeks, he had five interviews and eventually landed a better position than his old job—one with a higher salary, two weeks more vacation time, and only four workdays a week.

4. Let the Dark Night Pass

Going with the flow is not about giving up self-effort, but rather about accepting reality. It is about recognizing when it is time for action and when it is time to sit it out. After you have done all that is humanly possible during a period of crisis and the situation is still beyond your ability to remedy, you must anchor yourself with the spirit of endurance. Let the dark night pass.

One thing is certain in life: its ever-changing nature. The animals in the wild understand this well. After a lavish summer come the trying times of winter; then the spring follows. In the realm of God's creation, only human beings react with panic when change comes.

5. Do Not Display Your Vulnerability

During crisis, don't let outsiders in on your miseries. Even the most sympathetic people would rather be in the company of a winner. Outsiders feel helpless to lend you a hand solving your problems. And because of this they tend to distance themselves from you after the initial expression of sympathy in an attempt to escape from their own helplessness. To those who have contributed to and caused your crisis, do not give them the satisfaction of knowing that they have the power to hurt you. Let them know that your apparent crisis turned out to be a blessing in disguise. This is not a lie, but rather an affirmation. Be a good poker player, keep a straight face, and have steel for nerves.

6. Inactivity to Conquer Chaos

When drastic change and chaos occur in your life, a very effective antidote is inactivity. During the period of chaos, when everything you attempt to do to remedy a situation backfires, or your have to undo everything that has been done and start all over again, stop immediately and do nothing. Wait until the dust settles, and most likely you will see a clear path obviously laid in front of you.

Doing nothing is easier said than done, especially when one's life has been turned upside down. It requires tremendous power of endurance and the ability to act against every instinct of our nature, which continuously attempts to repair the situation.

When you immerse yourself in inactivity, you are also gathering and nurturing your inner strength. By doing so, without anxiety and with a detached spirit, you are able to focus yourself and thus create a force of powerful momentum and unshakable clarity. When you recognize the proper time to act, this newfound energy will aid you in realizing your desired result.

7. Live Your Life As If It Were Someone Else's

If your find your life unbearable, then imagine the life you are living is not yours, and that it belongs to someone else. Have you ever noticed that you are frequently quite good at solving someone else's problems? Next time during the period of crisis, instead of viewing the crisis as your problem, try to imagine that your life is someone else's. By doing so you will facilitate the solution and find tremendous freedom and relief.

You will fear no criticism and agonize over no defeat. You

will take chances that you normally would not. Suddenly, a multitude of opportunities will unveil themselves. You are experiencing unfamiliar ease in your business dealings; after all, it was not "your" life you were living. The problems belonged to someone else, and you were the temporary custodian of the situation. Your attitude will transform as your old and unbearable life receives a transfusion of new possibilities.

On my desk is a sign that reads, "Live your life as if it were someone else's." This helps me remember not to get too caught up in the drama of life.

I shared this thought with a friend of mine. The discussion prompted him to say to me, "As a matter of fact, the life you are living is not yours, anyhow. Most of us live out our life in our heads, and the person who lives in our head is not our true self. We live with our minds so full of hopes, fears, and fantasies that we basically don't experience most of our reality. The idea you've just expressed can free people from the limitations that they have set for themselves. Most of us are trapped by our sense of what and who we think we are."

Knowing how to handle adversity is a valuable skill. It is all about the state of mind—the state of Thick Face, Black Heart.

LIABILITIES AND ENDURANCE

The manner in which you interpret your liabilities determines how they affect you. Although I covered this in the chapter on negative thinking, I would like to reiterate it under the context of endurance. You cannot turn liabilities into assets unless you are able to endure the despondent, dark periods.

Our negative experiences in life are essential elements for us to fulfill our intended destiny. Unless we possess the power of endurance to live through the dark of the night, we will not see the glory of daybreak.

I was recently giving a lecture before a large African-American audience. My audience told me that since some of them were born black and poor, they felt that they already had a slow start in life from the beginning. I replied, "Look at Dr. Martin Luther King. If he had been born white and rich, what would he have made of himself? He'd be just another smart white boy." In fact, there is nothing you need to do to turn your liabilities into assets because destiny has already done the job for you.

Dr. King did not choose to be an African-American, but nevertheless he was. Thomas Edison did not choose to be burdened with a learning disability, thus making him unfit for school. Yet, because Edison did not receive standard schooling, in his world everything was possible: who and what he was were his assets.

That which separates those individuals who reap positive fruits from their seeming liabilities from those who are defeated by such liabilities lies in their ability to endure while learning to utilize said liabilities as the instruments that shape their success.

THE SWEET FRUIT OF ENDURANCE

Dick is working for a specialized custom design engineering company. His expertise is in robotics. Two years ago, he was employed by the company to create a robotic control system for industrial equipment. The company owner had a brilliant vision, which was to be the calling card of the company. As time went on, the complexity of the system generated doubts in the mind of the company owner as to whether the whole thing was even worth it. The more doubts the owner had about the project, the less important Dick became in the company's pecking order. He was first hired as manager of the project; later he was demoted to a regular engineer supporting other projects.

Many times Dick thought of quitting, but deep down in his heart he wanted the project finished. He believed it would be a revolutionary piece of hardware in the area of industrial manufacturing, so he stayed on. Each day, after he had finished working on other projects, he would work on his robotic control project. In the meantime, the company created another type of manufacturing hardware without any intelligent capacity. The owner began to sing a different tune — that what people really wanted was just dumb hardware that worked well.

One day the owner told Dick, "I am thinking about scrapping the whole robotic control project."

Dick had put his heart and soul into the project, and he knew the benefit of the hardware. He objected strongly, "If you don't want the control system, I will personally go out to seek buyers for different applications." The owner walked away saying nothing. Dick was left totally devastated, but he continued his work.

Two days after that conversation, a European manufacturing company came to the United States to see the demo of the company's hardware. The owner knew this was a long shot since the manufacturing company had already visited more than five companies all over the world. After three days of demonstrations, by accident, a manager mentioned that there was a robotic control system that was 95 per cent complete. The European buyers requested a demonstration the next day.

Dick was able to demonstrate his pet project. It was a hit. After the demo, the buyers talked of nothing but Dick's robotic control hardware. They said to the owner, "This is the highlight of our trip." The foreign manufacturing company purchased the full system, worth over two million dollars.

Dick endured the humiliation of being demoted and working on a system no one seemed to think was important. Finally, the company owner began to see that his original vision had been correct all along.

A STRATEGY FOR ROMANCE

The quality of endurance has infinite usage, not only limited to our traditional concept. For example, the problem with man-woman relationships is that when the man wants the woman, the woman doesn't want the man. When the woman wants the man, the man doesn't want the woman. The common relationships between the sexes are more like a game of tug-of-war than a storybook, poetic romance.

It seems that within many men and women lives an invisible hunter, a stalker who enjoys the exercise of the hunt far more than the warmth of intimacy. So the game goes on.

The next time you notice these hunter characteristics in your romantic interest, go ahead and create the hunt by first adopting the Thick Face, Black Heart detachment—play hard to get! Detach yourself from your instinctive need to get close and intimate. Hold back just enough so that you don't turn off the magnetism between you and your pursuer, and let the other person also have a little fun hunting you down.

However, you cannot adopt this strategy unless you are able to master the spirit of endurance and deprive yourself of the joy of being a hunter. The secret that enables you to endure the pain of this detachment is keeping your eyes on your objective. The objective will be different for each person. To some it will be a serious, entangled relationship, while others may simply want casual companionship. The point is that you've acquired this relationship and won your "prize" on your own terms.

Recently a friend of mine told me that he and his girlfriend were not doing very well. As a matter of fact, she had announced that she would like to see other people. My friend was devastated since he was horribly attached to her. I advised him to try something drastic because she was pretty much a lost cause.

He went back to his girlfriend and told her that it would be fine for her to see anyone she wanted, just not him. Three days later, they were married in Las Vegas. I'm not sure how long the marriage will last, but at least my friend was very happy that he got his "prize."

CONCLUSION

The spirit of endurance is one of the most powerful concepts we can learn. It can fulfill your objectives in life with no external effort. You do not have to conquer others, you only need to be tough with *yourself*. The ability to endure is your natural spiritual fiber. The strength that enables one to endure the unendurable is also the source of Thick Face, Black Heart.

SUMMARY OF KEY POINTS

- The spirit of endurance is an imperative quality in the expedition in our personal growth. This spirit was not a stranger to the early settlers and our founding fathers. Through endurance, this nation was born and made great.

- When one is destined for greater accomplishments in life, the preparation for such a journey can be extensive.

- Defeat is the mother of success.

- Endure by enduring—understanding the difficulties, enduring the hardships, predicting the risks, and tolerating the abuse, all ensure fame and success for such a person.

- What makes one truly great is knowing how to suffer the insufferable and how to endure the unendurable. Everyone knows how to thrive in the good times. It is the trying times that separate the one who has substance from the one who merely possesses the image.

- Through trials and tribulations, one endures by enduring. Thus the human spirit triumphs over itself.

- Thick Face, Black Heart is the foundation that supports you in enduring the humiliation of defeat and criticism, to rise above it and dare to do what is right in fulfilling your destiny.

- The Chinese word for crisis is made by combining two characters: crisis and opportunity. By observing life, the ancient Chinese wise men realized that the true nature of crisis is an opportunity in disguise. This is similar to the Western concept of "When God closes a door, He opens a window."

- Without the strength to endure the crisis, one will not see the opportunity within. It is within the process of endurance that opportunity reveals itself.

- Opportunity always exists within a crisis situation, but when we lose heart in a devastating crisis, we are blinded by our own emotion. When we can calmly endure the unendurable, the opportunity for a better alternative surfaces and reveals itself.

- Going with the flow is not about giving up self-effort, but rather about accepting the reality. You must learn to recognize when it is time for action and when it is time to sit out.

- When you immerse yourself in inactivity, you are also gathering and nurturing your inner strength. By doing so without anxiety and with a detached spirit, you are able to focus yourself and thus create a force of powerful momentum and unshakable clarity.

- Live your life as if it were someone else's. You will find tremendous freedom and relief. A transformation of your attitude will occur.

- Liabilities depend on how you see them; you can easily turn them into assets if you start to view your liabilities in a different light. However, a person will not be able to turn liabilities into assets unless he is able to endure the despondent, dark periods.

- Our negative life situations are essential elements for us to fulfill our intended destiny. However, unless we possess the power of endurance to live through the dark of the night, we will not see the glory of daybreak.

With what you get from others,
you make a living for yourself.
What you give to others,
makes a life for yourself.

—*HINDU MAXIM*

7

The Mystery of Money

Poverty is the greatest violence.

—*MAHATMA GANDHI*

Money is not the complete reward of a Thick Face, Black Heart practitioner, but to most people it is an important part of it.

THE WISDOM OF ANCIENT CHINA

As a child, I learned to write each Chinese character by endlessly repeating the strokes that made up the character until they were so indelibly burned into my memory that my hand could create them automatically. I learned the common meaning of the characters but never gave a thought to the deeper meaning of the symbols themselves. Now, as an adult, I am often struck by the poetic and sublime wisdom of the ancient scholars who created words out of simple pictorial symbols representing the basic elements of their lives and the world around them.

The Chinese character for money is composed of three symbols. One symbol means gold. The other two represent spears. The character for poverty is also composed of three symbols. The symbols depict a man standing at the bottom of a pit, bent as if under a great burden. These characters not only represent money and poverty, but also they say something profound and beautiful about them.

During my college years in Taiwan, a friend convinced me to accompany her on a visit to the local fortune-teller. After the old man told her fortune, she asked him to tell mine. He handed me a brush and a slip of paper and asked me to write a word. I drew the character meaning sky or heaven. He took the paper and studied the character. Beside it he drew the character representing money: gold flanked by two spears.

"Study this character carefully," he insisted. "It will reveal to you the mystery of money. Gold is tightly bound to struggle."

As I remembered the old man's words, I wondered why there were two spears connected to the idea of money. It seemed to me that just one would have adequately conveyed the idea that a struggle was involved in acquiring wealth. I drew the character and studied it carefully as the old man had commanded me to do. Quite suddenly I understood the mystery of money and the dual nature of the struggle that surrounds it.

THE OUTWARD BATTLE

The first spear symbolizes the outward struggle for survival. Although the earth contains abundance, its bounty is not equitably distributed among the billions of people who need to share in that abundance. From the beginning of civilization to the present day, one nation has battled another to acquire the other's resources. In the day-to-day struggle among individuals, the conflict is not often as direct and bloody as it can be among nations, but it is just as ruthless.

In the modern industrialized world, the principal struggle for survival takes the form of the struggle for money. Money plays an important role when it comes to furthering one's success. A well-managed business offering a superior product or service may still be overwhelmed by a less efficient competitor who is better capitalized. A brilliant and able politician will not accomplish his agenda if he is outspent and defeated for election by an inferior opponent. A ballet, play, or movie of great artistic importance will never be produced if its creators cannot attract the necessary funding. Anyone who wishes to accomplish his goals or claim a share of the earth's abundance must first be prepared to do battle for money.

Many times during my seminars, people will ask me: "If I have no money, how can I start a business and make it?" Nolan Bushnell founded the Atari video game company with only five hundred dollars. Four years later, he sold the company to Warner Communications for twenty-eight million dollars. With the twenty-eight million dollars he began numerous enterprises that cost him millions of dollars to support, and many of these ventures eventually went bankrupt. A worthwhile project can succeed through a grassroots effort when a person is willing to fight for the opportunity to manifest his vision.

It is never an easy path. If you don't have a worthy idea and superb execution, then money alone cannot save you. It can only prolong the time period before you lose it all. So the game of monetary success is not only about getting the money; it is also about having a great idea and being able to keep that money multiplying through worthy efforts.

THE BATTLE WITHIN

The second spear represents the battle within. Before one can fight and win the outward battle, one must win the battle within. Poverty is more a state of mind than an external condition. Most people struggle for small rewards because they are shackled by an unarticulated belief that they are not the kind of people who are worth the finer things in life. It is essential to transform your state of mind within yourself: you are worthy of whatever material rewards you seek, so long as you acquire them honestly and honorably.

Unclaimed Gifts

It was said that a holy man, because of his great virtue, was taken by the angels to visit heaven. As the angels were escorting him through the heavenly mansion, they passed through a great hall piled high with gifts of every kind. The man asked his guides why all these gifts were here. They replied, "These are all the things people prayed for but quit their prayers right before they were to be delivered."

Our Divine Maker never stops us from possessing worthy gifts. It is our own lack of faith in our worthiness to receive the gifts that prevents us from possessing them. Some just quit wanting them because they lose heart, convinced that they will never get what they want. For others, the objects of their desire are transitory. One day they want a new coat, the next day a new car. When the weather turns cold, they start wishing for a Hawaiian vacation. Their desires are little more than idle daydreams. If we are steadfast in our efforts to attain our worthy desires, they may come to us, but idle dreams seldom come true.

A Fair Exchange of Value

Money and wealth are obtained through interactions with others. You exchange your labor for money. In order to get a fair exchange value, it is necessary to convince the people with whom you do business that you can be of benefit to them. It is necessary for you to project a sense of your own worth. In order to do this, you must first have a strong inner sense of your own worth.

To have a sense of your own worth, you first have to do something that is worthy of your own respect. This includes hard work along with determination and perseverance. Concentrate your energy on the things that make you of worth to others: the competent and faithful performance of your duties, care in honoring your commitments, and the energy and creativity you bring to your tasks. Too often we dissipate our energy in resenting the success of others and railing at fate for keeping us from acquiring the wealth we seek. This is the battle within.

The Fruits of Poverty

Money may not buy happiness,
but it certainly will buy a lot of convenience.

—*CHINESE PROVERB*

Almost everyone thinks he wants to be rich, but in reality most of us are where we want to be financially. Obtaining prosperity is not about what you are willing to do to gain it; more importantly, it is about what you are willing to give up in exchange for it. This is an extremely important principle to remember. It is like the making of a superior athlete. The first thing the athlete has to confront is the question, What am I willing to give up to become a great athlete? Am I willing to give up the times that I spend with my friends? Am I willing to forgo the parties and fun times that my friends enjoy? Am I willing to forgo delicious, fattening food in exchange for a disciplined diet program? The list goes on.

Ruby is an apartment manager with a meager income. In an attempt to improve her financial situation, she works part-time selling real estate, but her hard work has never provided her any meaningful financial rewards.

As I watch Ruby, I realize that she is extremely attached to the fruits of her poverty. She is attached to the duties and the rewards of managing the apartment complex. By performing her job as apartment manager, Ruby satisfies her "psychological needs."

Ruby is the type of person we commonly label a "power tripper." A few months after a tenant moves in, Ruby starts acting more like a boot camp sergeant than an apartment manager. She thrives on the power she holds over her tenants, especially when she is on the "right" side in the list of dos and don'ts of the apartment's regulations.

Ruby thinks she wants to make more money through selling real estate, so she may give up her meager pay and long working hours as an apartment manger. But subconsciously her spirit feeds on the satisfaction and power of policing others as she performs her present duties. She could not possibly be content to give it up in exchange for an occupation that would require her to cater to the needs of her paying clients, even though it would mean a significant improvement in her financial status.

Ruby's mind sees no difference between the potential satisfaction that wealth can bring and the satisfaction experienced by staying in poverty. As a matter of fact, Ruby is subconsciously so attached to this specific advantage of being poor that she has great doubt about the value of trading a proven pleasurable experience (power tripping over others) for the unknown experience of being rich.

Ivan is a middle-aged businessman who has had numerous business ventures throughout his life. Unfortunately, he had a habit of taking his businesses to the top, only to watch them crash to bankruptcy with time. After twenty years of these ups and downs, Ivan finally discovered the cause of his failures.

Whenever he was on the top, he would live an extravagant lifestyle and at times would even sink into decadence. Deep down, Ivan is a pure-hearted, down-to-earth man. Therefore, his periods of decadent living would rub against his natural grain—the simple, harmonious lifestyle he truly felt comfortable with. This would eventually drive Ivan to unconsciously sabotage his own enterprises through a series of bad business judgments. When he finally realized the reason behind his downfalls, he was able to discipline himself and avoid repeating past patterns while thriving on the waves of success.

Squeeze Money Too Tight,
and It Will Slip out of Your Hands

Money is the element of life that inspires the greatest of emotions in individuals. It is tightly connected with the emotions of agony and ecstacy. When you have money, you never feel you have enough. If you have lost money, you wish you had appreciated it more when you did have it.

June, a forty-three-year-old Australian lady, is currently studying English literature at a Los Angeles junior college. She was referred to my friend Bob as someone who could assist him in editing a series of short stories he had written. June had never before edited fiction stories, but fifteen years ago, while she was in Australia, she had worked as a documentary film editor's assistant. She had a natural instinct for drama. During the past fifteen years in the United States, June had come upon rough times. She often had to earn her living by performing tedious labor at minimum wage. She had grown extremely bitter about the world, and her attitude toward money and people was very negative. Six months ago, she was fired from her used car sales job. She was unemployed once again.

Although June did not have a track record that demonstrated her talent, Bob sensed her natural intuition. After meeting with her, he decided to give her a try. Bob agreed to pay June the sum of three thousand dollars for three short stories. After working with Bob and finishing one story, June started to think to herself that perhaps she was working too cheaply. She thought she could change her working arrangement from a project basis to an hourly basis to earn more money. She presented her case to Bob, arguing and crying how she was being exploited by him for her cheap labor. Bob allowed that if June would accurately keep track of her working time, he would pay her twenty-five dollars an hour.

June was delighted because she had never received such a large hourly sum for her work.

June began working on the next story. She soon realized that after she eliminated her meal times, her fifteen minutes per hour of cigarette breaks, and the time she spent visiting about her life during working hours, her actual working hours were few. She spent only ten hours on the next story. This translated to approximately two hundred and fifty dollars per story. She realized she had just shot herself in the foot. Again she wanted to renegotiate with Bob. She cried to Bob that by her counting the hours, the love had gone out of their working space, and she wanted that love back. She wanted to go back to the original arrangement. Bob replied, "The love has not gone out of me. I have always had it within me. If the love has gone out of you, then it is up to you to get it back. To be more accurate, the whole thing to you was never about love. It was only about money. What happened here is because you wanted to get more money out of this situation. You squeezed the money too tight, and it has slipped from your hands." Bob then sent her home.

ACCIDENTAL WEALTH

The battle within must be fought and won not only to establish in your own mind your right to material wealth, but to develop within yourself the ability and will to go out into the world and fight for it.

Wealth is an uncertain thing. Every day, fortunes are made and lost. The person who has acquired wealth by successfully fighting the inward and outward battles is not so devastated by financial catastrophe as is the person who has acquired wealth by accident of birth or windfall. Misfortune may strip him of material wealth, but he still has the ability, will, and confidence to acquire it again.

My mother was born to great wealth. The only child of an only child, she inherited a huge estate that had not been dispersed over the generations to a number of heirs. Although she enjoyed all the comforts and privileges that wealth brings, she had been raised in a household of domestic discord. Her father had openly and lavishly supported a mistress and a second family. This was a cause of constant strife between my grandparents.

When it came time for my mother to marry, she decided that the best way to avoid flagrant infidelity was to marry a man of modest means. She chose my father, a poor but worthy distant relative. She then settled down into what she thought would be a tranquil and genteel life. But this was not to be.

After my parents were married, they moved to Tienjin. With my mother's monthly income from the land rental back in Manchuria, plus my father's salary, they were able to live lavishly in the British-governed section of the town. In early 1948, while the Communist forces led by Mao Zedong were steadily approaching Tienjin, my parents left their house to the care of the servants and moved into a newly purchased chateau in Shanghai's French territory. A year later, they were forced to leave all their wealth and flee to Taiwan. As we left our home in Shanghai, again my parents admonished the housekeepers to take good care of everything because we would return in a couple of months.

Forty-three years later, my parents are still in Taiwan. For years they waited for external events to restore their affluence in the same sudden way it had disappeared. While fortunes were being made all around them in Taiwan's post-Vietnam War prosperity, my father was content to take a government position that paid a modest salary. Neither he nor my mother ever made a serious attempt to become wealthy through their own efforts.

Great fortune had not done for my parents what they had expected it to do. Because neither of them had ever engaged in the inward and outward battles for wealth, they were unable to go out and restore their fortunes.

On the other hand, if you are fortunate enough to inherit wealth and not have the misfortune to lose it, that can sometimes be a curse as well. In *Circus of Ambition,* John Taylor describes how old-money families like the Rockefellers "felt imprisoned by their wealth": "By stripping them of the need to work, inherited wealth encouraged idleness and engendered feelings of worthlessness. Heirs to other great East Coast fortunes, such as the children of J. Seward Johnson of Johnson & Johnson, actually felt degraded by their money. Wealth, they came to believe, created a corrosive mistrust of others."

WEALTH AND TALENT

The Chinese character for wealth—the accumulation of money and other assets—is composed of two symbols: one is a seashell, the medium of exchange in very ancient times; the other is the symbol for the unique ability or talent that each of us possesses—the literal meaning of the symbol is "brilliance."

The path to wealth is not to chase money for its own sake, but to understand and develop your own intrinsic talents and inclinations. You must seek a livelihood that allows you to do what you were intended to do and brings you joy. If you do, the money will take care of itself. Too often we select a job because it pays well or offers security. But no matter how well a job pays initially or how secure it makes you feel, it will turn out to be a dead end unless it is in line with your own particular talents. It will eventually rob you of your enthusiasm and creative brilliance. At best, you will become mediocre, and your rewards will likewise be mediocre.

Because each of us possesses a spark of individual brilliance, every one of us is capable of accomplishing something in our own unique way that cannot be accomplished by anyone else. Striving to discover our niche in this vast human market is part of our conquest of life.

In most cases, life does not play hide-and-seek; rather, we are blind. Our unique abilities often display themselves in many situations in the course of our lives. Because we are so focused on making a living, we do not see anything else. In this case, for our own good, sometimes life will pull the rug from under us, so we are compelled to look around and discover new possibilities.

The Insignificant Reflects the Significant

In 1991, during Thanksgiving, I was working as a volunteer for the Thanksgiving meal at a church. I was assigned the work to fold seven hundred napkins, placing a plastic fork and spoon inside each. The job was very easy—any five-year-old could have done it well. Our team leader wanted all the napkins rolled very tightly so they would look very neat. This also was not difficult.

A lady sitting across from me was folding all her napkins terribly loosely. Even though she had been corrected many times by the team leader, her folding was not improving. She was going through the motion of folding, yet her mind and her heart were absent from the work. As some of the people she knew passed by her, I noticed that she would ask if they would like to make an appointment with her for a massage.

Although she was a professional masseuse, she had no takers.

Several hours later, she started to talk to me and asked if I wanted to have a massage from her. I told her I felt wonderful and that I didn't need a massage. For no obvious reason, she then asked me, "How can I get money without being greedy?"

Although the question came out of thin air, she looked sincere, so I told her, "By learning how to wrap your forks and spoons well." She looked at me, confused and puzzled by my answer.

The truth is, the manner in which we handle inconsequential work reflects our state of mind and our performance standards. If I had really needed a masseuse, I would not have used her, because I knew her performance would be equally inferior to her napkin folding. During our day-to-day lives, how we handle insignificant work broadcasts how we will perform significant tasks. All these are interconnected with our ability to obtain wealth.

Claim the High Ground

In the battle for material success, if you have trouble hitting your mark, try elevating your sights. You will have very little success with mediocre ambitions. Weak dreams inspire weak efforts.

One of the most important aspects of fighting the battle is choosing your ground. A very wealthy man, a self-made man who measures his net worth in hundreds of millions of dollars, gave me the best advice I have ever heard on the subject.

"The world is like a pyramid of people struggling with one another," he told me. "You don't have the choice of whether or not to join in the struggle, but you can choose where to fight. Don't fight your battle at the bottom of the pyramid. It is much too crowded down there. It is easier near the top."

In the struggle for money, it is often harder to scrape for a few dollars each day than to acquire an abundance of wealth. There is a common understanding among automobile salesmen, for example, that it is often easier to sell a luxury car than to pawn off a used, beat-up car to someone who can ill afford it.

DON'T BE A BEGGAR, BE A CHILD OF GOD

Next time you walk down the street and are approached by a beggar, watch what motivates you to reach into your pocket and pull out money for that beggar. Most of the time, you give because you feel sympathetic toward the beggar or you feel the need to make a connection from one human to another by helping him. My observation is that whatever your motivation may be, you rarely give a beggar money because you want to reward him for his skill in begging.

As spiritual beings, we often turn to our Maker to fulfill our desires magically. We do this by begging to God in our prayers. Actually, our prayers often sound more like shopping lists than devoted worship. Sometimes they read like a contract of performance: if you do this, then I will do that.

If our Maker did indeed grant every demand, then He would be more inclined to respond to your wishes if you approached Him not as a beggar but, knowing that He created you in His own image, as His child. What He has, you also have.

Since you are a child of the Divine who is made in His image and possesses all of His attributes, it is demeaning for you to beg for the fulfillment of your desires. As the child of God, you embody the full splendor of His finest attributes, and every "worthy" desire can be fulfilled through your God-given abilities. You are able to perform actions coupling wisdom with discrimination and undying determination to persist until you obtain all your heart's desires.

The more you explore your ability to bring forth your God-given attributes in attempting to fulfill your worldly needs, the more you will be able to sense His presence in your daily endeavors. The Divine image is no longer a painting of an old man with a white beard appearing in the sky among the clouds. His image is an ever-present, tangible force that reveals itself through your noble attributes.

ADAPT THE DIVINE TOUCH IN YOUR WORK

What makes a great artist great is his ability to recreate his Maker's creativity in his work. A good lawyer taps into his Maker's wisdom in delivering a convincing defense. In the same way, a good business manager copies, on a smaller scale, the Maker's ability to manage the vast universe. No matter what occupation you are in, the manifestation of your excellence is in direct proportion to the degree that you are able to bring forth the hidden divine qualities from within and apply these qualities to your daily tasks.

During an interview, Luciano Pavarotti, the most renowned tenor of our time, identified the practice of *yoga* as the single most important factor contributing to his singing excellence. The word *yoga* in Sanskrit means union. Pavarotti spoke of the union of the small individual entity with the universal entity and how this affects him as a singer.

The more you are able to manifest the Maker's qualities,

the easier it will be for you in your quest for self-fulfillment and your pursuit of rightful monetary rewards in your professional life. This is particularly visible among the creative occupations, perhaps because the artist is able to see the result of his work as a completed whole, whereas the businessman's work is an ongoing process. I have noticed that the difference between a great artist and a competent artist is not in technical ability but rather in the expression of soul. You see in the work of great artists the manifestation of that Divine force, just as if they were touched by God Himself.

A great dancer such as Baryshnikov transcends human limitations and brings us into the realm of the celestial world. The voices of Luciano Pavarotti and Joan Sutherland touch our hearts with overwhelming love and joy. The great artist Vincent Van Gogh painted works that not only copied nature but interpreted and glorified its mysteries. His paintings are more than just paintings. They are bridges connecting the human world to the world of the Divine, and we are willing to pay millions to possess his masterpieces.

OPERATE YOUR LIFE AS IF YOU HAVE ARRIVED

As you master your skill, this alone does not necessarily guarantee the rewards that come with success. Pavarotti is a wealthy man. Van Gogh made strangers who possessed his paintings wealthy, but he never enjoyed a decent living himself. The ability to bring forth the Divine touch in your work does not by itself guarantee financial reward.

There is another aspect to this mysterious puzzle. You need to perceive yourself as being successful and then operate your life as if you were. It is essential to uproot from your consciousness thoughts that somehow you are lacking and unworthy. Operate from abundance and self-importance. To some Thick Face, Black Heart practitioners this comes naturally; others have to work consciously at it. When Grace Kelly first appeared in Hollywood, she was a nobody, but she carried herself naturally, as if she already were a great star. When she actually was a great star, she looked and acted more like a princess than a movie star.

Before you can garner the external rewards, you first must inwardly experience that they already belong to you. In short, your inner reality will take the form of a self-fulfilling prophecy. Your actions will be unforced and much more effective because they are motivated from within, not because you are mechanically following a formula. Outer success will follow the actions and attitudes you manifest due to your experience of success as an inner reality.

TRANSFORMING YOUR ATTITUDE

The famous book *Think and Grow Rich* teaches us how we can think ourselves to riches. Throughout the years, I have carefully observed how people obtained wealth. It is not thinking, reading, or listening that transfers us from poverty to wealth. Rather, it is a switch of attitude from the center of our being. You can think all you want, you can affirm all you want, you can understand all you can possibly understand, but it will not necessarily change you or your circumstances.

These are necessary steps; however, your circumstances will not change until your knowledge and your understanding take on a living form from within. Because you have transformed, suddenly everything becomes possible.

This transformation has no fixed formula. It results from your willingness to do battle within and your unceasing courage to cultivate your inner strength to overcome your liabilities. Through this self-cultivation, you will eventually produce the magical fruit that will transform your attitudes in every aspect of your life.

A Transformation

In the mid-1970s, after a heartbreaking divorce, I decided to try my wings in the world of moneymaking. After looking around, I saw that the Southern California real estate market was booming and most of the realtors were driving prestigious cars. They seemed to have more than enough money. I too got my license and began to work in the world of real estate.

I was able to support myself in a small degree of comfort, but nothing impressive. During this time, I began to read many wonderful books in an attempt to transform my relationship with money. Besides reading about it, I practiced daily and lived the messages I read.

Later, I met a dynamic lady, Judy. I teamed up with Judy. We worked diligently for one month. We did everything we were supposed to do, but nothing happened. We didn't make any money. One morning we met as usual, but didn't have our normal enthusiasm; we were like two deflated balloons. That morning we were scheduled to see all the newly available properties. We felt too depressed to see anything, so we decided we would stop by an old Spanish church and just sit.

The church was completely empty except for the two of us. Judy took a seat on the right side of the church, and I took a seat on the left. The air was calm. The church walls echoed silently with the prayers offered over the past hundred years. I looked up at the altar and gazed at the limp Christ hanging from the cross. Sadness and love leaped out of my heart to him. I began my prayer in the form of a silent conversation with the Christ on the cross:

Since I was nine years old, I have loved you so. I was willing to do anything to be your champion. Do you remember that I used to lie in front of my family worship altar and pray for stigmata like St. Francis of Assisi? As I grew older, I realized you tested your followers in the trial of life rather than the dramatic miracles of stigmata. I was afraid I would not pass your test of life. Stigmata seem so much easier and more glorified than silently enduring the tests of living.

I remembered what you had done to Job in the Old Testament. You removed all of his wealth, then his health, then his basic human dignity. Only when he demonstrated his unshakable devotion did you restore everything to him tenfold. I am afraid of such a test. My flesh is weak. Deep down, I am always afraid to surrender myself. If I really surrender myself to you, you will turn me into a homeless bag lady, since I have no friends or relatives around. You will turn my life into a mess, just as you did Job's.

A gentle, clear voice from the depth of my being replied, "What was right for Job is not right for you. Job wanted the test for his own satisfaction. He wished to prove his love of me to himself. It was not I who needed the proof. There is no need for you to be destitute for my sake. I assure you I will be with you always. You are my very own. My blessing goes with you everywhere. You shall have no lack."

I wept uncontrollably for over half an hour. They were tears of relief and gratitude. The burden I had carried all my life dissolved in an instant; it disappeared like melting ice. At this time, I heard the sweet voices of the school students singing "America the Beautiful," echoing through the side door behind the altar. I thought to myself, it is not by accident that on the back of the American dollar bill is printed "In God We Trust." Whoever designed the dollar bill understood that the foundation of our money system was God's grace—therefore, "In God We Trust." Our founding fathers trusted God as the supporter and sustainer of our monetary system, yet I had so little faith. I wept even harder.

As I walked out of the church, Judy met me at the front door. Through her tearful eyes, I knew she had just had a similar experience. We looked at each other and simultaneously spoke out, "Let's go buy a house." We went to see the new houses on the market. We bought two houses within two hours.

I had no idea how I was going to pay for them. I didn't even have my share of the down payment. Judy and I were in an extraordinary state, though. We experienced no lack, only abundance. In that state of mind, anything is possible. I told her I only had a few thousand dollars in my bank account. I said it without guilt or apology. Judy said, "I will loan you the money."

Judy's husband had just been laid off a month earlier by Rockwell International and was temporarily out of a job. Rockwell gave him some stocks as compensation for his fifteen years of service. Judy sold the stocks, loaned me the down payment, and I became the proud (50 per cent) owner of two lovely homes in the prestigious neighborhoods of Studio City and Sherman Oaks in Southern California. We had a transformation of our attitudes about money.

Nothing had to make sense anymore. It was illogical for Judy to loan me the money and for me to own half the house; furthermore, she had no idea how I was going to pay her back, and neither did I. It was even more illogical for her to sell her only financial security while her husband was out of work. Engineering jobs were scarce; there were layoffs everywhere. But as your attitude changes, your relationship to your reality changes also.

After that day, everything we touched turned to gold. We performed our work with diligence and delight. Most of all, I knew I was a winner, and I knew I would never have to be fearful again of becoming a bag lady.

A few months later, besides being able to pay Judy back the money she had loaned me, I acquired three more properties, plus a beautiful home with a double lot, swimming pool, and full guest house. I moved in and furnished the place with everything new. My inner change of attitude earmarked the beginning of a new life for myself.

The Indifferent Attitude toward Money

Whether you have plenty of money or a little, remember, "Money is not part of who you are. You didn't bring it with you at birth, nor will you take it with you at death." Enjoy your money. Have money work for you and make it contribute to your life. See money for what it is, but no more. Don't let money take over your whole life, because money is fickle. Keep an indifferent attitude toward it.

FINE-TUNE YOUR UNDERSTANDING OF UNIVERSAL TIMING

For most of us, whether our desires are tangible or intangible objects, noble or ignoble pursuits, one thing is certain — we want to obtain them immediately. If our desires are not granted in a timely manner, anger, tension, and desperation will arise, and finally we will lose all heart and accept defeat.

We are like young infants who demand our milk bottles

with great urgency. If the bottles are kept from our mouths for a mere moment, we will wail in protest. In order to keep harmony, the mother must accept the baby's whims and adjust her needs to fit the infant's timing.

Unlike the human mother, our Divine Maker insists that we, His children, learn to fine-tune our understanding of His timing. We must learn to accept that the Creator gives according to His own schedule, regardless of our demands. When you learn God's timing, you learn how to live and work in harmony with yourself and others around you. Most importantly, you understand the art of communion with the silent voice of the universal will.

At the close of 1991, the mortgage interest rate plunged to almost a thirty-year low. A friend of mine, Sonya, grew anxious and upset because she and her husband could not raise enough money for a down payment on a house. At night she would dream about watching her children playing at a new home. Her expectations and thwarted desires made her accuse her husband of not being able to fulfill her most basic needs.

Recently she told me about her worries. I told her it does not matter how high or low the interest rate moves. When the time is right, the perfect house and the method to pay for it will reveal itself harmoniously and effortlessly. You must be content with whatever your starting point or financial condition is because that is your launch pad to begin your journey toward prosperity.

CONCLUSION

The mystery of money is not a one- or two-dimensional formula. Even the wealthiest people have no fixed formula to guarantee their own prosperity. In so many ways, prosperity is connected with our ability to bring forth every aspect of our Maker's qualities. In addition to the qualities mentioned here, the qualities of endurance, self-confidence, perseverance, self-respect, determination, discipline, love, compassion, generosity, joy, courage, righteousness, efficiency, and even ruthlessness should also be included. The more we can bring forth these qualities, the more we will tap into the power of our Maker. Ultimately, through our inner and outer battles, we will experience our connection with the Divine, the source of universal abundance.

For the practitioner of Thick Face, Black Heart this is a task that is never completed. Each day we experience a thousand successes and a thousand failures. Victory lies in perseverance. If we are steadfast in correcting our course, we can repeatedly recreate ourselves as the heirs to the abundance of the world. That is the mystery of money, the mystery of wealth: we do not have to beg; we need only claim that which is ours by right.

SUMMARY OF KEY POINTS

- The Chinese character for money is composed of three symbols: one symbol means gold; the other two represent spears. The character for poverty is also composed of three symbols: the symbols depict a man standing at the bottom of a pit, bent as if under a great burden. These characters not only represent money and poverty, but also they say something profound and beautiful about them.

- The first spear symbolizes the outward struggle for survival. Anyone who wishes to accomplish his goals or claim a share of the earth's abundance must first be prepared to battle for money.

- The second spear represents the battle within. Before one can fight and win the battle without, one must win the battle within. Poverty is more a state of mind than an external condition.

- Money and wealth are obtained through interactions with others.

- To have a sense of your worth, you have to do something that is worthy of your own respect first.

- In reality, most of us are where we want to be financially. Obtaining prosperity is not about what you are willing to do to gain it; more importantly, it is about what you are willing to give up in exchange for it.

- Money is the element of life that inspires the greatest emotions in individual human beings. It is tightly connected with the emotions of agony and ecstacy. When you have money, you never feel you have enough. If you have lost money, you wish you had appreciated it more when you did have it.

- The path to wealth is not to chase money for its own sake, but to understand and develop your own intrinsic talents and inclinations.

- Each of us possesses a spark of individual brilliance. Every one of us is capable of accomplishing something in our own unique way that cannot be accomplished by anyone else. Striving to discover what is our niche in this vast human market is part of our conquest of life.

• In most cases, life does not play hide-and-seek; rather, we are blind. Our unique abilities often display themselves in many situations in the course of our lives. Because we are so focused on making a living, we do not see anything else.

• The world is like a pyramid of people struggling with one another. You don't have the choice of whether or not to join in the struggle, but you can choose where to fight. Don't fight your battle at the bottom of the pyramid. It is much too crowded down there. It is easier near the top.

• You don't have to beg in your prayers for material prosperity. The abundance of the world is freely given to those who claim it as their natural birthright.

• Adapt the divine touch in your work. What makes an artist, dancer, lawyer, or businessman good is his ability to recreate his Maker's creativity in his work.

• Outer success will follow the actions and attitudes you manifest due to your experience of success as an inner reality.

• Money is not part of who you are. You didn't bring it with you at birth, nor will you take it with you at death. Enjoy money, but keep an indifferent attitude toward it.

*Means and ends
are convertible terms
in my philosophy of life.*

—MAHATMA GANDHI

8

Deception without Deceit

The word *deception* often has negative connotations due to the influence of the Western religious concepts of good and evil. From the Eastern point of view, the reality of life spans degrees of grey. Rarely is the reality of life solely black or white. In the same way, we seldom find someone totally pure and untainted by evil thoughts or someone rotten to the core without an ounce of goodness.

Deception, to the Thick Face, Black Heart practitioner, is a tool to be utilized to gain necessary advantages. Evil does not exist in deception itself, but rather in the user and uses. In Mark H. McCormack's book *What They Don't Teach You at Harvard Business School,* he states in the chapter on negotiating, "The game aspect of negotiation is saying and doing things which puncture those perceptions that come too close to reality while encouraging those perceptions which are furthest from the truth."

The 2,000-year-old Chinese battle strategy book, Sun Tzu's *Art of War,* is a guidebook for deception. Sun Tzu stated, "War is a game of deception.... If one is able and strong, then one should disguise oneself in order to appear inept and weak.... When you are ready to attack, you must convey the impression that you will not attack...."

An American client told me, "Compared to Asians, we are not very good at practicing deception. We refuse to acknowledge that we even practice it, as to do so would violently contradict our cultural belief system. Even though people in the Western culture are repelled by the idea of deception, in reality we are unable to escape it." While Westerners are practicing deception, they pretend that they are not, whereas Asians accept the reality of deception as a necessary element in their daily lives. They write books on and glorify the study of the art of deception.

THE UTILITY OF DECEPTION

As each one of us seeks people and conditions that can benefit his or her survival, sometimes it is almost impossible to accomplish a greater and worthier objective without employing some degree of deception. Our greatest president, Abraham Lincoln, understood the spirit of Thick Face, Black Heart: the fine art of deception without deceit.

In Abraham Lincoln's early, fragile political stage, he never expressed openly an intent to free the slaves and make them equal. His position was to follow the majority opinion, which proposed to segregate the blacks after they were freed.

After a decisive victory, Lincoln delivered his famous Gettysburg speech, in which he abandoned the position on segregation and stated clearly that all men are created equal.

Lincoln could not speak freely in the early stages of his political career. He had to use deception to secure the necessary votes to gain control of the presidency—only then could he do the greater good for the blacks in freeing them from the insufferable bonds of slavery and inequality.

Creating the Illusion of Utility

For thousands of years, Chinese masters who have practiced Thick Face, Black Heart have been documenting different methods of creating attractive "bait" to motivate their counterparts to act according to their secret agendas.

The worm is seen, but the hook is unseen. The outer appearance draws us, but the hidden catches us.

In the same way, when you wish to motivate others to participate with you on a personal or business level, you too need to create an attractive bait. You have to make the benefits obvious to attract your intended participants. If you cannot find a legitimate benefit, then create an illusion of one. By applying this principle, you will be able to entice your potential counterpart to participate with you. In time the benefits will, in fact, be realized by both. The following is such a story.

Deception without Deceit

Grass seed is a very important agricultural commodity in Oregon. The state supplies nearly 70 percent of the cool-season grass seed for the United States and fulfills nearly 50 percent of the world's seed demands. Oregon grass seed companies have always been interested in selling seed to China. The problem has been that as determined as Oregon growers have been to sell to the Chinese, the Chinese have been equally determined not to buy. As far back as the early 1980s, the American Seed Trade Association had pitched grass seeds to a touring

Chinese Vice Minister of Agriculture, only to receive a flat "no." In fact, given the Chinese idea of grass, the suggestion was ludicrous. It was tantamount to selling refrigerators to Eskimos.

In Chinese, the word *grass* is used pejoratively as a metaphor. A stupid person is said to have a container of grass between his ears. The Chinese have never planted grass for ornamental purposes. The Chinese consider grass a weed, and their idea of beautification is to pull grass out rather than plant it. My client, in trying to sell grass seed to the Chinese in the early 1980s, was suggesting that they expend precious foreign exchange to purchase more grass to pull up and throw away! The Chinese considered the idea of buying grass seeds a huge joke.

Still, in 1986, I took on one particular grass seed company as a client. Perhaps little could be done, I thought, but if anything could be done, I could do it.

I went to China and presented an intriguing picture to the Chinese government, outlining the overwhelming benefits to them, and portraying the Americans as naive. Since Chinese officials have always adopted a general attitude that foreigners are naive, my presentation was easily accepted.

I told the Chinese that the American company was looking for a low-cost production source. The American company would like the seeds to be produced in China, and would buy them back at the same price they were purchasing seeds from American farmers. In this way, the project would provide the Chinese government with the opportunity to earn much-needed foreign currency. I was welcomed with open arms and treated like royalty.

I knew China would not be able to produce quality grass seeds at a reasonable cost, given the weather conditions and agricultural methods. In order to sell it back to the United

States under terms similar to those given to American farmers, China would have to lose money.

As the Chinese enthusiastically began their grass seed production, I also began to visit China frequently. Accompanied by American technical personnel, I taught the Chinese the necessary production skills and advised them on the benefits of grass seed and how to maintain a plush green lawn.

A couple of years later, the Chinese ceased production of American grass seed because it was too expensive for them. However, in the process, they had learned the value of American grass seed. They began to buy directly from my client's company.

As I had initially anticipated, the efficiency and beauty of the American product was not lost on the Chinese, who hosted the 1990 Asian Olympic games. With seven thousand athletes participating in the view of thousands of international media and hundreds of thousands of spectators, the event was a showcase for modern China. They had used the superior American grass seed in their Olympic village stadium, and it was a great hit.

After the success of the Asian Olympic Games, the imported American grass seed became the hottest commodity and commanded as much as five dollars a pound as a result of supply and demand. (The same grass seed is selling for less than one dollar per pound in the United States.) Even though the average monthly income of a Chinese worker is twenty-five dollars, lawns are beginning to sprout in public places. The Chinese now see the nice, even, thick emerald-colored carpets as beautiful rather than undesirable. Now American grass seed even grows in the grounds of Beijing's ancient royal garden, which is presently the home and office of China's highest official, Deng Xiaoping, and also Jiang Zemin, the secretary general of the Chinese Communist Party.

In this incident, both the Chinese people and my American client benefitted from my deception by creating the necessary illusion.

THE PRINCIPLE OF UTILITY

Although we consider ourselves civilized and train ourselves to act with grace and good manners, after we remove this false façade we find that we are driven by the impulse of self-preservation, like all creatures. Everything we do is influenced by this instinct.

For example, the institution of marriage is often bound by this principle of utility. A husband and wife create an environment that nurtures one another. They depend on each other for emotional, spiritual, and financial support. If the couple no longer experience love and affection, they will remain together only as long as there are more benefits in staying together than in parting. These benefits could be financial security, the welfare of the children, or social status. The reasons for keeping a dead marriage afloat are countless, but the motivation is singular: self-preservation. When a man and a woman can no longer squeeze any benefits out of their relationship, they split.

The relationship between parents and children cannot escape this rule either. Mothers would not be able to love their children if our Maker hadn't implanted that love in them. Parents experience self-nurturing by unconditionally nurturing their children.

Some parents do not see their children as an expression of love. Instead, they see their children as punching bags: using the children as the object of their frustrations in life by abusing them physically, verbally, and emotionally.

The nurtured child stays with nurturing parents out of the

love they have for one another. The love they feel within themselves is like a spring shower, which softens and nourishes the other's heart.

Abused children stay with their parents purely out of the instinct for survival. Even bad parents are necessary for the children's physical survival. However, the children run away when the pain becomes unbearable.

The principle of utility dominates everything we do; we practice utility to support our survival. Even if we are doing selfless service for others, we always benefit equally or more than our benefactor.

In the business world, we spend time with those who can or will enhance our financial or social status. If a relationship is not mutually beneficial, we will spend very little time on it.

Recently, when discussing this utility principle with a friend of mine, he asked me, "Isn't this very negative, when you identify human beings with these traits?"

I replied, "No. If I told you that when you put your hand in the fire it would be burned, or if you didn't know how to swim and wanted to jump into the ocean, that you would drown, does that make me evil? Is it wrong of me to inform you of the nature of things? I don't believe it is of any virtue to insist on being ignorant of human nature."

Understanding the workings of human nature without pretense allows us to learn how to relate to each other more realistically.

UNCONDITIONAL SUPPORT

Around 2,700 years ago, in China, Guan was a noble prince whose ancestor's kingdom had been demolished prior to Guan's birth. His family had escaped to the neighboring country of Chi and fallen to the lowest social class. Bao, a wealthy scholar of regal birth, recognized Guan's intelligence and befriended the former prince. Guan's family was so poor that he did not even have money for meals; his livelihood was provided solely by Bao. Later, when Bao provided capital for a business venture by Guan, Guan spent it for his personal needs. Bao defended Guan by saying, "Guan is so poor that he has a great demand for cash. His intention was never wicked." Soon both had become the target of gossip for the nation. People were laughing at the stupidity of Bao and the ungratefulness of Guan.

Three times Guan was challenged by enemies to a duel; three times he fled. Bao would vindicate his cowardliness by saying, "Guan has an old mother at home. It would be against his filial duty to place his body in jeopardy." When Bao was selected to be prime minister, he deferred and insisted on Guan instead.

Guan proved himself to be one of the greatest prime ministers in the history of China. However, without the unconditional support and trust of Bao, Guan and China both would have been losers. Confucius remarked, "Without Guan's wise governing, Chinese civilization would have dissolved at that time."

Most of my life, I have followed the code of unconditional support set by Guan and Bao. Through the experience of life, I realize that Guan and Bao's relationship was the exception rather than the rule. The common human relationship normally has a different set of rules.

MUTUAL BENEFIT

When benefits are mutual,
then cooperation will follow.
Mutual cooperation results in benefits,
and thus leads to affection.

—*TAI GONG WONG*

Tai Gong Wong lived around 3,100 years ago and, at that time, wrote the first military text in the world. His philosophy was later adopted by countless Chinese military strategists; even the highly acclaimed *Art of War* by Sun Tzu was based on his work. His military strategy was not based solely on maneuvering and placing the troop formations, but rather on the understanding of human nature. Through his personal observations and studies of human behavior, he discovered that there existed unwritten laws mandating the principles of utility and mutual benefit that ordinary human beings unconsciously followed. By utilizing this understanding, he could predict the outcome of any given situation, thus maximizing his advantage. He was the first known Thick Face, Black Heart practitioner in the history of China.

As Tai Gong Wong stated above, "When benefits are mutual, then cooperation will follow...." This is the simple principle of utility. This principle applies in the international arena as well as our personal lives. The following stories illustrate my point.

Nelson Mandela in Japan

Nelson Mandela, the South African antiapartheid leader, visited Japan in late October 1990. He was disappointed and

rather surprised to learn that Prime Minister Toshiki Kaifu
had turned down his request for twenty-five million dollars
needed by Mandela to support the cause of the African
National Congress. The official reason Kaifu gave was that
the Japanese government did not support any political
groups.

Twenty-five million dollars was not a large sum of money
for Japan, one of the modern world's wealthiest countries.
The question was not about twenty-five million dollars;
rather, it was about "utility." If the Japanese government
could have realized how it could benefit from supporting
Nelson Mandela's cause, the financial support would have
followed.

Despite the fact that the Japanese government does not
openly support any political group, there have always been
many ways to get the job done. The Japanese government
could have encouraged donations from their private sectors.
Japan's large corporations have always had a close working
relationship with their government. After three days' effort in
fund-raising, Mandela walked away with only three thousand
dollars donated by private Japanese citizens who were sympathetic to his cause. This was not even enough to cover
Mandela's travel expenses.

The Japanese had followed the European communities in
canceling their trade relationship with South Africa. Even so,
Japan had traditionally enjoyed a friendly relationship with
the South African white ruling power. There were no visible
benefits to be gained by worsening an already deteriorating
relationship with that government. Furthermore, supporting
the battle against apartheid had never been a top priority in
Japan's international policy. The Japanese government in
general is not very sensitive to racial struggles.

When Japan chose to follow the world economic powers
in boycotting trade with South Africa, it was not motivated

by the human rights issue but rather was merely following its own agenda in creating its new world leader image.

When and if the Japanese government can identify the clear benefits in supporting Nelson Mandela's cause, then the financial support will follow.

The story above is not about political issues, but is meant to clarify the motivation behind the Japanese government's decision in refusing to support Mandela's cause.

A Strategy for Self-Preservation

In good times, bad times, ancient times, and today, there are always some young, up-and-coming individuals who exhibit extraordinary talent and capabilities in their chosen field.

Before they "arrived" at the top, while they were in the process of proving themselves and utilizing all of their resources to push themselves forward and upward, they were often labeled as "climbers." Interestingly, our society usually looks down on climbers. I believe we should lend a hand to those truly capable climbers. Unless we were born into the Kennedy or Rockefeller families, each one of us is on the way up to new plateaus. Today's nobody may become tomorrow's somebody. While you are on your way up, for your own sake, lend a hand to another climber.

Once during an interview, a reporter asked Gregory Peck why he would volunteer to share the leading role in the film *Roman Holiday* with an unknown actress, Audrey Hepburn. His answer was, "My motive was a selfish one. She was so brilliant, I knew when the film was released she would be an instant star. If I took the leading role alone, it would have made me a laughing stock. It's all about self-preservation."

Mr. Lin, a Taiwan business and political leader, told me,

"Years ago, the present Republic of China's presidential chief of staff, Y. S. Tsiang, 'voluntarily' removed himself from the political circle and started a teaching career. At that time, very few people came to visit him. Everyone thought he had no more future in politics. Since I had always admired his charisma, I would invite him to my house for dinner or tea. No one could even imagine then he would be holding the position of chief of staff today."

You can never understand or know the mystery of fate; We should always lend a hand to those capable individuals during the time they are on their way up. For the Thick Face, Black Heart practitioner, this is a good strategy for self-preservation.

The Key to Being Important

Mr. and Mrs. Smith are farmers in central California. They are just common folk performing their daily duties. They have no money or power to influence anyone or to change anything. Like most of us, they are not particularly "important."

Their daughter told me, "My father and mother are so opposite. My father's whole attitude toward others is to try and impress on them how important he is, because deep down he knows he is not. Conversely, my mother knows she is not important, and she accepts it. She never tries to impress anyone or prove a point to show how important she is. Beneath her quiet and gentle manner, she is very wise and down-to-earth. She understands the basic virtue of life—to serve your fellow man. Through service, she increased her value to her community. Therefore, automatically she became important."

On the other hand, Philip is a brilliant graphics designer.

His small studio is always struggling from month to month. It is not the quality of his artwork that jeopardizes his financial success but rather the quality of his personality. Like Mr. Smith, Philip felt a lack of self-importance. To Philip, the most important thing is not success in business or making money. The most important thing is to be "important" in others' eyes.

He is doing just the opposite of what Mrs. Smith did. Rather than make himself useful to his customers through excellent service, he is often having an ego competition with the very people he is supposed to be serving. Whenever a customer spoke to him in a tone of voice that he considered disrespectful he would turn down the work, even though his schedule was totally empty and he was desperately in need of money. Unfortunately, most of his prospective customers did not meet his standard of respect. I asked him why he felt so offended by these people. His answer was, "They think that just because they have a little money they can order me around."

Whenever people give him praise, he will soak it up like a dry sponge in a puddle of water. He can feast on that praise for days.

Although Philip is desperately seeking confirmation that he is "important," and craves to be respected, unlike Mrs. Smith, he does not understand that the key to being important is in making yourself useful to others.

The Distinction between the Con Man and the Businessman

A friend once stated, "A businessman and a con man both understand the value of deception. The only difference between the con man and the businessman is this: The businessman will ultimately deliver the benefits he has promised. The con man will not."

A good businessman has the ability to identify clearly to his customer the benefits of doing business with him. He convinces others that he is able to deliver such benefits. He makes others feel good about their wise choice in doing business with him.

Even when a businessman is misleading others, he does it with the intention of eventually delivering what he has promised. Sometimes, he may not be able to control all the elements, which may cause his failure to keep his own promise. On the other hand, when a con man misleads his victims, he never intends to make his promise come true.

There is a popular American phrase, "Fake it until you make it." This statement works well for a con man as well as a businessman. Both employ the skills of deception and make others perceive the benefits to be gained by associating with them. The difference between the con man and the businessman is not in their outward actions, but rather in the expression of their soul.

CONCLUSION

The idea of discussing the concept of deception may at first be repulsive to some, yet this is most definitely a beneficial tool in working with man's practical nature. It can assist each of us in avoiding needless setbacks and cause us to gain a winning edge.

SUMMARY OF KEY POINTS

• Evil does not exist in deception itself, but rather in the user and uses.

• Human beings will invest time and energy with those who can benefit them the most, now or sometime in the future. This is the simple principle of utility in everything we do; we do it for the benefit of supporting our survival. Even if we are doing selfless service for others, we receive the inner rewards. The giver always benefits equally or more than the recipients.

• A good business deal incorporates the following ideal: In my business I include your interest; in your business, you include my interest.

• We should lend a hand to ambitious and capable individuals for the sake of self-preservation.

• The key to making yourself important is to serve your fellow man. Through service, you will increase your value to others.

• The con man and the businessman both employ the skills of deception and make others perceive the benefits to be gained by associating with them. The difference between the con man and the businessman is not in their outward actions, but in the expression of their soul.

*When you work, you fulfill
a part of earth's fondest dream,
assigned to you when the dream is born.*

—Kahlil Gibran

9

Sixteen Noble Attributes of Work

Through the expression of work, we earn our monetary rewards. This book would not be complete without mentioning work. We predominately utilize Thick Face, Black Heart either with others or with ourselves during the period when we are performing our duties at work.

1. WORK: THE FONDEST HUMAN EXPRESSION

Work is a primary method used to express ourselves in fulfilling our obligation to support ourselves. Through work, we contribute to the collective good of society and the evolution of man. Work is an essential part of our self-expression and self-preservation. Only through work can the idea and the spirit of Thick Face, Black Heart take on a visible form.

2. PROVIDE FOR YOURSELF AND OTHERS

As a young man passed through a forest, he saw a lion taking a piece of meat to an injured tiger. The young man thought to himself, "God is good, He provides for all his creatures. Just look at that tiger—God also takes care of him. As I am the child of God, for certain, God will provide for me."

The young man went back to his small hut at the edge of the forest. He stopped hunting and waited for God to provide for him. A week passed and nothing happened, so he went hungry. Two weeks, then three weeks passed, and still nothing. Soon he was dying of starvation. A holy man passed by his hut and asked him what had happened. With the little strength he had left in his body, he told his story.

The holy man said, "When you saw the two animals, you should have learned from the lion, not the tiger. The lion provides for himself and also provides for others."

I salute all the world's entrepreneurs because they risk everything in their pursuits. Additionally, they are able to provide for themselves while creating jobs for others.

3. WORK AS SPIRITUAL UNFOLDMENT

There is no division between your daily work and your spiritual unfoldment. Every situation will accelerate your spiritual evolution. Your work is where your spiritual unfoldment takes place.

Through work, we encounter people and events that mirror our spiritual state. Through work, people and events either irritate us or uplift us. Whether it be irritation or inspiration, the universal intention is to utilize that particular situation to teach us a beneficial lesson.

Nothing in life happens by accident. If people and events in your life stir strong emotions, it signals the need to take a good look at yourself in that area.

4. WORK: THE GREATEST TEACHER

The purpose of labor is to learn.
When you know it, the labor is over.
The apple blossom exists to create fruit.
When that comes, the petals fall.

— *KABIR, A PROPHET*

Each time I write a book, I learn much more about the subject than I initially dreamed possible. For example, the concept of Thick Face, Black Heart has been in my mind for over twenty years. But as I describe Thick Face, Black Heart here, it has taken on a whole new dimension of clarity. It is no longer just a feeling in my heart. As I have laid it on paper and divided it into the different aspects of life, it has become tangible. Work is the greatest teacher.

5. WORK DOES NOT NEED YOU, YOU NEED WORK

He must perform his duty, however difficult it may seem,
for it frees him from the bondage of worldly life.
If he carries out the duty given to him
according to his nature,
he overcomes the bondage of living.

— *LORD KRISHNA*, BHAGAVAD GITA

God created this universe for us. The universe does not need us, but we need the universe. Similarly, the work we do does not need us, but we need the work. If any one of us disappears from this planet, the planet will continue to exist. If our planet disappears from this galaxy, the galaxy will continue to exist. If our galaxy disappears from the universe, the universe will continue to exist.

In 1990, a galaxy over a billion light-years from earth was discovered. Anything that is a billion light-years away is beyond my comprehension. It really puts our self-importance into a proper perspective.

Not long ago, during meditation, I heard my voice asking a question, "Does the world need a book on Thick Face, Black Heart?"

Another voice answered, "The world does not need this book, or any other book. But you need to write it." The answer surprised me. I thought I was writing this book because the world needed it. In contemplating this wisdom, I have discovered how profoundly true it is. In fact, I couldn't help doing it. I was driven from within. All great works are produced because their creators are driven involuntarily. The necessity to create is such a great force that it overcomes all human reason.

6. THROUGH WORK, DESTINY UNFOLDS

*Your work is to discover your work
and then with all your heart give yourself to it.*

—*LORD BUDDHA*

When you are true to your assigned work, your destiny will be true to you. If currently you are out of work, then make finding the appropriate work your full-time job. If you can't find work that suits you, it may be time for you to take the leap into the entrepreneurship that you always dreamed of. Before, you did not have the courage to quit your job and lose that regular paycheck. Often desperate situations provoke dramatic actions.

7. LIFE EVOLVES THROUGH ACTIONS

If you know all the great knowledge, but you sit and do nothing, your knowledge will be worth nothing to yourself or others. Even a philosopher needs to talk about his beliefs or write them down so others can benefit from his profound wisdom.

The universe is ever-changing and acts unceasingly. An individual is ever active, whether he is sleeping, eating, or just sitting. Even in the motionless, deep-sleep state, his internal body is ever active, supporting his life. As infants, we work unceasingly to learn the wonders of our new world. As students, we work to acquire basic knowledge and skill from our studies. As adults, we work to support ourself and others. As elders, we work to maintain the well-being of our physical bodies, and we contemplate the life behind us and the path before us, contributing our experiences and time to those who need guidance. The bottom line is, as long as you possess a body, you cannot escape work.

8. EMBRACE THE FARMER'S VIRTUE

We gain freedom
when we have paid the full price
for our right to live.

—*RABINDRANATH TAGORE*

Whenever work is mentioned, the ideas of procrastination and inertia arise instantaneously. There are many, many motivational books and tapes on the market. The objective of these books is to move people from nonaction to action, and eventually from action to effective action.

I have done extensive consulting work in agriculture, and during the years I have dealt with both American and Asian farmers. What American farmers have in common with the rest of the farmers of the world is their dedication to work.

The time for planting and the time for harvesting do not wait. If you procrastinate and miss the planting season, you will have no crop for the whole year. If you miss the harvesting season, you will have crops rotting in the field. If you miss the time for fertilizing the crops, you will have a poor harvest for the year.

A rich harvest is dependent on the farmer's timely dedication to his work. He does not have to read motivational books to overcome his inertia. Farmers understand the meaning of the saying, "The dictionary is the only place where success comes before work."

9. THE WORKING SECRET OF WOLFGANG AMADEUS MOZART

My faith in truth, my vision of the perfect,
help thee, Master in thy creation.

—RABINDRANATH TAGORE

The greatest natural musical genius ever to live, Wolfgang Amadeus Mozart, described how he composed his music.

When I am, as it were, completely myself, entirely alone, and of good cheer—say, traveling in a carriage, or walking after a good meal, or during the night when I cannot sleep; it is on such occasions that my ideas flow best and most abundantly. Whence and how they come, I know not; nor can I force them. Those ideas that please me I retain in memory, and am accustomed, as I have been told, to hum them to myself. If I continue in this way, it soon occurs to me how I may turn this or that morsel to account, so as to make a good dish of it, that is to say, agreeable to the rules of counterpoints, to the peculiarities of the various instruments, etc.

All this fires my soul, and provided I am not disturbed, my subject enlarges itself, becomes methodized and defined, and the whole, though it be long, stands almost complete and finished in my mind so that I can survey it, like a fine picture or a beautiful statue, at a glance. Nor do I hear in my imagination the parts successively, but I hear them, as it were, all at once. What a delight this is I cannot tell! All this inventing, this producing, takes place in a pleasing lively dream. Still the actual hearing of the total ensemble is after all the best. What has been thus produced I do not easily forget, and this is perhaps the best gift I have my Divine Maker to thank for.

When I proceed to write down my ideas, I take out of the bag of my memory, if I may use that phrase, what has been previously collected into it in the way I have mentioned. For this reason the committing to paper is done quickly enough, for everything is, as I said before, already finished; and it rarely differs on paper from what it was in my imagination. At this occupation I can therefore suffer myself to be disturbed; for whatever may be going on around me, I write, and even talk, but only of fowls and geese, or of Gretel or Barbel or some such matters. But why my productions take from my hand that particular form and style that makes them Mozartish, and different from the works of other composers, is probably owing to the same cause which renders my nose so large or so aquiline, or, in short, makes it Mozart's, and different from those of other people. For I really do not study or aim at any originality. (From *The Life of Mozart*.)

When we perform our work, we have to be silently in tune with our inner selves for guidance. Each person hears their inner silent voice differently. To some it comes naturally; others must cultivate that intuition through meditation and other spiritual practices.

10. USING INTUITION AS A BUSINESS TOOL

The definition of *intuition* according to the dictionary is as follows: 1. direct perception of truths, facts, etc., independently of any reasoning process. 2. pure, untaught, noninferential knowledge.

Intuition is a commodity that is extremely undervalued in the Western world, yet everyone who has ever succeeded in any extraordinary task has always drawn upon this power. A good trial attorney must be well versed in law and should research his case. However, he also needs to perceive intuitively the minds of the jury so that his presentation will sway the jury members in favor of his client.

I was told by a homicide detective that a good detective understands how to follow his instincts and gut feelings, whether he is seemingly on the right track or not. A good businessman, after examining his available data, ultimately will have to rely on his gut feelings to make the final decision.

Many revolutionary scientific breakthroughs often begin with an intuitive perception of unknown potential by a scientist. He then proceeds to prove his intuition through scientific experimentation and conclusions.

At age sixteen, Einstein asked, "If I moved at the speed of light, what would light look like?" This question was the seed for his theory of relativity, which he spent the rest of his life trying to explain to the world.

One of the foundation blocks of organic chemistry, the benzene ring, was revealed in a dream. The originator, F. A. Kekule, was trying to solve the puzzle of how carbon chains are connected. One night he had a profound dream in which he saw six snakes writhing, each biting another's tail. He immediately awoke and realized his subconscious had just given him the formation of the primary hexagon—a structure made up of carbon atoms that is the base of the benzene ring.

A year ago, I went with some friends to a racetrack for the first time in my life. Since I did not understand a thing about the horses and the races, I decided to rely on my intuition. Fortunately, I was sitting very close to the front and had a plain view of the horses as they displayed themselves prior to every race. As each horse came up, I would "tune in" to that horse and sense his condition and spirit at that moment. I was able repeatedly to place the top three horses in the order they came in. All of my friends couldn't believe their eyes. I have not been to the racetrack since. Maybe I didn't want to break my glorious betting record.

To put it simply, a well-developed intuition is a valuable tool in the workplace. The source of this intuition is the same as that which provided inspiration for Mozart's compositions.

11. WORK IN THE LIGHT OF GRACE

Our Maker's grace, the condition of being in His favor, is like sunshine. It indiscriminately showers light on all. Those who stand under the sun immerse themselves in the warmth of its rays and receive full benefit from them. Those who hide under the tree deprive themselves of the sun.

Through the power of our Maker's grace, the universe came into existence. Through the power of His grace, human beings are able to perform their daily duties and maintain their bodily functions.

In this same way, Wolfgang Amadeus Mozart learned how to listen to the music from his Maker. Such creativity is not through man's effort alone, but is a gift of your own soul — the Divine Grace.

Each one of us possesses that grace within. Some of us are in touch with it, while others are not. What made Mozart different was his ability to hear the music from "nowhere." As Mozart said, he merely dictated it according to the principles of composition in his time.

12. DISCOVER YOUR
NATURAL RHYTHM

With our Creator's infinite imagination, the world never ceases to provide us with wonders. Each one of us is unique. What works for one does not necessarily work for others.

For example, early to bed, early to rise is an acceptable norm for proper living. It is wonderful for those who enjoy the tranquility of dawn to rise early, but for others the norm might be detrimental. As I mentioned earlier, Salvador Dali, Winston Churchill, and Hugh Hefner all shunned a pattern of rising early each day and instead concentrated on working when they felt most comfortable.

This section is specially written for those who find it difficult to follow the nine-to-five schedule. If your natural working rhythm works best at night, try to find work that will allow you to do so.

13. REACH FOR YOUR
LIMITLESS LIMIT

A timber fit for pillars
should not be misused for chopsticks.

—CHINESE MAXIM

If you are capable, then stop selling yourself short by limiting your imagination. By the same token, if you are assigned an easy task and it is beneath your ability, then you are wasting your talent and will perform poorly.

In ancient China, a talented young man was assigned to govern a small, remote village because he had offended a powerful relative working in the royal court. After he arrived at his new post, all he did was drink and sleep. He ignored all work and let his tasks pile up. A year later, the court sent an auditor, who upon arriving heard the villagers complain about how the young man had neglected his duties. The auditor found the young man drunk, as usual, and questioned him about his disregard for duty. The young man replied, "Come back in three days, and everything will be done." Three days later, the auditor returned to discover a well-groomed young man in an orderly office with all his assignments completed. The young man had finished a year's worth of work in only three days.

The auditor later learned that the young man had been cast out to the remote village because he was the victim of a personal vendetta. When the auditor returned to court, he reported to the Emperor that a valuable talent had been misused, at a great loss to the country. The young man was summoned to court and reassigned to a worthy and honorable post.

14. THE THREE P'S OF WORK

The three P's of work are not a secret to most. Nevertheless, they deserve mention.

Purpose: purpose to work is like a flight chart to a pilot or a navigational map to a sea captain. You have to know where you are going and how to get there before you take off for your destination.

Perseverance: this was covered to a great extent in the endurance chapter.

Patience: nothing is possible without patience.

Unfortunately, in this physical world, time and distance are two elements that we have to make room for. Nothing happens just by snapping your fingers. Even simple tasks like my trips to Asia needed patience, since I sat on the airplane more than ten hours at a time. With patience, everything seems to glide along more smoothly. Without it, life seems more explosive and chaotic.

15. WORK: THE HIGHEST WORSHIP AND HIGHEST SACRIFICE

If you perform the sacrifice of doing your duty,
you do not have to do anything else.
Devoted to duty, man attains perfection.

—*LORD KRISHNA*, BHAGAVAD GITA

When duty is performed with a sense of detachment, the very work performed becomes a sacrifice and therefore a worship to our Maker.

What do I mean by detachment? Because we are made of flesh, it is necessary to receive a monetary reward to support our life. Being overly concerned with the reward will never enhance the outcome of our work but instead will interfere with our performance. When an archer's eye is on the prize rather than the bull's-eye, he surely will miss the bull's-eye as well as the prize.

What do I mean by sacrifice? Sacrifice is an act of offering—offering our labor to the One who grants us the ability to act. We perform our work without an attachment to self-gratification. Just by adopting this attitude, our efforts become a sacrifice to our Maker. Thus, the sacrifice serves as worship.

Treating your work as sacrifice and worship will not lessen your compensation. Whatever reward we deserve will come to us. In fact, this attitude will transform the ordinary task to something sacred. It will enhance your performance and lead to greater compensation.

16. THE HARMONY OF DIVINE WILL AND HUMAN WILL

Every morning in my affirmation I read the following: "Being attuned to the Divine will is the most important factor in attracting success. To discover through the right meditation how to be in harmony with the Divine will is man's highest obligation."

When human will is misguided, even success brings nothing but sorrow. A great being once said, "Human beings practice motivation blindly; they motivate themselves into action and often land at a place where they don't even belong."

In today's industrial society, people are compelled to keep up with the pace of the rest of the world. They need to be motivated constantly to work harder, longer, and better. They buy the newest motivational tapes and books, and if that is not enough they even will buy subliminal tapes to give them that extra push. All these "blind motivations" are attempted in pursuit of success.

There is nothing wrong with pursuing success. Whatever our life's objective might be, each one of us should reach out and try to touch the farthest star in our personal constellation. But when all our attention is placed upon motivation and actions as the means to reach success, we are missing an important ingredient: the guidance of the Divine will. Thus, we didn't enjoy what, in the beginning, appeared to be success, and ultimately we were disappointed.

I speak of this from firsthand experience. Years ago, I had a business that did very well for the first couple of years. After that, everything somehow went wrong. Even ordinarily easy tasks turned out unexpectedly wrong. It looked like a cosmic conspiracy against my business. But I thought my determination could overcome anything. I thought that I just needed to work harder and put more money into the business. I struggled for a couple more years with my partners. The more pressure I felt to save the business, the more I neglected praying and listening for the Divine voice. I didn't even need any motivational tapes or books because my blind motivation was driven by desperation. My determination to succeed and save the company was just about as strong as God's determination for me to change occupations. But it wasn't until every possible door was closed that I realized there is a will that is stronger and wiser than my will, which I must be in harmony with—the Divine will.

After closing the company, by chance I came across this profound passage: "Human beings practice motivation blindly...." If I had found this passage earlier, I might have saved myself much heartache. On the other hand, if I had read this before my devastating experience, I would not have recognized the depth of its wisdom.

SUMMARY OF KEY POINTS

- Work: The Fondest Human Expression. When you work, you fulfill a part of earth's fondest dream assigned to you when that dream is born.

- Provide for Yourself and Others.

- Your Work Is Where Your Spiritual Unfoldment Takes Place. Through work, we encounter people and events that mirror our spiritual state.

- Work: The Greatest Teacher. The purpose of labor is to learn; when you know it, the labor is over. The apple blossom exists to create fruit; when that comes, the petals fall.

- Work Does Not Need You, You Need Work.

- Through Work, Destiny Unfolds. Your work is to discover your work and then with all your heart to give yourself to it.

- Life Evolves through Actions. The bottom line is, as long as you possess a body, you cannot escape work.

- Adopt the Farmer's Virtue. The time for planting and the time for harvesting do not wait. If you procrastinate and miss the planting season, you will have no crop for the whole year. A rich harvest is dependent on the farmer's timely dedication to his work. He does not have to read motivational books to overcome his inertia.

- The Working Secret of Wolfgang Amadeus Mozart. Flow with the Divine Grace. Mozart did not study or aim at any originality.

- Using Intuition As a Business Tool. Intuition is a commodity that is extremely undervalued in the Western world. Yet, everyone who has ever succeeded in any extraordinary task has always drawn upon this power. To put it simply, intuition is your gut feeling. A well-developed intuition is a bankable commodity, and the source of this intuition is the same as that which provided inspiration for Mozart's composition.

• Work in the Light of Grace. Grace is like sunshine. It indiscriminately showers light on all. In the same manner, Wolfgang Amadeus Mozart learned how to listen to the music from his Divine Maker. Such creativity comes not through man's effort alone, but is a gift of your own soul—the Divine Grace.

• Discover Your Natural Rhythm. With our Creator's infinite imagination, the world never ceases to provide us with wonders. Each one of us is unique. What works for one does not necessarily work for others.

• Reach for Your Limitless Limit. A timber fit for pillars should not be misused for some small task. If you are capable, then stop selling yourself short by limiting your imagination.

• Three Principles of Work: Purpose, Perseverance, and Patience.

• Work: The Highest Worship and Highest Sacrifice. You perform the sacrifice of doing your duty; you do not have to do anything else. Devoted to duty, man attains perfection.

• The Harmony of Divine Will and Human Will. Being attuned to the Divine will is the most important factor in attracting success. To discover through the right meditation how to be in harmony with the Divine will is man's highest obligation.

*If one is able and strong,
then one should disguise oneself
in order to appear inept and weak.*

—SUN TZU'S *ART OF WAR*

10

The Advantage of Playing the Fool

The ancient Chinese classic *The 36 Strategies* is a manual on how to achieve victory without direct confrontation. This book has been studied by all Asian businessmen and politicians. Because *The 36 Strategies* was included in my previous publications, I will not go into details at this point. One can easily perceive the essence of these strategies just by examining the titles: "Pretend to be a pig in order to eat the tiger"; "Be wise but play the fool"; and "Escape is the best policy."

VICTORY THROUGH SUBMISSION

It is a fact of life that no matter how strong or ruthless you are, there will always be someone stronger and more ruthless than you. It is important to cultivate the sensitivity to recognize when you should fight back and when you should submit. It is even more important to develop the strength to endure this period of submission. When it comes to achieving your objectives, submission sometimes can be even more effective than fighting back.

Japan's economic success today clearly demonstrates the power of submission. After the country's defeat in World War II, Japan's status fell from being the master of half the world to that of an occupied nation. Japan learned the hard lesson that aggression does not always accomplish one's objective. After more than forty-five years of silent submission, Japan is thriving once more.

WHEN YOU WIN, YOU LOSE

"When you win, you lose." This great wisdom is from the teachings of St. Francis of Assisi. It is a profound insight, not easy to perceive at first, but the following story illustrates the point.

Years ago, I met a man in his early sixties who seemed to be without hope, as if he were trapped in a dark pit. He had been unemployed for over three years and had lost his life's savings.

It had all started five years earlier, when he entered the high-finance world of a lucrative overseas real estate venture. It turned out to be a total fraud. He lost over $270,000.

He was so upset about his loss that he started to pursue justice. His obsession forced him to take large amounts of time off from work, which finally resulted in his dismissal. After three years of legal battles and unemployment, he had devoured his remaining savings. By the time he won his court case, the offender had liquidated all of his assets, and the man was left empty-handed.

Countless small and large battles are fought in life. We all have to learn to choose wisely in which battle to fight and in which to accept defeat graciously and subsequently endure the humiliation of that defeat. Sometimes the price of ultimately winning can be so costly, you end up being the real loser. As Lee Iacocca said, "If competitiveness is reduced to simply 'who can produce it the cheapest,' then the biggest winner will be the guy who's willing to be the biggest loser."

DO NOT CROSS THOSE WHO CAN HURT YOU

Mr. Wong is a talented artist in Taiwan. He used to make a limited number of pottery objects and then sell them by word-of-mouth to his friends. He was making a meager living. By chance, Mr. Liu, an artist promoter, saw Mr. Wong's work, recognized his potential, and agreed to promote him.

Liu gathered one thousand sponsors. Each sponsor paid a membership fee equivalent to one thousand U.S. dollars. With a total of one million dollars, Liu began his promotional campaign, including private gallery showings, press exposure, and much more. Three years later, Wong's work became one of the most collectable of any contemporary artist in Hong Kong. His work now commands as much as one hundred thousand dollars.

Mr. Wong began to think, "Why should I pay Liu over half of my income? Furthermore, Liu is a dominating individual. Maybe it is better to get rid of Liu and go on my own." Wong discussed this with a distant relative, Mrs. Lam, a successful businesswoman.

Mrs. Lam's sincere advice was, "There are certain people you should never cross. Liu is one of them. Whatever your discontentment is with Mr. Liu, you should endure. Liu is a very powerful individual in the art community of Taiwan. As fast as he made you, he can break you even faster. You, as a rising artist, should never be on the wrong side of Mr. Liu. Through catering to Liu, you have obtained recognition beyond your wildest dreams. The world of art is purely about preserving values. You need Liu on your team." Mrs. Lam's advice was most prudent.

A struggling Hong Kong artist arrived in San Francisco and began to search for a gallery to represent his work—oil paintings portraying the lives of fishermen in his homeland. He labored without success before finding someone who recognized his talent. A prestigious gallery owner loved his work and vigorously promoted the artist through numerous showings. The owner published colorful coffee-table books displaying the pieces, and invested tremendous capital in positioning the artist as the gallery's main showpiece. Through the gallery's efforts, his first painting sold for twenty thousand dollars and the second for eighty thousand dollars. The artist, the gallery, and the collectors all profited.

However, a few years down the road, the artist was convinced by his friends that it was in his best interest to go out on his own. The end result: the gallery went out of business, the artist has a small shop selling nothing but his paintings, and his paintings have no tradeable value for the collectors. The artist does not gross anywhere near the amount he did when the gallery handled his work. Worse yet, all the people who invested in his paintings have lost money, and I am one of them.

THE ADVANTAGE OF PLAYING THE FOOL

Not long ago, a Taiwanese client of mine suggested that I contact Mr. Taro, a Japanese businessman, in Tokyo. Mr.

Taro was looking for assistance with his wholesale produce operation. I flew to Tokyo and met with Mr. Taro.

According to Mr. Taro, too much of what was shipped to him turned out to be inferior or spoiled because it was improperly handled at the source of production. This caused great concern, since he paid 10 percent duty on goods arriving in Japan, whether or not he sold them. Furthermore, he had to hire additional help to sort through the shipment, and he was losing money. What he wanted, he said, was somebody at the point of shipment to ensure quality. He was willing to pay 15 percent above his present cost for superior goods. To prepare for my new role, I toured his warehouses and listened to him while he explained his needs. The man was polite and thorough. Before my departure, Mr. Taro stressed the importance of providing him with current U.S. agricultural information.

As the faxes began to fly across the ocean, there was a curious lack of actual commitment on the part of my new client. He declined to place orders while at the same time requesting more information on the U.S. agricultural market.

Now, I don't mind giving information. The transfer of information is part of any business arrangement. However, that implies that there is a business arrangement in the first place and the transfer of information is an element in the deal. Thus far I had received nothing much of value from the Japanese businessman, yet I was sending information by the faxload. If I was to be an information service, I thought I should charge accordingly.

I decided to push the man: I asked him for a commitment. The Japanese dislike saying "no," as it disrupts a critical harmony implied in the Japanese way of doing business. When Mr. Taro faxed me back to tell me that he was not yet ready to commit, at least not without even more information, I suspected that I might have been taken for a ride.

It did not surprise me that Mr. Taro used me to gather information for him. It is a common practice among Asian businesses. What I found interesting was my response to being used. In the past, I might have seen two options: either I could chalk it up to experience, cut my losses, and move on to other things; or I could write the man to tell him that I was aware of his intentions and found them distasteful. The first option was practical, although a dead end. The second option, although also a dead end, would make my ego feel better.

I decided on a third option: adopt the spirit of endurance, play the fool, and do nothing. Since I had invested my time and goodwill, it seemed that I ought to find some advantage in the situation. I would accept him at his word—that he was an honorable man whose intentions to do business with me were bona fide, but that at present he had no use for my company's services. I would endure my humiliation of being outsmarted by Mr. Taro and divorce my ego from the situation, leaving open the future possibility of his business or assistance.

On the surface, the third option had the practical result of the first option. Both of them implied resignation and acceptance, but the third option in fact produced an additional result: suddenly I was in control. No longer had I been simply used unfairly and resigned to the role of "victim."

The moment I took the third option, I created an internal environment in which I was not only prepared to succeed, I had already succeeded. With the exception of possible material gain should Mr. Taro come back to me, nothing remained to be accomplished.

In this sense, I was not even truly waiting, because "waiting" implies "waiting for something," an outcome either good or bad. No, I was simply "available" should something good come along. Conversely, I was unavailable for anything bad to happen, the possibility of which I had already banished from my reality.

A year later, Mr. Taro called on me in the United States, and the end result of his visit was that he placed a sizeable order that also led to other business ventures. My tactic of "playing the fool" paid off.

SUMMARY OF KEY POINTS

- Victory through submission. If one is able and strong, then one should disguise oneself in order to appear inept and weak.

- It is a fact of life that no matter how strong or tough you are, there will always be someone stronger and tougher than you.

- It is important to cultivate the sensitivity to recognize when you should fight back and when you should submit.

- It is even more important to develop the strength to endure the period of submission.

- When it comes to achieving your objectives, submission sometimes can be even more effective than fighting back.

- When you win, you lose. When we fight a battle that we shouldn't, even if we win, we lose.

- We all have to learn to choose wisely in which battle to fight and in which to accept defeat and subsequently endure the humiliation of that defeat.

*Great spirits
have always encountered
violent opposition
from mediocre minds.*

—*ALBERT EINSTEIN*

11

Thriving among the Cunning and Ruthless

E ach one of us, in our normal state of living, attempts to ensure our personal interest and survival. The reality of living is that if you live your life with your heart and your wallet exposed, you have to be willing and prepared to be hurt and to lose your wallet as well. A saint walks on the street with a wallet. The thief sees no saint, but a wallet. To a thief the wallet is essential for his survival. To whom the wallet belongs is inconsequential.

The reality of this world is that thieves and robbers exist. In your world and mine, they don't just take your wallet. Worse yet, they will rob you of your faith and belief in the goodness of mankind and leave you bitter inside. Thus, it is essential to acknowledge the existence of brutality and shield yourself from harm with Thick Face, while using the spear of Black Heart to wage the unavoidable battles.

PRINCIPLES OF SELF-PRESERVATION

We Americans entered the 1990s to find ourselves worse off in our national economy and in our individual spending power than before. We have fallen from being the world's economic giant to being the world's largest debtor nation. An increasing number of people feel frustrated about their financial condition. As their frustration grows, some people become more difficult to deal with. The fact that former president George Bush was compelled to promote a new image of a kinder and gentler America tells us we are in fact going in the opposite direction, away from those graceful qualities.

In day-to-day interactions, the silent refrain "What have you done for me lately?" echoes. To the cunning and ruthless, gratitude for past kindnesses does not exist. Any past good deed is of little consequence. The only thing that matters to them is the question, "What have you done for me lately?"

In speaking of a gentler America, former president Bush tried to alter the nation's psyche. In the meantime, for the pupose of self-preservation, Thick Face, Black Heart practitioners should get acquainted with the following essential principles in preparation for mastering the art of thriving among the cunning and ruthless.

Guard Your Interest

Jim, a retired Northrop executive, once told me, "If you feel you are getting screwed, generally you are." In this world, most people experience that the nice guys always seem to be getting the short end of the stick. When we are too concerned with pleasing others and are too agreeable, we might be giving others an open invitation to take advantage of us. Recently, during a press conference, Colorado congresswoman Patricia Schroeder told the press that President Clinton was making favorable concessions only to those members of the legislature in both houses who had strongly opposed him, while ignoring the needs of his supporters.

If you don't stand up for what is rightfully yours, nobody else will. Even when you do stand up for your rights, many people will attempt to intimidate you. They will wish to take you down a notch and deflate you, so that you don't obstruct their forward motion.

Barbara is a news anchorperson for a network television station. She has been working with the station for over five years and her news program is currently getting number one ratings locally. But those five years getting to the top were not always smooth and easy.

Three years ago, when she had to negotiate her contract renewal with the station, she ran up against some serious resistance. The station management adopted the attitude that Barbara was barely pulling her weight and that she should consider herself lucky even to be offered another contract. She could hear the undertones quite clearly: "You are a girl. Girls should not be aggressive."

When she requested changes in the contract, the management was furious. Since her convictions about her self-worth were strong, she refused to compromise. Every day the news director called her into his office, excoriated her for her work, and ended each session by saying, "Sign this contract." Four months passed, and she still would not budge. Finally, the management granted Barbara every change that she had asked for.

However, before she went ahead and signed the contract, she took it to an attorney. The attorney suggested a few minor alterations in the wording. When she went back to the station and told them about this, they were shocked and infuriated once again. Her superiors made it clear that they considered her actions selfish and immoral. Even then Barbara did not back down. Eventually the contract was reworded to reflect a settlement that both parties could agree upon.

Barbara has recently signed another three-year contract at the same television station, and this time it was much easier. As she said, "Now they know how I work and that I mean what I say. A lot of people I work with told me I should have asked for more changes than what I really wanted in order to let them feel they had won something. But I don't believe in that. I asked them to change only the terms that I really couldn't live with. The changes I could do without I refused to ask for."

The point of this story is not about Barbara's negotiating tactics. There are no rules dictating whether you should ask for more than what you want or only for what you cannot live without. It's more important to notice and analyze the spirit that makes Barbara so strong. Day after day, she had to withstand the management's intimidation in the form of threats, abuse, and insults. Simultaneously, she had to get in front of the camera and announce the news cheerfully, with the professionalism of a seasoned journalist. She never let the emotions involved with the negotiations affect her work. Barbara had a strong sense of her own self-worth. She employed Thick Face, which shielded her from abuse and allowed her to fight for what she deserved. She used Black Heart to give her the toughness to stick to her convictions.

Know Your Value

Martha is an attractive real estate developer and a former film producer. She wrote a letter to one of the most prestigious industrial designers in the world about her real estate

projects. The designer came to visit her in California to discuss the possibility of acquiring her projects.

When I first met Martha during a professional conference,
she accompanied the designer and five of his entourage. At
that time, I had thought she was one of his paid staff as she
was interviewing me on camera for my impression of his latest project. A couple of years later, Martha became a close
friend. She told me then that she had been so ignorant and felt
she had been exploited and abused by this designer.

She told me the designer gave her the impression that he
was very interested in her real estate projects and had wished
to develop a long-term working relationship. Soon after, he
asked her instead to help him produce and conduct interviews
for a documentary video about himself, and he implied that
she was privileged to associate herself with him.
Additionally, she had to go to bed with him to sweeten the
deal. After one year, Martha walked away empty-handed.

She told me, "I did not know my own value. A whore at
least gets paid for her services. Worse yet, I knew he was a
married man."

The Vision of Discrimination

A dog's vision is full of prejudice and discrimination.

—*CHINESE MAXIM*

In China, dogs are not kept as house pets, but are used to
protect the home from intruders. A dog that does not bite is
of no use to a Chinese owner. But Chinese dogs are not
trained as watchdogs. The decision as to whom it should
attack and whom it should allow to enter is left to the dog's
instincts. A dog who lets a robber enter his master's home or

mistakenly bites an important visitor will come to an untimely end. The dog learns quickly to discriminate between welcome and unwelcome visitors according to a few simple rules.

1. Attack any poorly dressed or unkempt stranger who tries to enter the house. At best he is a beggar.

2. Attack any stranger who seems weak-spirited, furtive, or lacking in confidence. It is unlikely that any trouble will come of it. It is an easy way to demonstrate to the master that you are vigilant.

3. If a stranger is both poorly dressed and dispirited, don't hesitate a moment to attack. It is an easy victory with no risks attached.

4. Don't attack a well-dressed or well-groomed stranger. Chances are too good that he is a welcome visitor. Biting him could result in a beating from the master.

5. Don't attack a high-spirited, confident stranger. He might give you a good beating himself.

6. If the stranger is well-dressed, well-groomed, high-spirited, and confident, wag your tail and ingratiate yourself with him.

These simple rules of discrimination are common among the world's businessmen and political leaders, as well as among Chinese dogs. In deciding between whose favor they should curry and whom they should attack, they all tend to grovel before the wealthy and powerful and act viciously toward the poor and weak.

It is not only political leaders and Chinese dogs who operate this way. Sit in sometime on a corporate board meeting while the members are discussing potential targets for acquisition. You can be sure they will focus on the weakness and vulnerability of a corporation before they plan a takeover. Observe also what happens in a grammar school playground at recess. The bigger children will often single out the smaller ones and take advantage of them. Children understand the application of this principle intuitively without ever being taught because it is an inborn natural instinct.

A Hunter's Instinct

The behavior described above is true the world over. Those who are naturally cunning and ruthless will always find sweet and trusting individuals to take advantage of. In the kingdom of animals, the lion can always single out a sick or weak-spirited wildebeest among a herd of thousands. We humans also broadcast our inner state to others. As soon as others sense our fear and timidity, we become an instant target. This hunter's instinct is totally intuitive.

A friend of mine, Kevin, worked on a project with his partner for eight months. After he had spent all his savings and time and successfully completed the research and development part of his responsibility, his partner, who was in charge of marketing, secretly obtained another partner who could provide additional financing and coldly cut Kevin out. Since Kevin had spent all of his money in research and development, he now had no money even to hire an attorney in order to sue his supposed partner.

Kevin is a person who thinks the best of everyone. Just by being around him, you know he is a "nice" guy. As a matter of fact, he is too nice for his own good. Because of his blind but unswerving trust, he set himself up to be taken by his partner. He went ahead and did the work and gave the finished product to his supposed partner without a written agreement.

Kevin is not the world's only fool. Almost all of us have at one time in life trusted those who were supposed to be trustworthy and were found wanting. Through this process, we learn the necessity of becoming a warrior to fight skillfully for what we rightfully deserve.

Beware of the Biting Dog

Once there was a great Japanese Zen master who said, "Everything is God's love. Out of that love, the universe came into existence. God created the universe with no other substance but himself."

After one of his sermons, a disciple was so inspired by the talk that his heart was filled with love. As he walked through the village on his way home, a vicious street dog stood in front of him and started barking, showing all of his teeth. The disciple thought to himself, "My teacher has just taught me everything in this universe is created out of God's love. Since God created this world with his own being, I should love and respect all creatures." Intending to walk right past him, he smiled at the dog with great affection and love in his heart. But as soon as he came near the dog, the dog bit him.

The next day, he went to his teacher and told him about the incident. The teacher replied, "Maybe you knew you are made in the image of your Divine Maker and the essence of this universe is love, but nobody told the dog."

Like the young disciple, we desire to do good and see the best in everyone, but often our judgment of given situations is guided to a certain degree by ignorance, therefore inducing us to react inappropriately. The young disciple should have avoided this street dog or intimidated it, making it run away. It served no purpose to be bitten by the dog. This dog bites whomever comes across his path. This street dog is like the pickpocket, in that he does not discern the inner state of people passing by. As I've said before, when a pickpocket sees a saint, he doesn't see the saint; all he sees are pockets.

Safeguard Significant and Insignificant Advantages

Many Americans have told me that they think Asians are shrewd bargainers. This is said to be true whether Asians are at the international negotiating table or in the car dealer's sales office. Most Asians are trained unconsciously from a very young age that it is important to strive for a position of advantage. When they spend a penny, they expect a penny or more in return. Very rarely will they settle for half a penny.

My observation is that those who safeguard their interests in insignificant matters will also guard their interests in more important matters. This does not mean they become petty-minded and argue over every penny. More likely, they are extremely generous in giving or sharing their possessions with others of their free will. However, the key is that they act upon their "free will" instead of being taken advantage of involuntarily.

My friend J. J. is a wealthy lady in Taiwan. On her recent trip to the United States, she shopped for a new Volvo for her seventeen-year-old son who attends high school in the United States. She telephoned every dealer in town and finally paid cash for the car from the dealer who offered her the best discount. It was not so much that she needed to save the money; rather, it was a matter of her personal style. When I accompanied her to pick up the new car, the salesman, a fifteen-year veteran of his trade, told me that it is easiest to sell a car for its full sticker price to those who can least afford it.

During the whole process of shopping and bargaining for the car, J. J. had her son participate at all times. She told me, "He must learn from a young age the importance of striving for the best deal."

George has a consistent pattern in his life: he always gets taken. Although he is a chronic entrepreneur, in the past he also has been a chronic loser. Once he told me a very intriguing story. When he was six years old, he set up a stand in front of his house and sold food from his mother's refrigerator. He took the vegetables, fruits, and eggs and arranged each with a price tag. He sold eggs at one penny each when his mother had bought them for three cents. He quickly sold the eggs and vegetables at a loss. His doting mother thought it was so cute. She never mentioned to him that the objective of doing business was to make a profit.

Years later came the turning point of his bad deal-making. George was working at a flea market with his wife, Mary. One day he bartered with another exhibiting merchant and exchanged a product with a retail value of twenty-five dollars for a five dollar item. Mary had originally purchased this item at cost for fourteen dollars. After he told Mary about the incident, a red light popped up in her mind. George had again allowed himself to be taken.

Mary told George that the money difference was a small matter. What was important, however, was that George had to stop his pattern of making bad deals. At that moment, something extraordinary happened within him. For the first time, he saw how ludicrous he had been in the past.

He said to Mary, "I am going to break this losing pattern. I want to go back tomorrow and tell that merchant I made a bad deal and ask him what he is going to do about it." Mary

told him not to worry about it. Mary knew it would be difficult for George to go back, especially as the amount of
money involved in the transaction was so small. For the first
time in his life, George was determined to learn how to correct his past behavior. George said to Mary, "I realize I truly
have nothing to lose and everything to gain. The worst thing
he will say to me is no, and I can observe and learn from him
how to handle a confrontation like this." George went back
and renegotiated the deal successfully. He obtained additional items to make up the difference in the dollar amount.

All these stories may sound small and insignificant.
Nevertheless, whether we deal with intricate corporate negotiations or daily mundane encounters, we always operate out
of the same place—our strong or weak state of mind. The
manifestations may be different, but the sources of motivation are always the same.

Beat Ten Men in Combat by Using Your Spirit

"The only way not to be a victim is to be tough and ruthless along with the rest of the world." If that is your conclusion, then you have missed the subtle points I have endeav-
ored to make. As I have mentioned before, the world of business is like the animal kingdom, and each one of us transmits
our state of mind to others. We say either "I am available for
you to take advantage of me" or "Don't tread on me."

When contemplating the essence of Thick Face, Black
Heart, in time you will transform your spirit. The important
thing to remember is, it is not whether your words or actions
are tough or gentle; it is the spirit behind your actions and
words that announces your inner state. The sixteenth-century
Japanese sword master Miyomoto Musashi said, "You must
contemplate the Way of the warrior's skill so you will be able

to beat a man in combat by the use of your eye. With diligent training, you will be able to beat ten men in combat by using your spirit."

THICK FACE, BLACK HEART 101

For beginning Thick Face, Black Heart practitioners, it is most important to master the power of yielding. I have mentioned this before, but restate it here because it is an essential, potent concept that is unfamiliar to Western culture.

A mistake people may make when first studying Thick Face, Black Heart is that they become aware that in the past they have often been the victim of the cunning and the ruthless, so they instantly desire justice and seek to fight back. Through studying this book, you will come to realize that you have the power to make trouble and get your revenge. You will become eager and aggressive in confrontation while preparing to engage in combat. It is as if the clock's pendulum has swung one way all your life, and then you attempt to adjust its course with an opposite swing. As you begin to put your tough attitudes into practice, there are many good-hearted people who will be offended by your manner. In the process, you may turn yourself into a monster and offend everyone else along the way. Those who did not intend to take advantage of you will make you a target for the sake of self-defense. In this way, you will be victimized once again.

In order to protect yourself as you practice Thick Face, Black Heart, first acquire the power of yielding. Your outward action may seem to be submissive and nonthreatening, but inwardly, never lose sight of your objectives. When you can win a battle by maneuvering obliquely, why go for a frontal assault? When your opponent perceives you as no threat, he may not be moved to pull out his biggest guns when dealing with you. But if you forewarn him and overexaggerate your strength, he will be obligated to use his most effective weapons on you.

If You Don't Have to Trust Him, then You Can Always Trust Him

A few years ago, I was riding the train between Rome and Venice. On the train I ran into Roger, an American tourist. Roger was in his mid-forties. He had just lost a small fortune from his business due to his partner's embezzling three million dollars, leaving him with a huge debt. He was touring Europe, trying to get his head together to figure out what he should be doing next.

As our journey progressed, Roger became more comfortable talking about himself. He confided to me, "When I was in my early twenties, in San Francisco during the late sixties, I had a very small drug-dealing operation. I acted as the middle man, and after each deal was made, I would get paid my share of the commission. I never got cheated because I never trusted any of the people I dealt with. I followed a golden rule of mine: if you don't have to trust him, then you can always trust him. I had not considered my ex-partner as a threat, and therefore I ignored my golden rule." He further commented, "It is very difficult and frustrating to know where to draw the fine line of protecting your own interests versus trusting the higher and noble nature of another human being."

Do Not Underestimate Your Counterpart

All business relationships begin when people wish to combine their efforts to achieve mutually beneficial objec-

tives. As time and events unfold, however, the conflict of
interest within the original unity may begin to surface.

When a new venture begins, initially all parties are friendly and act noble. Because of this friendly atmosphere, many
have a tendency to expose too much of their private selves.
But, the seemingly harmless information provided can come
back to haunt them, and they will find themselves in a potentially vulnerable position.

Barbara and Jerry were respected professionals in the
same line of work. They decided to get together and develop
a project related to their field in their spare time. As they
spent most of their free evenings working on this project,
they got to know each other and their respective families
quite well.

A year and a half later, near the culmination of the project,
Jerry decided he wanted to be sole owner of the project.
However, he had a signed partnership agreement with
Barbara. Jerry sought to break their contract. After consult-
ing with an attorney, Jerry concluded that it would be almost
impossible to do. He had to find other alternatives.

Through family social gatherings, Jerry learned about
Barbara's marijuana smoking habit. He also found out that
her son was her supplier and that he was well connected with
illegal distributors. Jerry told Barbara that she should volunteer to abandon her project interest; otherwise, he would
make public Barbara's secret. Barbara quickly gave up her
entitled interest. She could not afford the scandal, especially
since she was a well-respected clinical psychologist.

Barbara made two big mistakes. The first is obvious; she
shouldn't have smoked illegal substances. The second mistake was that she grossly underestimated Jerry. She careless-
ly disclosed too much information about herself and consequently was made to pay for it.

The Thief of Peace and the Serenity Stealer

Keep a respectful distance from those who would steal your peace and serenity. In your daily life, you will run into this type of person around every corner. These people are not necessarily cunning or ruthless, nor are they a real threat to your career and personal objectives, but they *are* eternally annoying.

They operate by thriving on their own inferiority. Their actions and words are very cutting, even though people are nice to them. They also are gutless. On the one hand, they play up to the ruthless and cunning types who treat them like dirt, and yet they are mean to people who are decent and kind to them. These serenity stealers are people to be avoided. Life put them in a place that they resent because they feel it is beneath them. To get even with life, they react by attacking those who are nice to them, while being very agreeable to those who abuse them.

They cannot help themselves; their actions are involuntary. The serenity stealers steal into your heart and confidence with their sweet, charming exteriors. But after you allow them to get close to you, they will snap at you in order to diminish you in their eyes. They try to temporarily elevate their own inner power and feel good for a moment, but are usually remorseful afterward. They can't help themselves, and so the pattern continues.

It is important not to interact with them in a similar manner. If you do, they will make a lifetime career of attacking you. These people are masters of "death by a thousand cuts." You should always keep them at arm's length. Then they will eternally respect you and solicit your friendship. They will then transfer their troublesome energy to someone else.

You Don't Need to Win Them All

Human beings are very complex. You never know when your words and actions will be considered deeply offensive. Whether your intention is to offend or flatter, it will always be interpreted according to each person's private perception of himself, and your intention has very little consequence in his reality.

Mary Ann is a forty-five-year-old single lady. She grew up with a dominating mother and an abusive father. After twenty years of university schooling, she obtained three masters degrees in the areas of Urban Development, Asian studies, and Business Administration. However, she had difficulty in applying her schooling to the professional job market. She showed no interest in entering any profession for which she had studied. As a result, she worked as a part-time word processing clerk in an attorney's office for fifteen dollars per hour. Whenever I saw her, she would complain about how tough her life was, how much she needed more money, and how awful her living conditions were. I always encouraged her by praising her ability to obtain three masters degrees while others were having difficulty earning one. I told her everything would work out. It seemed my words always brightened her day.

On one occasion, while walking on the street with a friend of mine, I met Mary Ann. After the formality of introductions, I had the idea that my friend might be able to use Mary Ann in his office. Since Mary Ann only worked twenty hours weekly, she would be able to increase her income, thereby solving some of her financial problems.

With Mary Ann standing there, I proceeded to promote her abilities and encourage my friend to use her in his office. That evening when I arrived home, Mary Ann telephoned me. She was shaking with anger. She was totally insulted by my telling my friend that she was a skillful word processor. Never had it entered my mind that Mary Ann felt so deeply inferior about the job she had been doing for the past ten years that she had to hide it from others.

I didn't realize at the time that due to Mary Ann's lack of professional accomplishments, she harbored deep feelings of inferiority. She did not know how to alter her present circumstances and had consequently grown bitter. For people like Mary Ann, praise and acknowledgment are the only rewards that make life worth living. If anything is said or done to make them feel inferior, their sweet, gentle nature will instantly disappear into furious anger.

In the realm of human behavior, you can't win them all. In fact, you don't *need* to win them all. Utilize Thick Face, Black Heart to protect yourself from such insults and press on with your life.

The Theory of Polarity

We would like everyone we meet to love us, praise and support our work, and share our point of view. The reality is that no matter how holy or noble your task or point of view may be, you will never get everyone to agree with you. The secret is not to convince everyone but rather to understand how to have the world polarize its concept of you and learn to use this force for your benefit.

One of the most powerful and popular fundamental Christian ministers openly promotes polarization between different Christian sects and other religions that he considers pagan. Instead of having the controversies he has stirred up diminish his following, his ministry has grown by leaps and bounds through the utilization of his polarization theory. Even after a well-publicized scandal, he is still thriving and expanding. His secret power is to convince his followers to despise the other churches and religions so self-righteously that they become, by default, his eternal followers.

A former grand wizard of the Ku Klux Klan, David Duke, rapidly climbed the political ladder and became a serious contender for the Louisiana governor's office by utilizing the power of racial polarization. Although his political point of view is abhorrent to most Americans, he still drew the attention of the entire nation and an astounding number of Louisiana voters.

As long as prejudice and bigotry exist in our society, polarization will be a powerful tool. By utilizing the dark side of the human spirit and dividing people against one another, you can effectively generate a support base to promote your objectives.

Although the concept of polarization is usually frowned upon, in reality this venerated power is used by all levels of society. Therefore, we do not have the luxury of being ignorant of this force. It is important for us to learn the art of polarization in order to recognize it and avoid falling victim to it. Mastering this force will enable us to accomplish our worthy objectives.

The reality is that you cannot win over everyone's heart and mind. If you can get half of the population to support your cause, even if the other half despises it, you are assured of being on the path to victory.

The Unity of Violence and Nonviolence

The great apostle of nonviolence, Mahatma Gandhi, was a student of the *Bhagavad Gita,* which he studied daily. He once remarked that his five years in prison were not fruitless because they gave him the time to study and contemplate the *Bhagavad Gita*.

He followed the path of Krishna's instruction to Arjuna, which was to perform his duty with neither desire nor passion. Through such discipline, he gained an immovable, unshakable, and detached inner state. Gandhi was then able to formulate a nonviolent philosophy and a means of effective action against great adversity.

In the face of British domination, he led the Indian people in the practice of nonviolence in the form of sit-ins, marches, and other acts of civil disobedience. This precipitated barbarous acts of violence from the British, which enraged the world against their imperialism.

Gandi's detachment and dispassion enabled him to endure the violence inflicted on him and his people by the British while remaining true to his belief in nonviolence. To those who thought him passive or a coward, he said, "Most think nonviolence is not to fight. On the contrary, nonviolence is the strongest power. It conquers the power of violence.... My creed of nonviolence is an extremely active force. It has no room for cowardice or even weakness. There is hope for a violent man to someday become nonviolent, but there is no hope for a coward."

If Gandhi's adversary had been Hitler instead of the honorable British, he said he would have employed a different strategy. Gandhi said, "I make no hobgoblin of consistency. If I am true to myself from moment to moment, I do not mind all the inconsistencies that may be flung in my face. There is a consistency that is wise and a consistency that is foolish. A man who, in order to be consistent, would go bare-bodied in the hot sun of India or the sunless midwinter of Norway would be considered a fool and would lose his life in the bargain."

Mahatma Gandhi was a master of Thick Face, Black Heart at every level in its highest sense.

Harmony of the Lover and the Warrior

Recently, I began to have wonderful dreams in which everyone was full of love and compassion. No one had any evil intent to harm anyone else; all the people I met in my dreams were open and unpretentious. Money and social acceptance were irrelevant concerns. No one worried about abuse or harsh judgments because these concepts did not exist. We were all so open and free.

A female friend of mine appeared in my dream. In real life, she thrives on two emotions—envy and jealousy. She thrives on the envy from those who have less than she does, and she feeds on the jealousy toward those who have more than she has. But in my dream she didn't care who had the most or the best, and she no longer cared about her possessions. All she wanted to do was to love.

Then, in this dreamy utopia, I came upon a male friend of mine who had enjoyed powerful social status. He told me, "I cannot live without love; I want to leave my wife. I can no longer be bothered by society and politics, which have given me status and wealth. I want to give up everything. I want to love and be loved."

In my dream, everyone's heart was exposed and burning with the flame of love. When I woke up, I also felt my heart tender and sweet, full of love for everything and everyone. I didn't want to be a warrior wearing armor and carrying a spear. I only wanted to be naked in my emotion, without defense. I wanted to be a lover. Yet in the reality of the world, as Gandhi put it, "Violence is an inherent necessity for life in the body."

In our world, if a nation desires peace, it must arm itself. Without sufficient self-defense, peace is nothing but an unattainable dream.

Similarly, lovers cannot love others unless they feel

secure enough to love themselves first. If your life is full of the devastating emotions of anger and defeat because you have left yourself wide open for the taking, then it will be very difficult to have positive emotions toward others. You will begin to resent all people because, in your eyes, they are vicious and they are all thieves.

While the world may not have a shortage of the cunning and ruthless, there are also, as we can all attest, many noble and worthy beings. Protecting yourself from unnecessary harm allows you to cultivate that tender spirit of love. If you walk on the path of life armed with Thick Face, Black Heart, you can protect and nurture your noble emotions deep within.

THRIVING ON THE CUNNING AND THE RUTHLESS

Jim Brown, one of the greatest running backs in the history of American football, once said during an interview, "When people try to hurt me, it just makes me stronger. I take in that negative energy, run it through my system, and throw it back at them."

I am certain, if we think back, that each one of us has accomplished things that we ordinarily could not have accomplished if there had not been a strong oppositional force to challenge and stimulate us.

If we are strong within ourselves, do not accept defeat, and instead utilize the force of the cunning and ruthless to bring forth our hidden strengths and creativity, we will achieve the seemingly impossible.

Richard and Sam were working as software engineers in the same company. Richard's objective at work was to support his employer by producing excellent work in a timely manner. Sam, on the other hand, spent half his days doing what he was hired to do—write software—and the rest of the time reading every software publication available. Richard observed silently to himself that it is good to absorb new information, but this should be done privately and not on company time. Sam's study would be of benefit only to himself and his next employer. Since the company was so behind with its project commitments, most of its present customers were anxiously threatening to cancel their contracts if the work was not delivered within a reasonable time. Richard was quietly working a regular 50-65 hour week. Sam, on the other hand, was a social animal. He frequently made the rounds in the office, showing off how much he knew and, jealously, dropping a few destructive words about Richard.

Recently, Richard's project partner, Joe, had left the company, leaving Richard to clean up all the unfinished work. To make matters worse, Richard's original work was custom-tailored for a specific job. His work was now being adapted for a different project, which required complete recustomization. The new project was due in seven weeks. Everyone in the office thought Richard could not pull it off. Even Richard had his doubts. It looked like a new deadline would need to be renegotiated.

Richard silently began to study Joe's work and discovered that Joe's approach was incompatible with the way he would approach the project. The only hope to integrate the two software designs would be to junk most of Joe's software and start over, which meant that over six month's of Joe's work would be useless.

Richard's determination was strong. He would not give Sam the satisfaction of seeing him fail. Richard strove to achieve the impossible. As Jim Brown said, "I take in that negative energy, run it through my system, and throw it back at them." Richard's determination to overcome an impossible situation flared like a fire within him. He poured forth his creative energy, and in two weeks completed 70 percent of the project. There were five weeks left for the remainder of the work. Richard then leisurely finished the "impossible" task in a total of three weeks and delivered it to the customer.

The customer was delighted and remarked to the president of the company, "I didn't think that seven weeks was possible. I knew the software was complicated, and I was fully prepared to extend the deadline."

It is truly said, "Success is the sweetest revenge." I myself have lists of people that I have to give credit to for motivating me along the path to success through their ruthless actions toward me. Now that I have left them behind in the dust of my victories, they are no longer a threat to me.

The battle with the cunning and ruthless often is not about conducting a battle with outside forces. Encountering the cunning and ruthless stimulates the dormant strengths within us and allows us to bring forth extraordinary abilities that we are not in touch with under normal circumstances.

The Big Fish and Small Fish

If you swim with the sharks, sometimes they'll take a bite out of you. In life, you can choose to stay in the safe small pond or take your chances in the ocean.

The discovery of oil in the North Sea attracted the interest of many oil companies. Independent oilman T. Boone Pickens, Jr., also was looking at the prospects. After careful evaluation, he decided to take a chance because, as he recalled, "The British government was peddling its culls, and this prospect looked like a cull to me." After signing an agreement with the United Kingdom's Department of Energy to explore two sites, Pickens began the costly drilling operations.

Two years later, Pickens had a well operating on each site.

One site was bone dry, while the other yielded oil. But shortly after the North Sea discovery, Britain's new Labor government aggressively tried to get its hands on the oil reserves
in an attempt to save Britain's failing economy. In short, they
wanted to throw the foreign oil companies out, after the companies already had paid for the drilling rights. The government was asking for all the profit, even though the foreign
companies risked their money on costly exploration.

The government first passed a law requiring Pickens and
his partner companies to relinquish 20 percent of the producing oil field profits to the British National Oil Company (a
national corporation formed by the government). BNOC got
the profits but did not have to share any of the financial risks
or development costs.

The BNOC instituted another regulation that made the
companies pump the oil from the offshore rigs all the way to
storage tanks on land before pumping it back into tankers.
Pickens contended that the use of buoys to pump the oil
directly into the tankers at the offshore site would be
environmentally safer and, of course, cheaper. The inefficient
transport system eventually would cost the companies three
hundred million dollars.

Finally, Pickens had to sell the North Sea field, his biggest
discovery ever, to the British for a meager profit. He even
had to bluff and threaten the chairman of the BNOC to sell
his contract. The British Department of Energy would have
preferred that he just walk away from the field like a good
boy.

Beneath the regal image of the British, which Americans
hold so dear to their hearts, Pickens found nothing but common robbers. He remarked to Lord Kearton, BNOC chairman, "You guys are like Jesse James."

Then Comes an Honest Man

In a village of only naive men, if suddenly a deceitful, cunning, and ruthless man shows up, he is assured of victory. He will make victims of everyone. Many villagers will adopt his methods and will attempt to outdo each other. Then, if an honest man who performs his duty honestly comes into the village, he is like a breath of fresh spring air blowing into a polluted, foul-smelling room. People recognize his work and embrace him. He outdoes and outperforms all the cunning and the ruthless.

After a decade of foul air, driven purely by greed and selfish gains, we just may be ready for a breath of fresh air: liberation through honest, hard work.

Label Me "Cunning and Ruthless"

I remember, over fifteen years ago, there was a popular book by Robert Ringer, *Winning Through Intimidation*. In the book he said there are basically three kinds of people to look out for: those who know they are out to get you and say so; those who are nice people but due to their ineptitude cannot help themselves from victimizing you; and those who act like nice people but under their kind exterior are ruthless and cunning.

Whether you consider yourself to be one of the above or none of the above, I can assure you that you have been so labeled at one time or another by certain people who have crossed your path. These people, through their association with you, have set imaginary, unrealistic expectations as to what they would gain from your relationship. When the final results fall short, no matter how noble your motives may have been, you will not escape being labeled as a cunning and ruthless person who has heartlessly made them the victim.

In the past, whenever I was labeled unfavorably, I was bothered a great deal because I hold dear my image of myself as a just individual. Now, if I were to be labeled as cunning and ruthless, so be it.

Human beings create their reality according to their own individual perceptions. The reality does not change, but the perception is altered. As I previously stated, "If you feel you are getting screwed, you probably are." Actually, this statement should be qualified: you must be objective in order to reflect upon your experience properly. If a mirror is perfectly flat, then it can reflect the image without distortion. However, if the mirror is warped, then the image it reflects will be distorted. There is no doubt in my mind that most of us reflect our reality through a rather warped mirror. Therefore, very few of us can escape unfavorable judgment at times.

Exercise Disengagement

One of the powerful tools you can use when dealing with the cunning and ruthless is the exercise of disengagement: refusing to participate. If you suspect the people you are dealing with have no moral boundaries in acquiring their desires, don't get involved. The only reason you may be unable to sever your involvement is your anticipation of a lucrative outcome. When you can master detachment from your own greed and desires, you will eliminate much unnecessary heartache and loss.

Thriving in Yourself

A simple but important element to learn before you can thrive among others is the ability to thrive in yourself—your physical self. A tough mental state follows a well-conditioned physical body. Hindu teachings tell that the highest Dharma of an individual is the care for his body. This even takes precedence over the spiritual quest. Without the body, nothing can be achieved in the physical world. Put simply, the foundation to a successful life is being physically fit. Through exercise and a good diet, a sharp mental state will follow.

Sexual Indulgence Invites Fear

The different schools of Eastern philosophy—including the ancient cultures of India, China, and Japan—teach that sexual fluid is something so precious that one should not waste it needlessly. The fluid is an essence of a vital force, out of which springs a whole human being.

The Eastern tradition also has encouraged sexual moderation and restraint. When the sexual fluid is depleted, a mental weakness results. Creativity, vitality, and the fires of life dry up and leave a person feeling overwhelmed. So instead of riding life, life begins to ride you. These theories have no scientific basis but have been accepted widely for thousands of years.

Napoleon Hill, in his book *Think and Grow Rich,* relates a study which shows that the majority of men do not succeed in their early years because they tend to dissipate their sexual energies through overindulgence in the physical expression of sex.

Sexual energy, when not being utilized, can be rechanneled and transformed into a power that supports your business ventures and other worthy pursuits. A close link exists, according to Eastern thinking, between physical well-being, mental well-being, and sexual behavior. The relationship between them has been observed for thousands of years. After twenty years of my own observation, I, too, hold these relationships to be true. The proper channeling of sexual energy can give you just the edge you need to succeed in this fish-eat-fish world.

CONCLUSION

You are unable to stop others from attempting to take unfair advantage of you. You will therefore have to be ready with all of your faculties to defend your interests at any time against the ruthless and cunning. As one strives to be a just and noble individual, it is necessary to master the art of self-defense. A perfect lover is also a perfect warrior.

A Thick Face, Black Heart practitioner knows that in order to be tough with others, you first have to be even tougher with yourself and learn how to discipline your thoughts and your actions. Whether you are resisting or yielding, in pain or pleasure, in relaxation or effort, you must never lose sight of your intended target.

SUMMARY OF KEY POINTS

• If you don't stand up for what is rightfully yours, nobody else will. Even when you do stand up for your rights, many will attempt to intimidate you.

• Human beings thrive on competition, and the rule of competition is winner takes all.

• Only the strong will survive.

• Those who are naturally cunning and ruthless can always identify sweet and trusting individuals. Just as in the animal kingdom, the strong lion can always single out a sick or weak-spirited wildebeest among a herd of thousands.

• Respect a biting dog from a distance.

• Safeguard insignificant and significant advantages.

• It is not whether your words or actions are tough or gentle; it is the spirit behind your actions and words that announces your inner state.

• For beginning Thick Face, Black Heart practitioners, it is most important to master the power of yielding.

• While outwardly you may seem to be submissive and non-threatening, inwardly never lose sight of your objectives.

• When you can win a battle by maneuvering obliquely, why go for a frontal assault?

- If you don't have to trust someone, then you can always trust him.

- All business relationships begin when people wish to combine their efforts in achieving mutually beneficial objectives. However, as time and events unfold, the conflict of interest within the original unity may begin to surface.

- Any seemingly harmless information provided to your counterpart can come back to haunt you, and this will place you in a potentially vulnerable position.

- Keep the thief of peace and the serenity stealer at arm's length. These people are masters of "death by a thousand cuts."

- The secret is not to convince everyone to agree with you; rather, it is to understand how to have the world polarize its concept of you and to learn to use this force for your benefit.

- Mahatma Gandhi said, "Most think nonviolence is not to fight. On the contrary, nonviolence is the strongest power.... My creed of nonviolence is an extremely active force. It has no room for cowardice or even weakness. There is hope for a violent man to someday become nonviolent, but there is no hope for a coward."

- In our world, if a nation desires peace, it must arm itself. Without sufficient self-defense, peace is nothing but a unattainable dream.

- Similarly, lovers cannot love others unless they feel secure enough to love themselves first. If your life is full

of the devastating emotions of anger and defeat, it will
be very difficult to have positive emotions toward others.

- Jim Brown, one of the greatest running backs in the history of American football, said, "When people try to hurt
me, it just makes me stronger. I take in that negative
energy, run it through my system, and throw it back at
them."

- Then comes an honest man: after a decade of foul air,
driven purely by greed and selfish gains, the American
people just may be ready for a breath of fresh air—liberation through honest, hard work.

- Through their association with you, people have set
imaginary, unrealistic expectations as to what they
would gain from your relationship. When the final
results fall short, no matter how noble your motives may
have been, you will not escape being labeled as a cunning and ruthless person who has heartlessly made them
the victim.

- Human beings perceive their reality according to their
own individual perceptions. The reality does not change,
but the perception is altered.

- A Thick Face, Black Heart practitioner knows that in
order to be tough with others, you first have to be even
tougher with yourself and learn how to discipline your
thoughts and your actions.

- Whether you are resisting or yielding, in pain or pleasure, in relaxation or effort, you must never lose sight of
your intended target.

The killer instinct is not solely
reserved for the vicious and cunning;
it can benefit the virtuous and righteous as well.

—CHIN-NING CHU

12

Acquiring
the Killer
Instinct

To succeed in life in today's world, you must have the will
and tenacity to finish the job. Among bullfighters, there
are many who can work close to the horns, displaying great
bravery and brilliant technique, but the great ones are recognized by how they handle themselves in the moment of truth,
killing quickly and cleanly.

The courage to finish the job quickly and cleanly—that is
the killer instinct, the root of Black Heart. Every great man
and every great villain has it. This killer instinct can help an
individual accomplish great tasks to benefit mankind, and it
can propel an individual to bring destruction on earth. A
knife has great utility, and without it life would be extremely
inconvenient. Yet a knife is also a deadly weapon.

The killer instinct is another aspect of Thick Face, Black
Heart. It has ensured man's survival against the hostile elements of nature as well as from one another since the time of
the caveman. In today's civilized societies, the cruder elements of human behavior have been polished and refined,

and the killer instinct has undergone an outward transformation. But in some parts of the world, even today, the animal nature of the killer instinct remains intact. The application has varied, but the essence remains.

In this chapter, we will examine the efficacy of the killer instinct in action, rather than judge its moral value. Understand, however, that I am in no way endorsing violent behavior. The killer instinct that I am addressing here is not an outward action. Rather, it is the inward state that guides your will to direct your actions to accomplish your objectives. If we have any hope of correcting our timid nature, we must not turn our face away from the dark side of reality. If our enemies are incorporating the killer instinct and victimizing us, then we do not have the luxury of avoiding the topic. As the great military strategist Sun Tzu said, "Know yourself, know your opponent, one hundred battles, one hundred victories."

THE ASIAN PERSPECTIVE OF KILLER INSTINCT

To sacrifice the smaller for the larger is natural in Asian culture, whereas to Westerners this is barbaric and inhumane. From the Asian point of view, it is a natural course of action. This is why the Japanese never had any problems recruiting sufficient kamikaze pilots for their suicide missions during the latter part of World War II. Japan's only problem was that there were not enough airplanes.

Represented in China's five thousand years of recorded history are gigantic numbers of individuals who struggled endlessly for power and glory. The Chinese history books have become textbooks for learning and developing the art of the killer instinct. These books have been widely studied by the Koreans and Japanese, not for their historical value, but as guides to human behavior. They learned how the ancient Chinese heroes formulated their intricate strategies and, most importantly, how they executed these ruthless strategies to achieve their goals.

The heroes of Asia have, for the most part, been men who possessed the perfect killer instinct. At times, the killer instinct was utilized justly. At other times, it was abused. The following are stories from ancient China that demonstrate the application of the killer instinct to obtain specific objectives.

Liu Bang

One of the most documented rivalries in Chinese history was between Liu Bang and Xiang Yu. After the fall of the Chin Dynasty in the second century B.C., these two men battled each other for the control of China. Xiang Yu began with every advantage. He had the best troops, most of China was already under his control, and he was a great warrior and brilliant strategist.

During the three-year struggle, Xiang Yu fought countless battles and lost only one. But in losing one, he ultimately lost China to a man who was his inferior in every way except in the practice of Thick Face, Black Heart.

In one of his early victories, Xiang Yu captured Liu Bang. The throne was within Xiang Yu's grasp, yet he let it slip away. In acknowledgment of his admiration for Liu Bang as a great warrior, and according to his own sense of a soldier's honor, Xiang Yu honored his defeated foe by granting him living quarters instead of executing him. This misguided act provided Liu Bang the opportunity for escape, and he subsequently regrouped his forces and returned to conquer Xiang Yu's army.

On the surface, Xiang Yu's mercy might seem to have

been a noble action, but true nobility would have caused Xiang Yu to strike down Liu Bang when he had the opportunity. If he had done so, he would have ended years of chaos in China and untold misery suffered by millions of the common people.

Xiang Yu had personally taken on the destiny of becoming the ruler of China. It was for this purpose that he had launched the bloody civil war in the first place. He already had the blood of over one hundred thousand men on his hands; the blood of Liu Bang would have been merely one more. It was improper of him to forsake his objective at such a moment. The Chinese people just wanted to see one of them die quickly. They did not care who ruled China, they only wanted an end to this miserable war.

After Xiang Yu's one and only defeat, it was this same soldier's honor that prevented him from returning to his province to regroup. He could not face his people after losing so many of their sons. Instead, he took his own life.

Liu Bang's military commander, Han Xin, characterized Xiang Yu's weaknesses by saying that he had the benevolence of a woman and the valor of a peasant. Xiang Yu killed people ruthlessly on the battlefield, yet at the moment of truth when he stood before his defeated foe, he abandoned his objective and took refuge in a false image of his own nobility, masking his weakness as the "noblesse oblige" of one great warrior to another.

Liu Bang did not have Xiang Yu's accomplishments, but neither was he encumbered by Xiang Yu's concept of honor. During the years of their conflict, Liu Bang repeatedly lost battles to Xiang Yu, but he was never ashamed to return to his province to conscript another army. His heart was also blacker than Xiang Yu's. He could do whatever was required to fulfill his ambition without regard to the cost to others.

When Xiang Yu felt victory slipping away in their final

battle, he ordered Liu Bang's father, who had been his pris-
oner for many years, to be brought out and tied in front of a
pot of boiling oil. Liu Bang was commanded to retreat with
all his forces or see his father boiled alive. Liu rode to the
front of his troops and shouted, "You and I were blood brothers at one time, General Xiang. My father is also yours. If
you wish to cook our father, please share a cup of the broth
with me."

Liu Bang's Thick Face, Black Heart was not reserved for
his enemies. His closest companions also became victims.
During his struggle with Xiang Yu, Liu Bang was assisted by
three very able advisors: Han Xin, Hsiao Hei, and Zhang
Liang. It was largely through the efforts of these men that the
Han Dynasty, the ruling family of China for four centuries,
was established.

As the first commoner in the history of China to ascend to
the position of the Son of Heaven, Liu Bang was determined
that other ambitious men not get the idea that anyone could
make himself the Emperor of China. In order to secure his
position, Liu Bang found it necessary to rid himself of his
former comrades-in-arms.

Zhang Liang had an in-depth understanding of human
nature. After the final victory over Xiang Yu, he wisely took
his leave of the Emperor and retired to a life as a reclusive
monk in the forest. He knew that the very abilities that made
him valuable to Liu Bang during his years of struggle would
now guarantee his death if he remained at court.

Liu Bang's military commander, Han Xin, was the same
man who had been disgraced as a young man by being forced
to crawl through the legs of the ruffians. Despite Han's reputation as a coward, Liu Bang had taken him into his service,
and Han had served him faithfully all the days of his life.
After the defeat of Xiang Yu and Liu Bang's ascension to the
throne, Han became the second most powerful man in China.

His troops had placed Liu Bang on the throne; they could as easily depose him. But Han Xin could not forget that Liu Bang had lifted him from disgrace and given him an opportunity to become a great general. He did not wish to believe that he was locked in a life-or-death struggle with his long-time patron. Meanwhile, Han Xin was approached by other members of the court who were plotting to overthrow Liu Bang.

When Liu Bang invited Han Xin to court for a banquet, Han Xin thrust his doubts aside and left the safety of his military camp. The result of this gesture of trust was that, upon Han's arrival at court, the Emperor had his old companion minced up into a meat sauce.

During the years of warfare, it was Hsiao Hei's job to follow behind the army and see to the administration of the conquered territories. After his final victory, Liu Bang made Hsiao Hei prime minister. Hsiao Hei was a brilliant administrator. He created the concept of managing the affairs of government through a systematic delegation of authority and responsibility. This bureaucratic management system is still used today by governments worldwide.

Because of the efficiency and fairness of his administration, Hsiao Hei became so popular with the people that Liu Bang became fearful. The Emperor found a pretext to imprison Hsiao Hei until he was an old, broken man who no longer posed any threat.

In successfully accomplishing your life's objectives and ambitions, there is a direct relationship between the scope of your ambition and your ability to tap deep into your killer instinct. The greater your ambition, the more able and willing you must be to exercise your killer instinct. If your aim is to be the Emperor of China, then you must be totally willing to kill or be killed. Chinese history has proven that only those willing to go the distance in exercising their killer instinct see the final victory. The following story demonstrates this point.

The First Emperor of the Ming Dynasty

In 1368, Chu Yuan Zhang, a beggar from a peasant family, led the Chinese people in the overthrow of the mighty Yuang Dynasty, which had been established by the Mongols after their return from their victorious conquering of Europe. Chu established the Ming Dynasty which ruled China for three hundred years.

The peasants who had followed Chu in the revolution now expected proper rewards. If Chu had kept them in court and placed them in distinguished positions, these people would have shown him no respect because they still saw him as what he had been before, just another fellow peasant. Therefore, he would not have been able to rule with absolute authority.

However, if Chu sent them home with monetary rewards and did not grant them titles and positions, they would become discontented and possibly plot to overthrow him. So Chu decided to take action with the objective of securing his empire.

Chu invited all of his peasant friends from the war to join him in a great celebration of the establishment of the Ming dynasty. He set the date and carefully chose an isolated building. He ensured an abundance of food and an unceasing flow of wine to be provided there. At the height of the celebration, he secretly left, locked every exit, and lit a fire that killed everyone inside.

Leadership of Kung Ming

The killer instinct is not solely reserved for the vicious and cunning; it can benefit the virtuous and righteous as well.

Kung Ming, a great military strategist and benevolent leader, lived around 200 A.D. He has been praised by some Chinese historians as possibly being the wisest man to have lived during the five thousand years of Chinese history.

Kung Ming was very fond of General Ma, who was one of his talented young generals. Kung Ming recognized Ma's potential as a great military leader and hoped to cultivate Ma as his successor. With talent like Ma's, Kung Ming felt hope for his task of defeating his strong enemies and reestablishing the glory of the Han Dynasty for the overly young emperor.

In one of the decisive campaigns, Kung Ming ordered General Ma to a battle and repeatedly instructed him to occupy a certain small town to act as a decoy in order to tie up the enemy troops there. Kung Ming knew the brilliant, young, and arrogant Ma was like a highly spirited pony that needed time to be broken in. Kung Ming assigned General Ma two of his best advisors to ensure Ma a speedy victory with no unexpected surprises.

When General Ma engaged in battle with the enemy, he totally ignored Kung Ming's instructions. Despite objections from his advisors, General Ma led his troops to the top of the mountain. The enemy cut off General Ma's food and water supplies from below. He was quickly defeated, thus rendering Kung Ming unable to execute his overall battle plan.

Upon General Ma's return, Kung Ming ordered his execution. One of the respected old generals begged Kung Ming to spare Ma's life. He said, "Our nation is surrounded by strong, multinational troops. It is a shame to waste a talented general." But Kung Ming replied, "Law and order must be adhered to. In order to keep the discipline of the troops, I must set an example."

While weeping, Kung Ming beheaded General Ma.

A BANKABLE COMMODITY

Those who possessed a healthy dose of ambition in ancient China, coupled with the freedom to exercise their well-developed killer instinct, were often rewarded.

Not so long ago, Middle Eastern terrorists took Russian personnel hostage. KGB agents responded swiftly by kidnapping close relatives of the responsible terrorist leaders. The KGB cut off body parts of these relatives and sent them along with notes warning that the terrorists' wives and children would be the next targets of retribution if the Russian prisoners were not immediately released. The hostages were quickly released, and no Russian has been taken hostage since.

In our civilized world, most of us do not kill anyone in order to secure our personal interests. The tools for achieving one's goals have changed, but the guiding spirit remains the same, and the outcome on the victims is equally deadly.

In the last decade, the American financial world has become the ideal incubator, nurturing those who possess some degree of the natural killer instinct and eventually cultivating them into perfect killers in the world of high finance. Some of these people are motivated solely by greed. Armed with a perfected killer instinct and impeccable social standing, they are almost unbeatable. Even though a few are caught, many escape the hammer of justice. A Wall Street friend of mine told me privately that for every one caught there are ten more who are not.

In this country, wealth bestows a halo of dignity on those who possess it, and they are placed in the esteemed company of the most respectable entrepreneurs and dignitaries. Even though they may acquire this wealth by unconscionably robbing millions from the faceless public and leading many to their financial death, as long as they appear respectable and are not caught in the process, we Americans deify them.

It is sad but true that one who possesses and is willing to use a perfect killer instinct is, was, and always will be a bankable commodity.

THE SECRET OF ASKING FOR MONEY

While a healthy and well-developed killer instinct can aid the greedy, it can also assist us in accomplishing our worthy tasks or help us to overcome unexpected obstacles in life. Therefore, it is essential for us to explore the elements and the state of mind behind that perfect killer instinct.

The best way to examine this subtle state of mind is by looking at a particular experience that many of us have in common. A difficult thing for many sensitive people is to ask for money from others. Whenever we have to do so, there are conflicts of feeling that arise from within.

The large corporation can easily raise money compared with the small, starting business. Small entrepreneurs wishing to generate the necessary working capital often find it difficult to open their mouth and ask for money. Yet the ability to raise money is an essential skill for any entrepreneur.

T. Boone Pickens recalls in his biography that his jobs were mostly centered on raising money. In his early years, he was raising money either for land leases or for oil well drilling funds. He acknowledges that it is a never-ending task.

• • •

Don is a master when it comes to asking others for money. I have never met Don; yet, through a friend of mine, Edward, Don has become a living entity in my mind.

In the mid 1960s, Edward met Don. At the time, Don was wanted in thirteen states for fraud and embezzlement. Despite Don's moral shortcomings, you have to give him credit for his ability to "raise money." Without emulating his motives and moral standards, we can learn from him his perfect execution of the killer instinct in raising money.

Confucius said, "Whenever I walk among two other people, it does not matter their social status and accomplishments; at least one of them will be able to teach me knowledge that I do not possess."

Don sometimes raised money for projects that did not exist. Occasionally, he delivered what he promised. One time, Don asked for fifty thousand dollars for a "wonderful" venture from a group of people who had connections with the underworld. Immediately after he obtained the fifty thousand dollars, he took the money and hit the nearest bar. He bought drinks for everyone and blew over a thousand dollars. The next day, he invited Edward to Reno and gambled away the remaining money.

When Don's "investors" caught up with him, in front of Edward, they pointed a pistol at Don and demanded their money back. Don told the gangsters, in a composed, collected, and detached manner, that a rival gang had stolen their merchandise. Then he smoothly proceeded to state that the only chance to recoup the lost money was for them to provide him with an additional five thousand dollars. Don was like a skilled bullfighter standing calmly in front of the angry bull and skillfully delivering the final kill. Edward could not believe his eyes—these toughies actually lowered their guns and gave Don another five thousand dollars.

One time Edward asked Don, "What is your secret of ask-

ing for money." Don replied, "You ask by asking." Edward
said, "But I have difficulties opening my mouth. My mind
has many considerations that leave me unable to open my
month." Don looked straight into Edward's eyes and said,
"You cannot worry about that. You have to ignore totally
whatever your mind is telling you and whatever you're feeling. Just focus wholeheartedly on your task: asking for the
money."

That is the state behind the spirit of the killer instinct. The
sixteenth-century Japanese sword master Miyamoto Musashi
said: "Whatever state of mind you are in, ignore it. Think
only of cutting."

Don possesses the killer instinct naturally. It is part of who
he is. However, his talent is terribly misguided. If he devoted his talent to fund-raising for worthy causes, he would be
an invaluable asset to himself and others. Nevertheless, his
words are profound. He described a state of mind that is totally detached from all considerations except the completion of
the immediate objective. A totally focused state of mind is
the essential driving force behind the perfect killer instinct.
Without it, your actions and words are powerless and ineffective.

Never Go to Bed without Collecting First

At one time, I worked for an American company on a
retainer basis to develop its market in China, Hong Kong,
and Taiwan. Wally and I reached an oral agreement that his
company would pay me a monthly fee plus a percentage of
the sales.

Shortly after I began working with Wally, I presented my
regular working contract to him. We worked together on
some minor wording problems, and Wally promised to have

the contract retyped. As I got to know Wally better, I was charmed by his integrity and professionalism. Because of this, I neglected to follow up on the unfinished contract. If there was one person I could trust, Wally was the one. Before I even noticed, three years passed by and the contract had not been signed. I wasn't worried though.

Then Wally sold his 50 percent interest to his German partner. I was still not concerned about my unsigned contract. After all, Wally's son-in-law, Peter, was staying on as the president of the company, and Peter knew how hard I had worked for my money. Besides, I was good friends with Peter's wife and in-laws.

After Peter took over the Asian project, I mentioned my unsigned contract to him. He repeatedly told me he would take a look at it, and that he didn't see any problem.

After working with Peter for one year, I decided I would like to resign from my responsibility and unload some of my professional burdens. I told Peter that I would like the contract signed so I could continue to receive the entitled percentage. Peter said, "Well, we have to look at how many years you will continue to receive this commission. It may be three years, or five years." I reminded him that the original agreement had no termination.

After six months, my negotiations were getting nowhere. The problem was, I had no leverage with which to bargain. I was at his mercy, and he would rather keep his money than be merciful. He was demonstrating his newfound power and trying to prove to himself what an excellent deal maker he was.

Peter acted like a high-spirited bull standing in front of a bullfighter with a broken sword. I felt powerless, angry, and humiliated. Then I remembered the words of Japanese sword master Musashi, "Whatever state of mind you are in, ignore it. Think only of cutting." I thought to myself, "Peter is acting tough, but if I can find his jugular vein, I can come in for the kill, even with my broken sword."

I telephoned him and made it quite clear that if he did not settle this matter with me in a timely manner, I would have no choice but to inform all of the Asian customers I had introduced him to that he was trying to cheat me out of my entitled financial interests. I assured him that this was not an idle threat but rather a measure of desperation. I delivered my punch and then proceeded to speak to his sense of honor, because Peter valued himself as a devoted Christian.

"Peter, I am in a totally powerless situation and am at your mercy—somewhat like the prostitute who doesn't collect her money before she goes to bed with the customer. When all is finished, she wants her money. If the customer does not honor their agreement, there is nothing she can do about it. The customer already has what he wanted. I am in the same situation as that prostitute, asking you to honor an agreement from which you have already reaped the benefits. I am threatening you because I have no other alternative; I have no other cards to play. When you corner a dog and give him no way out, he will jump over the wall, whether he wants to or not."

Well, it worked. Peter realized that my humiliation was so great that I might do anything to take my revenge. The possibility of destroying his personal reputation and that of his company among the Asians was very real. We worked out a compromise that he would pay my commission for an additional twenty-one years.

At the end of our conversation, he asked me, "What is the topic of the book that you are working on?"

I told him, "How not to get screwed by others."

He laughed and said, "You haven't lost your sense of humor." In fact, he didn't know how literal my statement was.

I MUST BE CRUEL, ONLY TO BE KIND

The next element I want to discuss digresses slightly from the focus of this chapter, but the chapter would not be complete without it. The question is, while we are dealing with the topic of killer instinct, when do we stop exercising the killer instinct and express our inborn human compassion?

As William Shakespeare said in *Hamlet,* "I must be cruel, only to be kind." You should never stop exercising your compassion. Have love in your heart, but be smart and express your compassion with restraint and detachment.

Every human being has the desire to be abundantly generous and to give freely. This includes love, compassion, respect, and material possessions. Deep down, as children of our Divine Maker, we all wish to perform our labor free of charge, solely as an expression of love. At the same time, we wish to reward others with an abundance beyond their possible expectations. Yet, the reality of daily survival causes too many people to feel contracted and fearful. Nevertheless, at one time or another, we have shared our resources with the needy beyond our reasonable capability.

In time, we notice, it is much easier to be compassionate and provide for the nameless and faceless needy persons than for those we consider to be our "special ones." This is because, through experience, we see our compassionate generosity often abused. It seems to some, the more you give them, the more you should give. These people act as if you owe them. Out of your desire to be kind, you expose yourself without a protective shield.

Strange but true, we often abuse those who support and love us the most.

Beth and Lisa have known each other more than twenty years. Lisa is a divorced woman and has lived alone for over ten years. Recently, Beth was informed by her husband that he wanted out of their marriage. Beth moved in with Lisa while Beth's house was being sold.

Lisa was sympathetic to Beth and wanted to help her all she could. She let Beth stay with her free of charge, in order to cut down Beth's living expenses. Lisa opened her arms and heart to a wounded friend. She catered to Beth's every need. Beth moved out six months later, and the two of them have not spoken since. Lisa feels hurt and abused by this incident. She told me, "I opened my heart and my wallet too quickly and without reserve. I gave everything up front. I could not top my own performance, but Beth's expectations were ever-rising."

In order to be kind, we have to be cruel. A Thick Face, Black Heart practitioner learns the necessity of restraint and controls his desire to be overly expressive of his compassion. Compassion is a state of mind, not a blind competition over how much you can do for others. Often, in order to be kind, we have to control our desire to do too much. Along the same lines, good parents learn the importance of controlling their urge to overly indulge and pamper their children. They know that they must be cruel, only to be kind.

ACQUIRING THE KILLER INSTINCT

The killer instinct is one aspect of Thick Face, Black Heart. Without it, Thick Face, Black Heart would be nothing but good intentions without the power and ability to act.

The killer instinct is the power that propels us to take proper actions in spite of ourselves, keeping us on the path to our objectives. This killer instinct is within each one of us as part of our genetic coding. Due to our social programming, the idea of an inborn killer instinct is repugnant, and we have suppressed it. Because this instinct is within us, we merely have to reacquaint ourselves with it.

Remember when you first learned to flip a pancake in a frying pan? You started by rocking the pan to create a momentum that allowed the pancake to slide up and down inside the frying pan. Then with one throw into the air, the pancake turned and you caught it with the pan.

When you are too timid and concerned about whether the pancake will fly too high and miss the pan, the result is that your pancake will go up in the air a few inches, but won't have the height to turn. When it lands, you'll have a mess inside the pan. On the other hand, when you are too concerned that the pancake will not turn over, you use too much force, and the result is that your pancake will probably land on the stove, outside of the pan.

When you learn to flip a pancake, you need to explore your own inner realm, to be in touch with the state of mind that gives you perfect strength, perfect control, and perfect detached courage. Carefully observe your inner state. Watch for the moment just before you throw the pancake high in the air to make that perfect landing. When you find that state of mind, recreate it often. It will help you to cultivate your perfect killer instinct.

Learning to flip a pancake seems easy and not particularly profound. Yet, the truth of life is hidden everywhere equally. The lesson of acquiring the perfect killer instinct is not only in the drama of bullfights and the high finance of the business world; it also exists in its entirety in the flipping of a pancake.

The state of mind that aids us in performing the mundane task of flipping a pancake is the same state of mind that executes the perfect killer instinct. When I speak of flipping a pancake, it is not about the pancake; it is about being in touch with that something inside of you that provides you with the courage to overcome your inner timidity and considerations. It is about tapping into the state of perfect strength, perfect control, and perfect detachment in fulfilling your worthy objectives.

The Surgeon's Strength

I once spoke with a young surgeon who had served in Vietnam. He told me, "Medical school ill prepared me for the horrors of war and mutilations that human beings are capable of inflicting on one another. During my time in Vietnam, I performed my duty only because my devotion to my fellow men and sense of loyalty to my duty were stronger than my fear. That loyalty transformed my fear into pure courage and strength in spite of myself."

Recently, I underwent a minor operation to have a benign tumor removed from my breast. The doctor gave me only a local anesthetic, so I was conscious during the whole procedure. Although I couldn't feel any pain, I could feel my breast being pulled very strongly from every direction, as if the surgeon were cutting up a rubber doll. She performed her work with dispassion and detachment, but this attitude did not disturb me.

On the contrary, I found great comfort in it. While she was working, I felt a tremendous affection pouring out from her hands. This affection that I experienced came from her dedicated detachment in accomplishing the objective. Consider a child who has a thorn in his hand. What would be the greater kindness, to pick gingerly at the thorn so that it remains in the wound and festers or to remove it with assurance even though you may cause the child a moment of pain?

The circumstances that brought forth the inner strength of the two surgeons were different, yet both were true to their professional objectives. Within this detached strength lies a signpost to the mystery of the killer instinct—the root of Thick Face, Black Heart.

SUMMARY OF KEY POINTS

- To succeed in life, you must have the will and tenacity to finish the job.

- The courage to finish the job quickly and cleanly—that is the killer instinct, the root of Black Heart. Every great man and every great villain has it.

- The killer instinct can help an individual accomplish great tasks to benefit mankind, and it can propel an individual to bring destruction upon the earth.

- A knife has great utility, and without it life would be extremely inconvenient. Yet a knife is also a deadly weapon.

- The killer instinct is another aspect of Thick Face, Black Heart. It has ensured man's survival against the hostile elements of nature, as well as from one another, since the time of the caveman.

- If we have any hope of correcting our timid nature, we must not turn our faces away from the dark side of reality.

- If our enemies are incorporating the killer instinct and victimizing us, we do not have the luxury of avoiding the topic. As the great military strategist Sun Tzu said,

"Know yourself, know your opponent, one hundred battles, one hundred victories."

• It is sad but true that one who possesses and is willing to use a perfect killer instinct is, was, and always will be a bankable commodity.

• I must be cruel, only to be kind. You should never stop exercising your compassion. Have love in your heart, but be smart and express your compassion with restraint and detachment.

• The killer instinct is one aspect of Thick Face, Black Heart. Without it, Thick Face, Black Heart would be nothing but good intentions without the power and ability to act.

• The killer instinct is the power that propels us to take proper actions in spite of ourselves, keeping us on the path to our objectives. The killer instinct is within each one of us as part of our genetic coding.

• The truth of life is hidden everywhere equally. The lesson of acquiring the perfect killer instinct is not only in the drama of bullfights and the high finance of the business world; it also exists in its entirety in the flipping of a pancake.

• The state of mind that aids us in performing the mundane task of flipping a pancake is the same state of mind that executes the perfect killer instinct.

- Flipping a pancake is not about the pancake; it is about being in touch with that something inside you that provides you with the courage to overcome your inner timidity and considerations. It is about tapping into that state of perfect strength, perfect control, and perfect detachment in fulfilling your worthy objectives.

You don't manage people,
you manage things.
You lead people.

—*GRACE HOPPER,*
  U.S. Navy Admiral, retired

13

Thick Face,
Black Heart
Leadership

Each one of us, in large or small ways, is a leader. Some have an official title for their roles as leaders, while others may lead their brothers, sisters, or friends on the playground. Leadership is a state of mind—what you do to yourself, not what you do to others.

Recently, many Americans have been voicing discontent about our present political system. The problem is not so much that the system needs reform (although it does); more importantly, we desperately need to overhaul the standards of integrity among our political leaders. A nation, a corporation, a small business, or a family's well-being is tightly intertwined with the quality of its leaders.

LEADERSHIP: AN ESSENTIAL ELEMENT OF SURVIVAL

The ancient Chinese were convinced that the quality of their leaders was directly related to national survival. The code of leadership has been addressed in many ancient art-of-war books. Among these books, *Kung Ming's Art of War* most extensively deals with the question of leadership. Kung Ming, mentioned in an earlier chapter, is considered to be the greatest leader to have lived during the five thousand years of recorded Chinese history. His book, which is relatively unknown to Western readers, defines in detail what constitutes a great leader and a poor leader.

Kung Ming's description of a great leader shows a great deal of similarity to a Thick Face, Black Heart practitioner. The ancient Chinese always placed tremendous value on their leaders' spiritual and philosophical merit. Even today, the Chinese place virtue over technical ability when evaluating a corporation employee or government official.

A person with great abilities who lacks spiritual depth will not be a benefit to his organization, but will be a threat to himself and others. People will naturally follow a person who possesses strong spiritual qualities in addition to his professional aptitude. As the Chinese are fond of saying, "For a worthy leader, one will walk across boiling oil and raging fire to support his leader's objective."

Kung Ming's book is intended for military use; however, the principles that guided the ancient military leaders are interchangeable with those that guide today's political or business leaders. I have provided a literal translation from *Kung Ming's Art of War* so that you may see the unique flavor of his writing.

Kung Ming said:

POWER AND RESPONSIBILITY

Power and Responsibility are the two faces that share one physical body, and they cannot be separated. A leader who is the central power of a nation must at the same time be fully responsible for the success and failure of that nation. Power is the force that supports one to command and lead. This force communicates its presence by the manner in which that individual carries himself. A leader who is skilled in command is like a strong tiger who possesses wings. He possesses total freedom in expressing himself, and his action meets no obstacles. A leader who is inept in command is like a fish out of water. Although he wishes to ride the force of the waves, he is unable.

UPROOT THE WICKED

The reasons for the failure of any organization are rooted in the following people.

1. He who is fond of creating clusters among the mediocre-minded people so that he may focus the group's objective to annihilate the proficient individuals

2. He who is enslaved by his extravagant spending habits

3. He who devotes all of his attention to faultfinding, thus stimulating the group's discontent, all for the benefit of his selfish aims

4. He who only focuses on his personal losses and gains, and whose actions are solely based on the principle of winning at all costs

• • •

The above-mentioned are malicious, hypocritical, and wicked. One must keep away from them.

METHODS TO RECOGNIZE THE INDIVIDUAL'S TRUE CHARACTER

The most difficult thing is to detect someone's true nature. One can be outwardly kind, yet vicious inside. Others seem sincere, yet evasive. Some are brave in expression, yet cowardly. Others are hardworking, yet untrustworthy.

The following are seven methods to detect an individual's character.

1. Debate with him to know his viewpoints on life.

2. Challenge him verbally to watch the changes of his inner state.

3. Discuss strategies with him in order to observe his wisdom.

4. Enlighten him as to the difficulties and dangers ahead, thus to know his courage.

5. Cause him to be drunk, then observe his real nature.

6. Make him handle money, then know his virtue.

7. Assign work to him, then discover his competence.

In addition to the above, the following are methods provided from other ancient books.

1. During the time of his misfortune, observe whom he befriends.

2. During the time of his prosperity, observe who receives his charity.

3. During the time he is holding high offices, observe whom he employs.

4. During the time of difficulties, does he act unethically?

5. During the time of poverty, can he be bribed?

6. Tempting him with lustful sex, observe his steadiness.

SIX DIFFERENT TYPES OF LEADERS

1. *The compassionate leader:* He guides his troops with a virtuous heart and supervises them with strict standards. He knows his troops' difficulties and appreciates their devotion.

2. *The virtuous leader:* He who does not reject responsibilities. He is never concerned about his personal interest. To him, there is only the glory of death, not the shame of living.

3. *The wise leader:* In good times, he is self-restrained. In victory, he is not self-satisfied. He is wise, yet yielding in expression. He is strong, yet humble in manner.

4. *The strategic leader:* In planning, he is creative and original. In action, he is resourceful and imaginative. He is able to turn disadvantage into advantage and defeat into victory.

5. *The courageous leader:* Place him in an ordinary situation and he seems unimpressive. However, the bigger the challenge, the more courageous he becomes.

6. *The great leader:* When he meets a proficient individual, he treats him with great respect. He has the capacity to accept criticism and suggestions. He is tolerant, yet firm. He is courageous and brave, and also skilled in strategies.

THE EIGHT CHARACTER FLAWS AMONG LEADERS

1. Greed

2. Jealousy of others' competency and proficiency

3. Being easily influenced by others' gossip and opinions and taking delight in praise

4. Focusing only on understanding others, yet knowing nothing about oneself

5. Indecision

6. Being enslaved by the pleasures of the senses

7. Malevolence and cowardice

8. Evasiveness and deceitfulness; only paying lip service; lack of sincerity

The following are additional points presented in other military books, which are important to include.

1. Lacking competence, yet possessing a great sense of self-importance

2. Taking action hastily

3. Inertia and laziness

4. Lacking courage

5. Being competent but lacking the physical well-being and strength to carry out one's ideas

6. Cruelty

7. Lack of charisma

THE NINE ESSENTIAL ABILITIES OF A LEADER

1. The ability to recognize the situation of his opponents

2. The ability to recognize the methods of advance and retreat

3. The ability to know the limitations of his resources

4. The ability to recognize favorable timing for actions

5. The ability to utilize the natural geographic elements and understand the advantages and disadvantages inherent in any given situation

6. The ability to exhibit originality in strategic planning and provide his enemy with total surprise

7. The ability to hold his plans in total secrecy

8. The ability to create harmony among his troops

9. The ability to generate common objectives among his troops

YIELDING AND OVERCOMING

A good leader is strong, but not brittle. He is flexible, but not indecisive. He understands the principle of the fragile overcoming the strong, of the delicate conquering the forceful. He knows that if a person's character is genuinely weak, he will perish. When a person's character is overly forceful, destruction is waiting for him. A good leader should be neither forceful nor fragile; this is the Tao of leadership.

THE TWO STANDARDS OF GOOD LEADERSHIP

1. A good leader should not be arrogant. Arrogance will lead him to forget his manners. Due to his lack of manners, he will lose the respect of his troops, who then will reject him and cause his army to disband.

2. A good leader should not be miserly. This will cause him not to reward deserving individuals properly. When the soldiers have not been rewarded accordingly, they will not devote themselves to the cause wholeheartedly. This will

eventually threaten the national security. (In ancient China, switching allegiance from one nation to another was done as easily as we change jobs today.)

ONE WHO IS SKILLED IN DEFEAT WILL NOT SEE DESTRUCTION

This point has been addressed extensively in a previous chapter.

A NATION WELL PREPARED IN SELF-DEFENSE WILL HAVE NO WORRY OF INVASION BY OTHERS

Self-defense is essential for national survival, just as the bee and scorpion have been equipped by nature with poison for the protection of their survival.

THE FIVE ASSETS AND EIGHT LIABILITIES OF A LEADER

Five Assets

1. He possesses a majestic air and the ability to motivate others

2. He respects his elders and is benevolent to his brothers

3. He is faithful and loyal to his friends

4. He is tolerant toward the masses

5. He is diligent in the execution of his duties to accomplish his objectives

Eight Liabilities

1. He is unable to judge right from wrong

2. He does not employ proficient individuals

3. He does not strictly execute the laws

4. He does not perform charitable works for the needy

5. He is unable to project future outcomes

6. He is unable to prevent the leaking of top-secret information

7. He does not, or is unable to, recommend deserving individuals for appropriate promotion

8. He is unable to take full responsibility for his defeat

THE THREE MUST-HAVES FOR A PROFICIENT LEADER

1. Heart and stomach: The heart and stomach are the most essential parts of our physical body. They are dear and close to us. A proficient leader must surround himself with wise and trustworthy counselors. He needs them as he needs his own heart and stomach. Without these people, it would be as

if he were walking in the dark of night without proper directions.

2. Ears and eyes: A proficient leader must have additional pairs of ears and eyes who are devoted to him. Without these people, he would be in the dark and isolated. Knowing is power.

3. Claws and teeth: The claws and teeth are essential when you need to scratch and to bite others. A proficient leader needs to have people who are specialized in executing his killer instincts. Sometimes it is necessary to do some biting and scratching in order to accomplish one's just objectives, and these people are also useful for one's own self-defense. Without these people, he would be like a hungry man who has eaten poison: his death is certain.

THE ORGANIZATION OF THE TROOPS ACCORDING TO EACH INDIVIDUAL'S NATURAL ABILITIES

Each individual should be placed where his talents are utilized best. An individual who can move swiftly and skillfully should be assigned to a regiment carrying out a sneak attack, while a slow but strong warrior might be suited best for a longbow regiment.

FIFTEEN CODES OF LEADERSHIP

1. Understand the importance of espionage.

2. Be diligent in obtaining the enemy's information.

3. Be fearless when facing superior enemy forces.

4. Be not tempted by bribes.

5. Display absolute fairness.

6. Show endurance.

7. Exhibit big-heartedness.

8. Be trustworthy.

9. Respect competent individuals.

10. Do not allow personal judgment of people to be affected by others' criticism and gossip.

11. Be truthful and sincere.

12. Show benevolence to the troops.

13. Be loyal and faithful.

14. Understand personal limitations.

15. "Know thyself and thy enemy."

THE FOUR FUNDAMENTAL RULES
OF LEADERSHIP

1. Be very clear that your troops know your expectations of them. Make sure they understand what is expected of them when you ask them to march, and what is expected of them when you ask them to retreat, and what constitutes disobeying an order.

2. Guide them with benevolence and virtue, and they will adopt the concept of proper conduct.

3. Promote competency and inspire the capable, thus motivating the troops to their peak performance.

4. Be faithful to your standards of punishments and decorations. Let your troops know that you mean what you say. Establish the trust that your word is golden.

THE OMENS OF VICTORY AND DEFEAT

Omens of Victory

1. The proficient are exalted, and the incompetent are removed.

2. The troops enthusiastically carry out the commands.

3. The troops are motivated and high in spirit.

4. Punishments and decorations are carried out in strict manner.

Omens of Defeat

1. The troops' spirits are low, and they are listless in carrying out their daily duties.

2. The troops feel insecure about their position. The
   slightest rumor causes great uneasiness.

3. The leader overestimates or underestimates the enemy's strength.

4. The troops are overly concerned with their physical
   comfort.

5. The leader betrays his duty by obtaining secret profits.

THE PROPER ATTITUDE OF A LEADER
TOWARD HIS TROOPS

In ancient times, a great leader was one who treated his
troops as if they were his children. When danger and difficulties arose, the leader marched forward in an attempt to solve
the problems.

When there are rewards, the leader steps aside and lets the
troops enjoy them. He comforts the wounded and buries the
dead with utmost respect. He shares his food with the hungry
and removes his clothing to clothe the needy. He invites the
wise ones to serve him with greatest respect and rewards the
brave ones with decorations and awards.

THE FIVE FORMULAS TO MOTIVATE YOUR TROOPS

1. Attract extraordinary talents by assuring them prestigious titles and generous salaries.

2. Treat your people with respect and trust their ability to perform.

3. Set clear standards of expectations for their performance, and praise or reprimand them accordingly.

4. Inspire your people by setting performance standards.

5. Notice all the "little right things" they have done, then praise them. Acknowledge their outstanding performance with bonuses or promotions.

Thus, your troops will work enthusiastically to reach for their personal best.

The wise man hears of the Tao
and practices it diligently.
The average man hears of the Tao
and gives it thought now and then.
The foolish man hears of the Tao
and laughs aloud.
If there were no laughter,
the Tao would not be Tao.

—*LAO TZU*, TAO TE CHING

14

Thick Within,
Black Within

YOU CANNOT OBTAIN WHAT YOU
ALREADY HAVE

The secret of how to obtain the state of Thick Face, Black Heart is that there is nothing to obtain because Thick Face, Black Heart is your natural state. You cannot obtain anything that you already have. You merely have to remove the barriers and discover that which you already possess.

A tiger need not learn how to be fierce. The ocean need not learn to be oceanic. The fire burns the forest without asking, "How do I burn?" So, too, human beings need not take lessons on how to be natural beings. Our Maker has implanted the perfect intelligence inherently within the essence of all things.

Through our "proper" social upbringing, we have disfigured the intuitive understanding of the natural law of winning that is within each one of us. We have distorted the natural ability of Thick Face, Black Heart, which was intended to support our spiritual and material growth. Now our task is to rediscover and recover what we already possess.

THE BLESSING AND THE CURSE OF FREE WILL

I am able to love my God
Because He gives me freedom to deny Him.

—RABINDRANATH TAGORE

Each human being is fully embodied with free will—a total and complete divine intelligence imparted by our Maker to use as we see fit in fulfilling our highest good. Through our free will, topped with a healthy dose of ignorance and confusion, we often handle our lives like a blind man driving an automobile. The only way we manage to stop is by crashing.

The gift of free will that our Maker has bestowed upon each of us is the greatest blessing, as well as the greatest curse.

SEVEN STAGES OF UNFOLDING

The degree to which you understand the universe in which you live is in direct proportion to the degree of understanding you have of your true self. Additionally, the success of your accomplishments is in direct proportion to your ability to overcome the obstacles along the path of your life's journey.

In order to discover your natural state of being, you must

undo the wrongs that have been imposed upon you since your birth. The first step is self-reflection and self-discovery.

Following are the seven stages of self-unfoldment in the state of Thick Face, Black Heart.

1. The Desire to Do Right

You feel the intense desire to do good, to do the right thing. At this stage, you also feel helpless. Your life is filled with conflicts within and without. In your experience, good people and good actions may be rewarded spiritually, but in the real world they always seem to be getting the short end. You see the only reward for being good is good itself. Because of this, you feel desperate, dejected, and disheartened.

At this stage, you have no tolerance for Thick Face, Black Heart. You think that it is only for sinister-minded people.

2. Confusion and Negativity

Eventually, you begin to gain insight. Up to this point, you think you have been making a noble sacrifice, when in fact you have not been sacrificing at all. Rather, you have been denying and depriving yourself, afraid to acknowledge your needs.

Before you are a son, daughter, husband, wife, employee, executive, politician, entrepreneur, lawyer, or policeman, you are a human who possesses natural and basic human needs. By ignoring your individual needs and totally catering to the needs of others in accordance to the role you are playing, you have betrayed your inner nature and sacrificed your well-being. In fact, you have victimized yourself through self-denial. This was done under the noble pretense of self-sacrifice.

You begin to feel anger and resentment, and at the same time you feel guilty about these despicable emotions, which are unfit for people of your character.

At this stage, you are confused. You begin to reevaluate all of your previous concepts of repulsion toward Thick Face, Black Heart.

3. The Battle for Surrender

You finally reach the conclusion that it is too painful to live your life without the liberty of self-expression and self-nurturing. You cannot contribute to anyone if you cannot contribute to yourself. The pain of living under others' standards has become intolerable.

By now you are persuading yourself to accept your "despicable" emotions. Anger and guilt fill you and are part of you for the time being. You have reached the conclusion that life is just as painful whether you practice self-denial by living up to others' expectations or practice self-expression and feel guilty about it. At least, you feel, the latter option creates the opportunity for movement within you.

4. Acceptance of Your Imperfect Perfection

You are evolving to the point where you are less judgmental about your anger and resentment. You start to see yourself as imperfectly perfect. You experience love for your perfection and your imperfections. You begin to be aware that a great courage exists within you, the power of courage that enables you to acknowledge your own existence and

your own needs. Your need for self-nurturing is more important than the expectations others have set for you.

You begin to break new ground and set new standards for
yourself. At this point, all the people who know you will realize you are changing, certainly for the worse. They will think
you have become totally self-centered and inconsiderate of
others. You break all the expectations of the old and familiar.
You are responding to the screams from within: "If I have
one life to live, I want to live as me."

You are in ecstacy over the possible new realms that await
you, but also in agony over the abandonment of the old. As
at the moment before parachuting from an airplane, you are
full of fear and excited anticipation.

Yet this transition period will be painful at times. This is
the stage when Arjuna is confused and overcome with grief
about waging battle against his beloved people. Most of all,
he is forced to uproot his limited concept of goodness and
embrace the expanded virtue.

5. The New Possibilities

Eventually, the old and unworthy will fall by the wayside.
They will drop from your life. Like a magnet, you will draw
new and exciting events and people because like attracts like.

At this stage, you have begun to develop the natural
power of Thick Face, Black Heart. This power gives you the
strength to stand up against your automatic, habitual actions
and thoughts and venture into new frontiers. As each event
crosses your path, you will not react automatically according
to your old ways. You will take a moment to reach within
yourself for guidance and discover the best course of action.

At first, this is a slow process, and often your habitual
response gets ahead of your conscious effort. Through prac-

tice, you are more aware of this inner state of Thick Face, Black Heart. In your business and personal encounters, you become steadier and more centered.

6. The Inner Harmony

By breaking through your notion of others' standards and expectations, you find a new surge of inner harmony: the unfamiliar emotion of peace and tranquility.

You begin to experience genuine compassion for others — not because you are supposed to or because you feel guilty if you don't, but rather through your own love for yourself. You recognize that the flame of love burning within you is equally present in others, even though they may not perceive it themselves.

At this stage, when others slap you in the face, you no longer feel like a victim of your sense of morality. You have a choice: to slap back twice or turn the other cheek. The decision of how to react will be in accord with the result that you are looking for. Thick Face, Black Heart has become the constant companion of your thoughts. Through practice and contemplation, Thick Face, Black Heart transcends from an indefinite idea to an integral part of your natural state.

7. Detachment: The Power Source of Magnetism

The highest code of living is detachment. There is no power higher than the power of detachment. When one masters the state of detachment, he becomes the embodiment of dispassion and fearlessness. At this stage, nothing he possesses will possess him. He becomes the master of his possessions, rather than being possessed by them. He becomes the master of his universe.

Detachment is the secret key to obtaining everything you "want." Have you ever noticed when you *stop* wanting something, the object of your desire comes to you naturally? You cannot keep it away from you. This is the mystery of how the world works. This mysterious principle somehow works for material objects as well as for people.

At this stage, you are to the world as the lotus blossom is to the mud pond. Though it has grown from the mud pond, it is yet untouched by the mud. In terms of material possessions, have and have not are no longer so different; they look more the same to you. You are in the world, but you also transcend the world. At this stage, your state of mind regarding material success is that of satisfied dissatisfaction. You will challenge your limitations for the pure joy of challenge, for continued expansion is the natural expression of your own divinity.

MAN'S THREE QUALITIES

According to Eastern thought, human nature can be divided into three qualities. Everyone possesses all three in different degrees. However, each individual is dominated by one of the three which influences his character and directs his behavior the most.

These three qualities are called "the three gunas" in Sanskrit. Although all human beings are created equal, their accomplishments in life are different. The reason is due to their natural temperament and their proficiency in self-effort in relationship to the three gunas: tamas (inertia), rajas (activity), and sattva (wisdom). The source of these gunas is the karmic impression (impressions left by past actions) and various kinds of understanding we have acquired through our life.

Tamas

The qualities of tamas include inertia, obstruction, ignorance, and ego domination. When one is in this state, one feels physically sluggish, lethargic, and inactive; mentally foggy; dull and heavy, with a tendency to procrastinate; spiritually unenthusiastic, unresponsive, and bored. In this state, when one does act, the guiding force for action is dominated by solid ignorance.

The thirteenth-century prophet Jnaneshwar described the state when tamas guna predominates our psyche:

The body decays, there is little desire for work,
and a person yawns continuously;
as a falling stone cannot turn itself over,
he remains unable to change in his posture.
Even if the earth were to descend into the nether regions,
or the sky fall down on him, it would not occur to him to
rise.
He would like to sleep for as long as the earth exists,
for he has no other desire.

This state was also described in *The Philokalia*, a prose anthology of Greek-Christian monastic texts, compiled during the eighteenth century: "Physical weakness and heaviness enter the soul through laziness and negligence and bring faintness of soul." When one is in this state, one is in a state of "living death."

Rajas

Rajas represents activity and struggle, influenced by the ego. In this state, one is actively performing one's tasks. The mind is agitated, excited, struggling, and sometimes in pain. The spirit is often restless. Activities may bring momentary pleasure, yet the nature of this pleasure is fickle.

Rajastic people are go-getters. They aggressively partici- pate in the process of making money. They thrive on the excitement of activities. Their actions may lead to the results they seek; however, the pleasure of success may not last, because the motivational source of the action is ego-centered and self-serving. Most of the activities in today's business world are centered on rajas gunas.

Through the actions of the rajas guna, money follows and pleasures are purchased, but rajas do not provide inner satis- faction, because the nature of rajas is not satisfaction, but rather pain and struggle. When you have no satisfaction, you feel you need to do more in order to make more money so you can buy more satisfaction. The cycle goes on. You become enslaved by the need to act in order to sustain your life. The driving force of the rajas guna is the same force that motivates us and causes us to land in places where we do not belong.

This is the reason, from ancient times to the present, that true teachers do not teach the quick method of hyping one's enthusiasm as a solution to human development. They take the solid path of guiding us, and delve deeply into the source of our Divine enthusiasm. The objective of many human motivational books, tapes, and seminars is to inspire the par- ticipants to be enthusiastic about their lives and to move them from a state of inertia into a state of activity. These tools are useful but incomplete.

A sick soul is the source of a weary mind, which leads to feeble performance. These motivational techniques are inad- equate to move you to the state of sattva, the divine satisfac- tion. They may move you from the tamasic state (inertia) to the rajasic state (activity), but the fruit of your work provides no nectar. When you move from inertia to activity in any focused area, there will be visible improvement in the quality of your life. For many, it is enough to have moved from the state of "living death" to the state of active living. However, because these activities are influenced partially by the ignorant human ego, their success is often short-lived or mixed with pain and struggle. Your hard work and activity ultimately become the source of your misery.

Even your work is divinely ordained; however, due to your lack of understanding the *art of detachment* while performing your work, your work engulfs you, and that very work will be the source of your betrayal.

The example of a few great successes of recent times will make it clear that action alone may bring success and pleasure, but the ultimate result often leaves you disillusioned and dissatisfied.

President Lyndon Johnson, after he devoted his whole life to diligent public service as a champion for the poor and the needy, was "voluntarily" retired from the White House. After his retirement, according to his close friends, he felt so disheartened that he literally drank himself to death.

President Nixon's ego-oriented actions led him to fall at the peak of his political career.

Former British prime minister Margaret Thatcher, who struggled all of her life and held the seat of prime minister longer then anyone else in the history of Britain, was removed from office by her own party in the middle of her elected term.

The power of rajas is dynamic. It provides riches and glory, yet its fruits are fickle and not without pain and disillusionment.

Sattva

The nature of sattva is expansion, pleasure, knowledge, and wisdom. One acts by being in tune with the guidance of that inner wisdom. In public, he is energetic and purposeful. In private, he is humbly cautious. He questions whether his actions are in line with the law of Dharma. Thus, the results of these actions are always beneficial for the greater good, as well as for his personal destiny.

The state of sattva is pleasure dictated by actions that are guided by wisdom and knowledge. One acts with purpose and detachment. He understands that the essential reward of action is the joy of action itself. The material reward is frosting on the cake.

Although he welcomes all the glory the world has to offer, he has transcended the ego-driving expectations. The possibility of failure does not crush him. He is indifferent to pain and struggle. The situation might be devastating, but he is not devastated. He graciously rides the waves of life through glory and disgrace.

Shakespeare's *Hamlet* is considered a play of human tragedy. Yet I see it as a celebration of the human spirit triumphing over itself, victory over the struggle between man's lower nature and his higher nature. Hamlet goes through the transformation from the tamas (ignorance) to rajas (participation), then dies in the state of sattva (expansion).

A Thick Face, Black Heart practitioner is dominated either by the qualities of rajas or sattva, depending upon the person's natural temperament. However, the state of sattva is the aspiration of each individual.

Mimic the Virtues of the Four Forces

"There's nothing,"
and we think there's nothing at all;
but listen, that echo really answers.

—*JAPANESE ZEN SAYING*

The state of sattva exists in its entirety within the manifestation of nature, and it is the ultimate state of Thick Face, Black Heart. By observing and meditating upon nature, we catch a glimpse of this state, as did the greatest Catholic saint, Francis of Assisi, in his most moving prayer, *The Canticle of the Creature,* in which he praises the natural working of God's world.

> *Praise be to Thee my Lord for Brother Wind, for air and*
> *clouds, clear sky and all the weathers through which*
> *Thou sustainest all Thy creatures.*

> *Praise be to Thee my Lord for Sister Water. She is useful*
> *and humble, precious, and pure.*

> *Praise be to Thee my Lord for Brother Fire, through him*
> *our night Thou dost enlighten, and his is fair and merry,*
> *boisterous, and strong.*

> *Praise be to Thee my Lord for our Mother Earth, who*
> *nourishes and sustains us all, bringing forth diverse*
> *fruits and many-colored flowers and herbs....*

Nature follows the perfect law. This law manifests itself as the perfect discipline, perfect justice, perfect strength, perfect surrender, perfect detachment, perfect giving, perfect sacrifice, perfect conquest, perfect harmony, and perfect ruthlessness. Nature is the embodiment of Thick Face, Black Heart.

The law of nature is the state of sattva and the perfect expression of Thick Face, Black Heart. By contemplation upon natural forces, one obtains the state of Thick Face, Black Heart.

The elements of nature are indifferent to human judgments. They are uncompromising with human standards. They possess freedom and the courage of action. This action can be submissive or aggressive, ruthless or gentle, compassionate or dispassionate, yet it always remains vigorous, active, and disciplined. It always remains true to its Dharma, and it is ever detached.

DEVELOPING GODLIKE EGO AND GODLIKE HUMILITY

Ego is considered by the Eastern philosophies to be a human's worst enemy. Western psychologists credit it for all the achievements of mankind. The Easterner wants to get rid of the ego; the Westerner wishes to nurture it.

Godlike Ego

Recently, an associate of mine asked me, "You do a lot of speaking publicly. What do you do not to be intimidated?"

I replied, "I was never intimidated. I don't know why. Maybe because I have an extraordinarily arrogant spirit."

The question of ego is not whether we should kill it or keep it, whether it is good or bad for us. The real problem of ego is that we do not have the right kind. The only kind of ego worthy of contemplation is the kind of ego that our Creator possesses: absolute, ultimate, gigantic, and huge. Once this godlike ego enters your consciousness, it naturally destroys petty-mindedness and expands awareness. Your ability to obtain the state of Thick Face, Black Heart has a direct relationship with your ability to incorporate this god-like ego state into your awareness.

Godlike ego is not something I can describe to you, just as I can't describe a piece of exotic fruit I once ate in Thailand. It can only be obtained through direct experience. Possessing a godlike ego is the result of our small human ego touching the Divine.

Godlike Humility

Lately, when I have run into friends, the words *getting out of the way* kept popping up in different circumstances. One thing these friends all have in common is the way they use these words in the context of getting their small ego out of the way so their life will work. If you can detach yourself from your "small ego," your pettiness, and instead understand the nature of your relation to the Divine, then you can allow your life to unfold naturally. You free yourself from trivial concerns and find the peace you seek in the "bigger picture."

The other side of a godlike ego is godlike humility. This is also an objective of a Thick Face, Black Heart practitioner: to be able to get petty-mindedness out of the way and simultaneously master ultimate humility and frailty. In strength, he is unconquerable; when frail, he is invincible.

I have often thought to myself how humble God truly is. This is particularly apparent whenever I have a late meal and then want to sleep, or whenever I shove too much food into my stomach and demand that my stomach do its job. My stomach may feel pain and discomfort, but it never refuses to perform its duty to the best of its ability. If our Creator had not implanted his humility within our organs to serve us unconditionally, our organs certainly would have the right to go on strike and refuse to function unless we treat them with more respect.

Although the East and West may not agree on the terminology and definition of the word *ego*, they both agree on the importance of developing that awareness which supports our sense of connection to our Maker and assists us in manifesting a strong sense of who we are in achieving our highest good. At the same time, they also agree that we should uproot our inferior and unworthy qualities from the depths of our soul.

THE UNIVERSALITY OF THICK FACE, BLACK HEART

Thick Face, Black Heart is the intangible weapon of one's inner strength, which defends, supports, and protects us in our business encounters and daily life. The source of this strength and the mental toughness of Thick Face, Black Heart lies within that unshakable center deep within our spirit.

The quest for Thick Face, Black Heart is a spiritual matter. Once we locate the source of Thick Face, Black Heart, we may freely apply the concept to every aspect of our lives.

During my studies, I have seen no diversity, only unity, among the teachings of the East and West. East and West may have different metaphors and symbols, but the differences are only in the wrapping, not in the essence.

The works of the sixteenth-century Spanish mystics such as St. John of the Cross and St. Teresa of Avila, as well as of the thirteenth-century mystic, St. Francis of Assisi, all speak of the same divine state that is found in the recordings of the

Hindu and Buddhist doctrines. The description of the seven stages of spiritual progress by St. Teresa of Avila, in her book *Interior Castle,* is identical in detail to the Hindu recordings of the spiritual journey through the seven chakras (spiritual centers within one's body) toward the goal of Divine Union.

I have repeatedly demonstrated, both at practical and mundane levels, the universality of Thick Face, Black Heart. Lao Tzu, Abraham Lincoln, Mahatma Gandhi—these people all speak of Thick Face, Black Heart. Although they were divided by culture, time, space, and nationality, their state of mind is one. The world manifests itself through infinite forms; we are all, in essence, the children of One Maker.

SUMMARY OF KEY POINTS

• Thick is within, Black is within. We cannot obtain what we already have.

• Through our "proper" social upbringing, we have disfigured the intuitive understanding of the natural law of winning, which is within each one of us. We have distorted the natural gift of Thick Face, Black Heart, which was intended to support our spiritual and material growth. Now our task is to rediscover what we already possess.

• Seven Stages of Self-Unfoldment

   1. The Desire to Do Right. The intense desire to be good, to do the right thing. At this stage, you have no tolerance for Thick Face, Black Heart.

   2. Confusion and Negativity. The realization that you have been victimizing yourself through self-denial and the pretense of self-sacrifice arouses anger and resentment within you. You are confused by the despicable emotions you are experiencing.

3. The Battle for Surrender. By now you are trying to persuade yourself to accept your despicable emotions.

4. Acceptance of Your Imperfect Perfection. You begin to see yourself as imperfectly perfect. You begin to break new ground and set new standards for yourself.

5. The New Possibilities. At this stage, you have begun to develop the natural power of Thick Face, Black Heart. This power gives you the strength to stand up to your automatic habitual actions and thoughts and venture into new frontiers.

6. The Inner Harmony. By breaking through your notion of others' standards and expectations, you find a new surge of inner harmony: the unfamiliar emotion of peace and tranquility.

7. Detachment: The Power Source of Magnetism. The highest code of living is detachment. At this stage, nothing you possess, possesses you. You become the master of your possessions, rather than being possessed by them.

    Detachment is the secret key to obtaining everything you "want." Have you ever noticed when you *stop* wanting something, the object of your desire comes to you naturally?

    At this stage, you are to the world as the lotus blossom is to the mud pond. Though it has grown from the mud pond, it is untouched by the mud.

• Man's Three Qualities
  1. *Tamas:* inertia, obstruction, ignorance, ego domination.

When one is in this state, one feels physically sluggish, lethargic, and inactive; mentally foggy; dull, heavy, with a tendency to procrastinate; spiritually unenthusiastic, unresponsive, bored. In this state, the guiding force for action is dominated by ignorance.

2. *Rajas:* activity, struggle, influenced by ego. In this state, one is actively performing his tasks. His mind is agitated, excited, struggling, and sometimes in pain. His spirit is often restless. His activities may bring momentary pleasure, yet the nature of this pleasure is fickle.

3. *Sattva:* expansion, pleasure, knowledge, and wisdom. One acts by being in tune with the guidance of that inner wisdom. In public, he is energetic and purposeful. In private, he is humbly cautious. He questions whether his actions are in line with the law of Dharma. Thus, the results of his actions are always beneficial for the greater good, as well for the good of his own destiny.

• Learning the Virtues of the Four Forces. Nature follows the perfect law. Nature is the embodiment of Thick Face, Black Heart. Through contemplation of the natural forces, one obtains the state of Thick Face, Black Heart.

1. Sister Water: gentle, submissive, humble, and ruthless

2. Brother Fire: useful, strong, fierce, destructive, purifying

3. Brother Wind: formless, strong, fierce

4. Mother Earth: giving, sacrificing, and sustaining

• Godlike Ego. The only kind of ego worthy of contemplation is the kind of ego that our Creator possesses: absolute, ultimate, gigantic, huge. Once this godlike ego enters your consciousness, it naturally destroys petty-mindedness and expands awareness.

• Godlike Humility. When you get your "small ego" out of the way, your life can unfold naturally. The other side of a godlike ego is godlike humility. This is also the objective of a Thick Face, Black Heart practitioner: to be able to get petty-mindedness out of the way and simultaneously master ultimate humility and frailty.

• Although the East and West may not agree with the terminology and definition of the word *ego*, they both agree with the importance of developing that awareness which supports your sense of connection to your Divine Maker and assists you in manifesting a strong sense of who you are in achieving your highest good. At the same time, they also agree that we should uproot the inferior and unworthy qualities from the depths of our souls.

• During my spiritual studies, I have seen no diversity, only unity, among the teachings of the East and West. East and West may have different metaphors and symbols, but the differences are only in the wrapping, not in the essence.

*Most of our efforts are in vain
while we try to satisfy the
unquenchable thirst for life.*

—CHIN-NING CHU

15

Paths to Thick Face, Black Heart

Oh man, the jewel is in your bosom;
why look for it everywhere else?

—*JAPANESE ZEN POEM*

THE GENETIC CONNECTION

In January 1991, I spent six weeks in Australia, enjoying a magnificent winter, sunbathing under Sydney's summer sun. Besides reading books and watching the waves, I often fell into a natural meditative state.

In one of these states, I had a glorious vision. I saw the whole universe filled with golden sparks of energy. These golden sparks came from every direction, rushing down with immense force into a tiny, tubelike hole. Inside this hole was a mighty gravity that nothing could escape. Every golden spark was genetically programmed to rush into this tiny hole.

When I came out of this state, I realized that the small hole was the center of my being, the Divine origin of my soul and the source of all strength and all joy. I understood that we alone, as human beings among all the creatures of the universe, were genetically coded to be drawn to this Divine force. When we violate this natural human state, all elements in the universe, including ourselves, work against us.

Everything in life—whether it be starting a business, making money, getting married, having children, getting divorced, changing jobs, finding a new girlfriend or boyfriend, drinking, smoking, or taking drugs—is motivated by our basic desire to "feel good," to experience the connection with that Divine source within each of us.

Although our actions may be guided either by ignorance or wisdom, producing negative or positive results, our motivation is always noble: the constant desire to be immersed in that godlike, blissful state.

Most of us use the only method that we know to be in touch with this inner joy: our outward activities. If falling in love or getting a new spouse satisfied our craving for this state, then we would change our mates often. If changing jobs brought that new and exciting feeling, then we would change jobs often. Ignorant people chase after this inner bliss, as a dog chases after its own tail. They are always in action and never satisfied.

WHERE IS LIFE'S OPERATING MANUAL?

How does one go about finding this inner bliss? Some people hold our Maker responsible for the way we have mishandled our lives, because they believe our Maker has forgotten to deliver them a copy of the operation manual. I used to feel this way, but now I see it differently. Our Maker did not leave His children without a manual; rather, we simply do not know where to find this manual or how to read it.

When we discover where this manual is located and how to read it, then we will attain the state of Thick Face, Black Heart.

This mysterious operating manual is written without paper or ink. It is ever within you and without you. There is no place or time in which this manual is not present.

THE BUSINESS MANUAL VERSUS LIFE'S MANUAL

Business is a major part of our life. One who has the requisite skills for life will also be skillful in business. This is because business is based on interaction with people — all people, even ourselves. Life is about relating to people, others and ourselves. The foundation for acquiring the skill of relating to other people is rooted in the degree to which we are able to understand and relate to ourselves.

I have spoken of the practical value in adapting the power of Thick Face, Black Heart when we cross paths with others in the world of business or casual relationships. I have emphasized repeatedly that the source of Thick Face, Black Heart is within us as the natural state of our soul. Now we are ready to embark upon a journey that will allow us to directly experience the source that supports the dynamic of Thick Face, Black Heart.

THE DYNAMIC FORCE BEHIND THICK FACE, BLACK HEART

The power source of Thick Face, Black Heart is also equally present elsewhere in the universe. This force, toward which all existence rushes, is the source that brings about the reality of creation.

After developing the theory of relativity, Albert Einstein devoted most of his life to working on proving the unified field theory. He was convinced that there is a single force in the universe that binds all the diverse elements of creation together. Many scientists, then and now, have criticized Einstein's "simple" view of the universe. Einstein may not have been able to prove his theory prior to his death, but his intuition about a unified field theory is in harmony with all the oriental views of the universe.

The Merit of Unlearning

A Zen monk lived in sixteenth-century Japan under a bridge. He expressed his simplistic principle of life in a few profound words: "Most people try to know more to become more clever every day, whereas I attempt to become more simple and uncomplicated every day."

The story exemplifies the burdens we place on ourselves in everyday life. At the moment of birth, we are born naked but possess a natural dynamic force—the root of Thick Face, Black Heart. As we grow older, we deplete this natural force by conforming to man-made virtues, ideals, and principles.

These artificial standards encumber and distract us, so in order to obtain Thick Face, Black Heart, there is not so much to learn as there is to unlearn.

Live the Knowledge

We are shaped by our thoughts;
we become what we think.
When the mind is pure, joy follows,
like a shadow that never leaves.

—*BUDDHA, THE DHARMAPADA*

It took me over a year and a half to finish writing this book. In the beginning, this book was a notion in my mind and a feeling in my heart. As I kept on clarifying this "feeling" and putting it on paper, I became clearer about my own state of mind regarding Thick Face, Black Heart. After living with the information every waking and sleeping moment, I experienced a great transformation within me.

I am no longer the same person who started this book. My spirit is more centered, my mind is more focused on my objectives, my execution is more effective, and my emotions are more controlled. As I occasionally travel through the valley of the shadow of death in the competitive game called "making a living," I focus myself and recall the information in this book, from which I find great strength. Words are not merely words, they are the embodiment of power.

The ideas communicated in this book are genuine and truthful. I promise that you will arrive at a different dimension as you unceasingly contemplate the principle of Thick Face, Black Heart and let it support your every professional and personal endeavor.

THE SEVEN CENTERING TECHNIQUES

Man goes to great trouble
to acquire knowledge of the material world.
He learns all branches of mundane science.
He explores the earth,
and even travels to the moon.
Yet he never tries to find out
what exists within himself.
Because he is unaware of the enormous power
which lies hidden within him,
he looks for support in the outer world.

—ANCIENT HINDU TEXT

On January 6, 1992, *Newsweek* magazine's cover story was about how Americans pray to God. The report revealed that 91 percent of women pray, as do 85 percent of men. More than 78 percent of all Americans pray at least once a week, and more than 57 percent pray at least once a day. Just about all Americans, regardless of their religious denomination, agree that the source of all power, knowledge, creativity, and wealth lies within our mighty Maker. By being in touch with His power, we are empowered and renewed.

Through prayer, we bring forth the spirit of the Almighty, and He lives within us. As the Bible says, "The kingdom of heaven is within." God does not reside in the marble structures of the church or temple. He lives within the human heart.

In order to talk to God, we need to listen for God. We need to learn His language: the language of silence.

The following are techniques to center and calm one's mind. The aim of introducing these techniques is not a religious one. Calming the mind allows us to behold the power within, the root of Thick Face, Black Heart. When the mind is calm, all mysteries are revealed and God's hidden power within us naturally radiates forth.

Depending upon each person's nature and beliefs, one method may be more suitable than another. These techniques are not mysterious; they are practical and have proved effective for thousands of years. For example, have you ever wondered why rocking chairs enjoy such popularity? The secret is not in the chair, but in the motion of rocking. As the chair rocks, the human mind becomes calmer and the spirit feels more serene.

The ancient Hindu scripture *Vijnanabhairava* describes 112 different methods to calm the mind. One describes swinging one's body slowly while sitting in a vehicle or practicing a self-induced swinging motion, which results in a tranquil mental state.

The following techniques are useful for anyone, especially busy workers living a hectic life. The techniques are simple, yet potent.

I. Practice the Presence of God

Rejoice evermore,
praying without ceasing.

—*First Thessalonians V, 16–17*

Practicing the presence of God and invoking the power of the Divine inspires you to identify with your Creator. To practice his presence, simply repeat the name of the Divine unceasingly. Among all the methods of calming the mind and recharging it with vitality, this is the easiest for the present age.

Repetition of God's name is not only practiced in Eastern traditions; it is also common among Western spiritual seekers. St. Francis of Assisi, for example, promoted this practice among his followers.

The mind is easily distracted; it loses its focus and becomes restless. If it is not directed positively, its power will be diffused.

While we feed the body, we often starve our mind. By our not providing the proper diet and discipline to the mind, it becomes irritated and increasingly restless. Because of our natural genetic coding, our mind will not cease to trouble us until we provide it with what it craves: to be touched by its Creator. By uttering the name of the Divine continuously, you will touch Him and He will touch you back.

When you initially practice this repetition, your mind may resist. You will be unaccustomed to the practice, but with time and experience you will learn to immerse your mind in the pool of the Divine presence. You will float in ecstasy, while your heart bursts with joy. Through the repetition of the Divine name, your intellect will sharpen and your mental strength will toughen.

Practicing the presence of God can be done silently while you are going about your worldly duties. Counting rosary beads can also be beneficial, since holding the rosary will act as a reminder to the mind to focus on the Divine. When Gandhi was assassinated, he was uttering the Divine name of "Ram, Ram." Even at the moment of sudden death by gunshot, Gandhi's mind was absorbed totally in the nectar of the Divine.

II. The Art of Breathing

In Sanskrit, breath is called *prana,* the vital force. In Chinese, it is called *chi.* Breath is closely connected to the well-being of the mind. Watch your breath. You will discover that when your breathing is short and shallow, your mind is restless. When you breathe deeply, your mind will become calm and tranquil and your intellect sharp and focused.

In the *Essene Gospel of Peace,* Book Two, Jesus said, "We worship the Holy Breath which is placed higher than all the other things created. For lo, the eternal and sovereign luminous space, where rule the unnumbered stars, is the air we breathe in and the air we breathe out. And in the moment betwixt the breathing in and breathing out is hidden all the mysteries of the Infinite Garden."

The same thing is recorded in *Vijnanabhairava* (24): "The exhalation goes out and the inhalation goes in. By steady fixation of the mind at the two spaces between the breaths, one may experience the full nature of God."

Today, Catholic Trappist monks commonly adopt a breathing technique to center their mind and focus on God.

The following are a few simple steps for practicing the art of breathing:

1. Select a quiet, serene place in your home, preferably a room dedicated for prayer and meditation. If that's not possible, assign a corner used for this purpose only.

2. Wear natural fabric when meditating: silk, cotton, and wool are recommended.

3. Wear the same set of clothes during your regular breathing and meditation session.

4. Establish an altar, and if you prefer worship of a specific form, place the image of your chosen deity there to inspire your devotion.

5. Candles or fragrance can also be used to create a serene

mood. It is advisable to select the same fragrance each time, so you associate the fragrance with your meditation.

6. Sit quietly on a wool mat on the floor, or on a chair covered with a wool mat, with your back erect, body relaxed, and stomach empty or not too full. (Always using the same wool mat will help you associate it with meditation.)

7. Close your eyes. Bring your attention to your breathing.

8. Watch your breath naturally go in and out of your body.

9. Listen to the sound of your breath. When your breath comes in, it makes the natural sound *ham;* and as the breath goes out, it makes the sound *sa.* Humans breathe in and out 21,600 times a day, and each time the breath repeats *hamsa.* Jesus said, "The Holy Breath is placed higher than all the other things created." Listen to your breath silently as you breathe in and out, watching the space between the inhalation and the exhalation.

10. With your mind, follow the breath within you and observe the space where inhalation meets exhalation, approximately twelve fingers distance from the nostril. Behold the space between the breaths, for it is the gate to the mystery of this universe and beyond.

11. At first, sit for five minutes each day. As your mind becomes calmer, prolong the sitting time to a half hour or longer.

III. Invoking the Inner Music

At any stage of the above meditation process, while the mind is calm and serene, you may naturally drop the effort of attempting to harmonize your breathing. As the mind gets calmer through diligent practice of sitting peacefully, one will hear an inner music, sounds that may be different for each individual: buzzing bees, gurgling water, the whisper of a celestial flute, the chime of distant gongs, the blowing of a horn, or a mixture of all of them in a tranquil and harmonious arrangement. Just sink into the ecstacy of the inner music. But do not force it. If you don't hear anything, just sit and enjoy the silent void.

Years ago, in the middle of a working day, I stopped at a church, just to sit. As my mind gradually calmed, I heard the ring of the most beautiful Zen bell. The sound of the bell ringing through me was as though the fresh spring rain had washed away all of my day's fatigue and bathed me in the pool of exhilaration and jubilation.

After I left the church, I told my partner, who was sitting next to me in the church, how beautifully the bell rang. My partner told me there was no Zen bell ringing whatsoever. Then I realized that the bell I heard was my inner music of Divine delight. I had heard the inner music often before, but never had it been so loud.

In fact, the Zen Buddhist and Christian bells, the Tibetan long horn, the Hindu conch, and all other spiritual ceremonial instruments are an attempt to recreate the inner music that is heard during meditation.

IV. Unlocking the Inner Vision

As you practice the breathing centering technique, you might see divine visions in the form of shimmering white light, or blue lights, even stars, or galaxies.

Be very careful. The goal of meditation is not to hear and see the phenomena. These are merely road signs to indicate that you are on the right track. The spiritual experience will unfold as it is right for you, depending upon your temperament, so do not worry if your meditative experiences are not similar to those of others. Simply enjoy the presence of the Divine in a blissful and expanded state.

For the meditator, the experience during meditation is private. One does not make it public without good reason. I have been sharing some of my experiences in order to assure you that the effort you put forth will not be wasted.

Five years ago, I spent over six months at my mountain property in Mosier, Oregon. The land is nearly four thousand feet high, and my closest neighbor is forty acres away. I spent a great deal of time in deep meditation. The longer I was alone, the more my inner and outer states merged. It came to the point where I could literally see my mind working, see it pulsating and sparking with energy.

Sometimes at night I traveled to the center of the Milky Way. The stars were dazzlingly white, some glowing individually against black space, others clustered so that their light bled into one another and formed a brilliant tableau.

On other nights, though, the stars shifted to a red color. I did not know exactly how or what signaled the change. Since it is a fact that spiritual states are closely tied to physical reality, I looked for an explanation for the change of colors in nature. I asked around and learned that in astrophysics there is a phenomenon known as the red shift, which is a lengthening of the wavelength of a star as it diverges from another body, causing its visible light to shift from white to red. On those nights when the stars appeared red, I was moving ever inward to new, unexplored states.

V. Contemplating the Vast Open Space

When you are gazing into the sky, the open desert, or the ocean, imagine these vast spaces as expressions of the Divine and then let this image dissolve in your head. As your mind merges with the vast open space, the reality of outer and inner becomes one. At that moment, you will experience the whole universe bathed in the Light of the Divine.

Everyone is familiar with the feelings brought about by gazing into the sky or the ocean; a sense of tranquility rushes over us. Even though you do not experience the ultimate state immediately, the benefit to the mind is obvious.

The following two techniques are unconventional, but I am listing them specifically for the benefit of the unconventional.

VI. Courting Blissful Oblivion

The euphoria of sex mirrors the bliss of the Divine. What I am about to reveal is not a statement to encourage indulging in carnal pleasure. It merely points out that God's bliss is present everywhere, and we can gain a glimpse of it during our sexual encounters.

1. While locked in an embrace with a lover, one is totally dissolved in the feeling of oneness (unity) and loses all sense of anything external or internal. Similarly, when the mind is dissolved in the Divine Energy, one loses all sense of duality and experiences the delight of unity-consciousness. At the time of sexual intercourse, an absorption into your partner is brought about by excitement, and the final rapture that ensues at orgasm betokens the delight of the Divine. This delight, in reality, is your own Divine bliss. This sexual absorption is only symbolic of your absorption in the Divine Energy.

2. During the time of orgasm, instead of focusing on the joy of the orgasm, focus on the source of that orgasm. By tracing it back to the source, one discovers that the source of all delight is the delight of the Divine. This delight does not come from an external source. The lover is only a catalyst for the manifestation of the delight.

3. Even in the absence of a lover, there is a flood of euphoria, simply by the intensity of the memory of sexual pleasure. Since sexual pleasure can be obtained by memory, even in the absence of a lover, it is evident that the elation is inherent within.

4. On the occasion of joy arising from seeing a friend or relative after a long time, one should meditate on the joy itself and become absorbed in it. The mind will then identify with the source of the joy.

VII. Soliciting Joy from the Pleasure of Eating

When one's joy swells at the prospect of savoring a good meal, one should meditate on the condition of this joy itself. Supreme delight then will follow.

Once a student asked his teacher, "What is the state of Buddha?"

The teacher answered, "When you eat, you eat; when you sleep, you sleep; when you work, you work." This is a similar concept to one Mahatma Gandhi expressed, "No matter where you are, make sure you are there." Whenever your mind is totally absorbed in whatever activities you are performing, your mind will remain calm and content, and the bliss of God will reveal itself.

THE TWO WHEELS OF THICK FACE, BLACK HEART

The two wheels of Thick Face, Black Heart are the knowledge and experience of spiritual matters combined with the awareness of the practical sciences of survival.

Spiritual contemplation benefits one's spiritual life as well as one's capacity to handle the mundane world. Such contemplation sharpens and polishes the mind and makes it fit to accomplish objectives; it improves the ability to concentrate; it makes one indifferent to outside judgments and influences; it grants the power for compassion as well as divine vengeance. All of these traits, combined with pragmatic worldly skills, are what enable one to operate efficiently in our shrewd and competitive world. Together these form the complete dimension of Thick Face, Black Heart.

SUMMARY OF KEY POINTS

• Our Divine Maker did not leave His children without an operation manual; however, we do not know where to find this manual or how to read it. This mysterious operating manual is located within as well as without each one of us.

• Everything we do in life is motivated by our basic desire to "feel good," to experience the connection with the Divine power within each one of us. Because our actions are guided by either ignorance or wisdom, the consequences produced are either negative or positive. Nevertheless, our motivation is a noble one: the desire constantly to be immersed in that blissful state.

• Man goes to great trouble to acquire knowledge of the material world, yet he never tries to find out what exists within himself. Because he is unaware of the enormous power that lies hidden within him, he looks for support in the outer world.

• Seven Centering Techniques

  1. Practice the Presence of God. Invoking the power of the name of the Divine inspires identification with the Divine. Among all the methods of spiritual practice, this is the easiest for busy people.

  2. Prana Yama, The Art of Breathing. Breath is closely connected to the well-being of the mind. When we master our minds, we master our world.

     a. Sit quietly on a wool mat on the floor, or on a chair, with your back erect, body relaxed, and stomach empty.

b. Close your eyes. Bring your attention to your breathing.

c. Watch your breath naturally go in and out of your body.

d. Listen to the sound of *hamsa* as you breathe. When your breath comes in, you hear the natural sound *ham;* and as the breath goes out, *sa*. Watch the space between the inhalation and the exhalation.

e. With your mind, follow the breath, observe the space where inhalation meets exhalation, approximately twelve fingers distance from the nostrils. Behold the space between the breaths, for it is the gate to the mystery of this universe and beyond.

3. Invoking the Inner Music. While the mind is calm and serene, sit quietly and listen for the inner music. One may hear the sounds of buzzing bees, running water, the celestial flute, the hitting of gongs, the blowing of a horn, or a mixture of all of them in a tranquil and harmonious arrangement. Just absorb yourself in that inner bliss.

4. Unlocking the Inner Vision. As your mind becomes calm, you may see Divine visions, such as white light, blue light, stars, or galaxies.

5. Contemplating the Vast Open Space. When you are gazing into the sky, open desert, or the ocean, imagine these vast spaces as expressions of the Divine. Then let this image dissolve in your head. As your mind merges with the vast open space, the reality of outer and inner

become one. At that moment, you will experience the whole universe bathed in the Light of the Divine.

6. Courting Blissful Oblivion. The bliss of sex mirrors the bliss of the Divine. God's bliss is present everywhere, and we can gain a gleam into the source of His divine bliss during our sexual encounters.

  a. At the time of sexual intercourse, an absorption into your partner brought about by excitement and the final delight that ensues at orgasm betokens the delight of the Divine.

  b. During the time of orgasm, instead of focusing on the joy of the orgasm, focus on the source of that orgasm. By following the source of the orgasm, one discovers the source of all delight: the delight of the Divine.

  c. Even in the absence of a lover, there is a flood of delight, simply by the intensity of the memory of sexual pleasure.

  d. On the occasion of great delight being obtained, or on the occasion of delight arising from seeing a friend or relative after a long time, one should meditate on the delight itself and become absorbed in it. One's mind will then identify with the source of the delight.

7. Soliciting Joy from the Pleasure of Eating. When one experiences the expansion of joy, or savors the pleasure arising from eating or drinking, one should meditate on the perfect condition of this joy. Then there will be supreme delight.

• The two wheels of Thick Face, Black Heart are the knowledge and experience of spiritual matter combined with the awareness of the practical sciences of survival.

Those most skilled in warfare
are those who conquer the enemy without fighting battles
who capture cities
without laying siege to them

—*SUN TZU'S* ART OF WAR

16

How a Piranha
Eats the Shark

A ccording to some economists, the standard of living in
America has not improved for the last three decades. In
fact, it has deteriorated. The reasons seem mysteriously elu-
sive to most experts. It is my opinion that in order to reverse
this dilemma, each one of us needs "to turn ourselves
around." In general, a transformation of any kind begins with
a single entity. We as Americans need to get back to the basic
elements that originally made America great.

In this book, I have repeatedly pointed out the value of
Thick Face, Black Heart, which each one of us embodies and
our founding fathers, the early pioneers, also possessed. We
have not lost this source of inner strength, we simply need to
rediscover it as part of our transformation.

336 CHIN-NING CHU

A SALUTE TO AMERICAN
ENTREPRENEURS

Arnold Schoenberg, the great twentieth-century composer, once stated that the problem with modern man is that he has no tolerance for discomfort. Schoenberg would have been appalled to see the extravagance of the 1980s.

In light of the shortcomings of our present society, thank God for American entrepreneurs. When others are indulgently extravagant, these individuals are obsessively bent on manifesting their visions into material reality.

A friend of mine once said that the entrepreneur is a person who, in order to avoid working eight hours a day, works sixteen hours a day. As I see it, the solution to American growth is a simple one. Our system should support and encourage our greatest natural resource: the American entrepreneurial spirit. These entrepreneurs fight with great strength and determination against all odds, risking their financial security and their family's well-being, while swimming in a vast, shark-infested ocean, yet never losing heart and sight of their objectives.

Recently, I received a phone call from a reader, a young entrepreneur who is developing a device that will dispense natural fragrances into buildings to enhance the quality of the air. He told me how much he had enjoyed my previous books and wondered if I had thought of writing a new book dealing with ways in which small entrepreneurs might effectively compete with the bigger and more powerful companies. I told him that *Thick Face, Black Heart* would provide the tools needed to accomplish his objectives and that I would also add a chapter entitled "How a Piranha Eats the Shark," to provide additional practical strategies applicable to the world of "big fish eats little fish."

I. THE FOX BORROWS THE TIGER'S PRESENCE

The fox is a very intelligent creature who, due to his lack of physical strength and size, is placed at a disadvantage. The fox receives no respect in the woods, and no one really takes him seriously. In order to overcome this, one of the solutions for the fox is to convince a tiger to be his friend. By closely associating himself with a strong and respectable tiger, the fox can walk next to this great cat through the jungle and enjoy the same fearful respect accorded the tiger. Even when the tiger is not next to the fox, the knowledge that the fox is closely related to the tiger is enough to ensure this fox's survival in the wild.

If a fox is unable to befriend a tiger, then the fox should create an illusion of close association with the tiger by carefully trailing behind the cat while boasting of the deep friendship they share. In this way, he creates an impression that his well-being is of great concern to the tiger.

The fox and tiger are merely metaphors and in reality can represent many things. The following are some possibilities.

1. The tiger is a powerful and influential individual who shares your vision and is willing to aid your cause.

2. The tiger could be a powerful individual willing to lend his hand for purposes of mutual benefit. In a similar vein, have you ever noticed that multitudes of birds ride on the backs of huge water buffaloes? They provide relief for the buffaloes by eating the ticks and mosquitoes from their backs, while the buffaloes provide shelter and protection for the birds.

3. The tiger could be an organization or association that

shares your vision and point of view. By joining forces with others, you can create the necessary presence of a tiger.

4. The tiger could be your political connection. By supporting the "right" candidate, you can create a powerful partner. For this reason, the rich often generously donate large sums of money to have their own "pet tiger."

5. The tiger could be your position or job title. A single individual is often unimpressive. However, if you are working for a powerful and influential employer, you are no longer just a powerless, single entity.

People in government service understand this concept well. When you are representing a state or federal government during a visit to a foreign country, you will be treated quite differently than if you were traveling as a private citizen. You have automatically empowered yourself through your association with the American government. A CEO from a giant corporation receives special treatment wherever he goes, due to the fact that his authority extends over the resources of his entire company.

Senators, congressmen, and presidents of the United States glow with special importance during their terms in office. After they are out of their respective offices, this glow diminishes.

6. The tiger could be your talent or your work. If Isaac Stern had never played the violin, he would never have become the Isaac Stern we know today. Through his ability to master the instrument, Isaac Stern became world renowned. By the same token, whatever your field of expertise, your work can be your "tiger."

7. By marrying the "right" person, you will have your

tiger. This is the oldest tactic to achieve instant recognition and power.

II. BEFORE HITTING A DOG, FIRST IDENTIFY THE OWNER

In ancient China, a dog in the street was an unwelcome sight because many citizens were bitten. If you saw a suspicious dog looking unfriendly, you would take off your shoes or find a stick to hit the dog, causing it to flee. Before you did so, however, you would ask around and discern to whom this dog belonged. If the dog belonged to a wealthy and powerful family, beating such a dog could be unwise. If the dog belonged to a poor man or was homeless, then you could freely beat it. This Chinese maxim is used to describe the way humans operate. If you don't want to be bitten, then associate yourself with the rich and powerful.

The essence of this story is similar to that of the tiger and fox. Understanding this concept is vitally important. This is the reason people learn to "name-drop." One time a publisher asked my agent who my clients were and who I knew. This publisher did not mean he wanted to know how many John Does and Joe Blows I had for clients; he was looking for recognizable names.

III. COLLECT THE SMALL FORCES

Expand your forces from singular to multiple. One piranha alone might not have any impact; however, hundreds of piranhas will surely overcome the shark. Mothers Against Drunk Drivers was created through a single mother's grassroots effort. One mother was able to organize all the other mothers who shared her view. Utilizing collective force, MADD was strong enough to overturn the outdated drunk driving laws.

IV. DECEPTION IS THE ESSENTIAL

Deceiving a predator by employing camouflage is vital for survival in the animal kingdom. As I have mentioned before, when facing a strong opponent, why attempt a frontal assault when you can utilize manipulative warfare?

The following are popular Asian concepts of business: The marketplace is a battlefield. The essence of war is deception. When you are ready to attack, you must create the impression that you will not attack. Keep plans as dark and impenetrable as night. The highest form of victory is to conquer by strategy.

Japan has adopted these concepts in its economic warfare with the United States. Japan appeared to be "no threat" and pretended to be a docile pig (as previously referred to in *The 36 Strategies*) in the '60s, '70s, and '80s. Now, in the '90s, it is feasting on the "tiger": the American government and taxpayers.

Japan, along with Asia's four newly risen dragons—Taiwan, Hong Kong, Korea, and Singapore—all utilize these basic strategies. The concept of "deception" is the essential element when the small need to compete with the large and strong. As Sun Tzu said, "If one is able and strong, then one should disguise oneself in order to appear inept and weak." After attempting military supremacy in World War II and failing, Japan has now chosen to conquer the world economically. If she had made this intention clear, her victory would never have been possible. The secret of Asian economic success is worthy of America's respect and fear. Most of all, we should learn to adopt their winning strategies to enhance our own victory.

V. HITCHING A FREE RIDE TO SUCCESS

Once there were a hare and a crab in the woods. The hare challenged the crab to a race, and the crab accepted. When the race began, the hare swiftly bolted away. As the hare took off, the crab jumped up and grabbed onto the hare's furry tail. The hare ran furiously toward the other end of the woods, not knowing the crab was getting a free ride. A few steps before the hare reached the end zone, he stopped and thought, "Wait a minute, I am running against a crab. Why am I running so fast?" He looked back and saw that the crab was nowhere in sight. Suddenly the hare heard the crab shouting, "I won, I won." He turned around, and a few steps away saw the crab standing on the finish line.

Again, for one of the classic examples in our time of how a piranha eats the shark, we can examine Japan's economic success. Japan, like the crab, is riding on the tail of America's industrial research-and-development efforts and is beating America at the finish line of economic competition. Without detection, the Japanese have been reaping the benefits of America's ingenuity. In the past decade, Japan has accumulated half a trillion dollars of trade surplus from the American consumers. Along the way, Japan has totally wiped out the American consumer electronics and computer memory chip industries and is presently threatening to wipe out another: the automobile industry.

VI. ATTACK THE VULNERABILITY OF YOUR OPPONENT

According to Sun Tzu's *Art of War,* the most essential factor in determining victory is to know yourself and know your opponent. Sun Tzu did not mention that the size of the army is the deciding factor for victory, nor did he claim that the most well-equipped army will ensure victory. If either had been the case, America would have been the indisputable victor in the Vietnam War.

It is especially important to know how to identify and attack the vulnerability of your superior opponent while you protect yourself from exposing your own weakness. Some popular ancient Asian strategies were:

Remove the Firewood from under the Cooking Pot

When you are facing a pot of boiling water, the force of the boiling water is fierce and unmanageable. Instead of dealing with the hot water, you should step back and discover the *real* source of the water's force: the firewood. Once the source is discovered, you can easily remove the firewood from under the cooking pot, and the water will lose all its might. *Remember, what may appear to be the source of one's strength can often also be the source of one's weakness.*

I employ this strategy when the situation becomes "unmanageable" and it becomes necessary to remove the "firewood."

One time I represented an American client who was marketing his product in China. I was facing one strong competitor who had a special log burning under his boiling water. My competition's president, Mr. Jones (a fictitious name),

was serving as international director of his industry's association. He was spending sizeable sums of money, providing
many fringe benefits to the Chinese through the association's
international marketing budget. However, he never made
clear to the Chinese that the money he spent was derived
from a public fund. All the Chinese officials thought that Mr.
Jones was a man of great vision to be willing to invest such
sums of money, hoping to build a solid relationship for the
future. They believed that no reasonable businessman would
"throw his money away" as Mr. Jones did.

As I have mentioned, strength is often vulnerability in disguise. This may not always be the case, but certainly it was
true in this incident.

During one of my visits to China, it became necessary to
divulge the fact that the money Mr. Jones was doling out did
not derive from his company's marketing fund. The money
he used was supposed to promote the industry as a whole, not
benefit any particular individual company. Mr. Jones misled
the Chinese. Furthermore, Mr. Jones' term as the international director would soon end. Since this position is rotated in a
yearly election, it would not be a wise move for the Chinese
to favor Mr. Jones's company, especially when many
American companies were discontent with his unorthodox
handling of public funds. These considerations led the
Chinese to believe that it was in their best interest to keep a
respectable distance from Mr. Jones, especially since the
Chinese had already reaped the benefits.

Display Your Forces in the East and Attack in the West

When you discover that your opponent's vulnerable
defense is at the west side of the city wall, you should open-

ly display your forces at the east wall, making ready for a frontal assault while secretly attacking the west.

VII. MASTER THE ART OF RETREAT

If you are small and wish to take on the big, the first step you need to plan before you wage your challenge is your path of escape. Unlike the Japanese, who believe death in combat is a great honor, the Chinese prefer to survive by retreating, thereby living to fight another day. In fact, the Chinese see retreat merely as another form of advance.

VIII. EFFECTIVE EXECUTION

When you are small and face overwhelming opposition, you must find a way to spend half the effort to obtain twice the result. The following are several effective ancient Chinese strategies.

Sails Follow the Wind

In every success story, there are many winds to contend with. Before your journey, observe the wind carefully, detect its direction, and then follow it. You will get to your destination twice as fast with half the effort.

Asian martial arts are all based on this strategy. The art of defense is not about force against force but rather the idea that you flow with the force of your opponent. When he delivers a punch, you should avoid his blow, causing him to fall from his own force. While he is off balance, you can quickly and effortlessly deliver your blow. In essence, you will learn to tune in with the situation and learn to *react* instead of to act.

In this book I have revealed many small strategies that I have "designed" to gain certain advantages during my business encounters. The truth is, however, I never really sit down and plot out the strategies. I merely flow with the situation and then react accordingly.

One Arrow, Two Birds

You only have one chance to shoot into a group of birds clustering in a treetop. If you miss, you will frighten all the birds away. Before you shoot, you need to calculate your angle and your aim carefully, so your one shot will yield two birds.

Logan is a business psychologist who provides consultation to businesses involved in solving their internal personnel conflicts and increasing productivity. Logan was planning to expand his client base through the traditional avenues of direct mailing and advertisements in regional business publications. While he was contemplating the effort and costs of such an enterprise, a sudden inspiration came to him. Rather than sending out mailers to his targeted potential customers, he contacted the local television stations and presented them with his idea for a three-minute segment on business psychology to be inserted into their news programs.

Eventually, Logan's concept was accepted by a network-affiliated morning news show. Now, instead of Logan having to chase down his clients, they have started to contact him. Furthermore, this exposure enabled him to set himself apart from the rest of his competitors as a renowned authority (after all, he was on television!) and also saved him a sizeable sum of money in marketing and promotional expenditures.

IX. BEWARE THE SMALLEST

Success in life often comes from accumulating a stronghold of small victories. Failure is often caused by overlooking insignificant events.

One time during a lengthy business encounter with a Korean company, negotiations were not going very well. Every time we thought we had an "understanding," everything would fall apart. After investigating, I discovered that the source of the problem lay with the Korean company's translator. He was unwilling to admit that he couldn't understand the subtleties of the English language for fear that he would be demoted to a less prestigious position. Whenever he was not clear about the intent of the American company, he would make things up. This action had created a tremendous misunderstanding, and it appeared that both companies had irreconcilable differences. Later, I spoke to both the boss and the translator on two separate occasions. I explained that the English language is full of subtle nuances, and if a translator must ask for clarification, it does not reflect on his competency. Both were satisfied, and the companies reached an agreement.

X. THE NEW LEAPFROG THEORY

If you have a large, perfect diamond and you take it to the village marketplace, you will have a tremendously hard time trying to convince the junk peddlers to give you five dollars for it. However, if you circumvent the village peddlers and the small-town shopkeepers and go directly to the most reputable diamond dealer in the nation, you would not have to waste your energy attempting to convince him. Your merchandise would speak for itself. You wouldn't even need to open your mouth, and he might offer you five hundred thousand dollars for it.

If you are a true gem, do not waste your energy trying to undersell yourself to the common village peddlers. You will annoy them and waste your time. It is much easier to sell valuable goods to those who recognize the value than to those who do not.

In 1985, shortly after I took up residence in Portland, Oregon, I was appointed to assist the Oregon state government in hosting a group delegation from China. I was not aware that there had been numerous contenders for this assignment. Whoever was chosen would quickly get to know these officials well through three weeks of extensive statewide traveling, thus leading to many lucrative business ventures. Many of the influential Oregon business organizations and individuals strongly supported their consultants and were resentful when I was chosen. My dramatic entrance into the Oregon political and business circles unknowingly created some strong enemies.

I quickly grew tired of playing petty games with these self-proclaimed enemies. Instead of continuing to battle with my opposition, I decided to adopt the "leapfrog theory."

I started to write books. Due to the enthusiastically positive reviews in the *London Financial Times, USA Today,* and many other papers and magazines, I was placed in the position of an undisputed authority on Asian business culture. I no longer had to prove myself to those annoying "small" people who constantly undermined my efforts.

When you are dealing with ignorant people, don't attempt to convince them of anything. Instead, leap to the top, gain endorsement from established authorities, and ally yourself with the powerful and the wise. The "leapfrog theory" only works if the direction of your "leap" is toward your association with the "tiger."

XI. ALTERED REALITY

We measure our reality according to our experience. As our experience expands, our reality is also altered

When I was in Taiwan, I remember that my elementary school and high school were enormous and had large playing fields. In a recent visit, I went back to both schools. What I had remembered as huge grounds were actually very small schoolyards. My impressive schools had suddenly shrunk. In reality, the schools and their playgrounds have not changed, but I have. My perceptions have changed; I have seen the world.

In the same way, your opponents seem big, while you feel small within. As you grow bigger inside, suddenly, those huge, powerful "sharks" shrink. As a matter of fact, they were not really sharks at all but rather normal-sized fish who are making a huge disturbance in the water.

XII. FROM VICTIM TO VICTOR

Everyone understands the importance of not being a victim; how being a victim leaves you powerless. For some, it doesn't matter how many books they read and how much they understand the importance of being in charge of their emotions. These people just cannot help thinking that somehow their state of mind has a direct relationship to the fact that others are able to hurt them physically or emotionally. They can read and understand a thousand times, but the idea never *really becomes a part of them.*

After your unceasing struggle, somehow, out of nowhere,

mysteriously, the concept of not being a victim transforms itself from an idea to a conviction.

Recently, I felt betrayed by a close associate and was hurt by the experience. I felt that my inferior state of mind had a direct connection to the incident and the person who caused it. As I lay in bed, mindlessly watching television, my mind frantically attempted to seek a harmonious resolution. Although I had no power to change the incident, I was hoping somehow I could view this dreadful experience from a different perspective. However, I did not know exactly what I was looking for. I had always understood that I shouldn't be a victim of my emotions and outer circumstances, but convincing your heart with your head can be difficult. Suddenly, in an instant, I saw that there were three separate elements: myself, my emotions, and the incident. I had thought that these three elements were connected, but in reality I am the one who controls how I wish to feel within. A never-before-experienced sense of freedom engulfed me.

This transformation was not caused by any particular thought. My transformation was not a change of attitude, but rather a realization. A spark had been ignited within. Instantly, everything lit up within me, and I didn't know how it had happened. Something deep inside me just switched on. I remembered something I had read one time in an ancient text that held the secret of such transformations: "Struggling, struggling, one day, behold, the great goal."

Immediately, I attempted to capture that "moment." What element had ignited that transformation? What thoughts within me triggered that sudden burst of light? I was unable to identify the cause.

Thick Face, Black Heart practitioners strive unceasingly for the transformation from victim to victor. When the piranha experienced such a self-transformation, he brought forth inherent attributes of which he was never aware. At that instant, he realized that all the time that he thought he was small and insignificant, in fact he was as mighty as the mightiest. This is an indescribable transformation. Yet those who experience the phenomenon know it is real.

Epilogue

The applications of Thick Face, Black Heart are infinite. The only limitation is your ability to translate and adapt these principles in your daily endeavors.

Throughout this book, I have analyzed the different components of Thick Face, Black Heart. These individual and seemingly separate components are like the facets of a diamond. Without the facets, a diamond is merely a rock. It is important to remember that without the specific attributes of each component, there is no Thick Face, Black Heart.

The wisdom of Thick Face, Black Heart is not my creation. I am merely a vehicle, bearing the concept to you. These doctrines are from the timeless wisdom of natural law.

Who I am, the life I have lived, and the knowledge that I have been able to absorb have all contributed to my realization of the wisdom of Thick Face, Black Heart. As with most people, some aspects of Thick Face, Black Heart come to me as second nature, some are learned easily, and yet there are those that I have to ceaselessly struggle with to master.

Writing this book has been difficult as well as easy. The difficulty was that Thick Face, Black Heart is an abstract concept that exists within each of us. The challenge of dividing this idea into chapters and paragraphs has been a soul-searching experience with countless false starts.

Once the work was finally on course, the topics of each chapter seemed to appear miraculously in my life or the lives of my close associates. These experiences were directly relevant to what I wrote each day. Many times, people would come out of nowhere to tell me dynamic stories about themselves and then vanish from my life. Each time I needed a quote, I would effortlessly reach for just the right book and turn immediately to the page I wanted. Even casual conversations with friends would end up supplying me with the missing piece needed for a chapter.

So I salute the Universal Will. Through His providence, this book has been realized. As the great composer Johann Sebastian Bach said, "Soli Deo Gloria," only to God the glory.

Appendix:
Thick Black
Theory

L   ee Zhong Wu was a social philosopher and critic. He did
    not set out to teach a method of achieving one's goals.
His purpose in writing *Thick Black Theory* was to describe
the symptoms of an illness in Chinese society. In the course
of his inquiry, he described the methods by which men obtain
and hold on to power: how they use their power and wealth
to accumulate more power and wealth. He analyzed the
methods they used and the lengths to which they would go to
achieve their own ends.

THE UNLIKELY MACHIAVELLI

The methods he described in such detail were offered
without apology, as they were descriptions of the way people
interacted in the real world. Lee did not initially propose
these methods as principles to be followed in achieving one's
own ends. He only wished to make people aware of their

existence. Lee was intrigued about the idea of translating his work into other languages; however, his close associates were concerned that the hostile Western powers in China would combine two radical Chinese inventions, gunpowder and Lee's Thick Black Theory, to further victimize China. They did not want it in the hands of non-Chinese.

Though he understood the principles of accumulating wealth and power, Lee was an inept practitioner. He was a poor man and a lifelong failure by common standards of measurement. Though he wrote a treatise on how to obtain an appointment to an official post, and another on how to keep the post and use it to one's best advantage, he was dismissed from the only official position he ever held. He emphasized in his essays that the primary reason to strive for an important appointment was to be in a position to accumulate wealth through bribery and corruption. At the time of his dismissal, he was so destitute that his friends had to take up a collection to pay his fare home. During his tenure in office, his most notable acts involved drastically reducing his own salary and then closing down his own office because he felt there was no real need for it.

One of Lee's close friends characterized him as a monk who carried his monastery within. Though his body lived in the world, his heart renounced the worldly life. Lee himself, when chided about his inability to use the Thick Black Theory to improve his own life, replied that he was the explorer, the one who spent his time on uncharted ground. Like Moses, Lee's destiny was to point the way but never to live in the promised land. It was only natural that those who followed would be able to refine and make better use of his discoveries.

But Lee was not truly a failure, nor did he truly renounce the use of Thick Black Theory. He simply had a different agenda. Lee could not have written as he did, nor persisted in the face of the furor stirred up by his writing, if he had not had Thick Face. He was convinced of the value and the truth in what he wrote, and he did not care if the whole world thought him mad. Lee thought of himself as a great teacher like Confucius, and this self-image carried him through the years of scorn and public condemnation unscathed.

Lee successfully practiced a form of Thick Face, Black Heart that was primarily concerned with self-discovery and was bound up with his sense of mission.

THE PUBLICATION OF
THICK BLACK THEORY

Thick Black Theory was first intended to be published as a series of essays in *The Chengdu Daily* in 1911, but the violent reaction to the publication of the first installment caused Lee's publisher to cancel the series. It was instead published in a single slim volume by friends of Lee in Beijing. It went through several printings before being banned by the government.

It was banned because too many people were made uncomfortable by the truth in Lee's observations. They were not used to seeing the ruthlessness and hypocrisy underlying many Chinese institutions laid bare. They felt that by merely mentioning these things, Lee was at best muckraking; at worst, they felt he was advocating the immorality he depicted.

It did not help that Lee was an outspoken critic of the new revolutionary government, the Republic of China. Although Lee had been an early follower of Dr. Sun Yat-sen, the guiding force of the revolutionary struggle in China, he quickly became disillusioned with the new government. He maintained that the only difference between the barbaric ways of the Ching Empire and the enlightened government of the Republic was the use of euphemisms to excuse the excesses of power. He explained that in the old days when you ran afoul of a powerful official, he would simply send his thugs to beat you and drag you off to prison. In the new Republic of China, if you ran afoul of a powerful official, he would first accuse you of disturbing the social order, then he would send his thugs to beat you and drag you off to prison.

As a consequence of having been banned for so long, *Thick Black Theory* is largely unknown to the current generation of Chinese. In Taiwan, it was banned during the thirty-eight years of martial law from 1949 to 1987 and has not been widely read there even since the lifting of martial law. In Hong Kong, however, it has been continuously available and is somewhat more generally known. Despite the fact that most contemporary Chinese are not aware of Lee's work, the phraseology of "Thick Black Theory" has become part of the Chinese language. The Chinese use Thick Black Theory when referring to ruthless behavior without attributing the source of this idea to Lee Zhong Wu.

THE EYES OF LEE ZHONG WU

The writings of Lee Zhong Wu are obscure. His examples are drawn from the world of provincial China at the turn of the last century. In many ways they are not relevant or even completely understandable to the modern Western reader. Still, Lee's observations are touched by genius, even if it is a genius that is difficult to convey across the twin barriers of language and culture.

In this Appendix, I will attempt to give the interested reader the flavor of Lee's thought by discussing a few of his writings.

SIX WAYS TO OBTAIN AN OFFICIAL POSITION

In Chinese society, holding a position in the government bureaucracy is the only prestigious occupation. A high-ranking government bureaucrat is at the top of the social and economic order. Consequently, almost everyone is constantly trying to obtain an appointment to some official position. Lee discusses the six steps involved in getting appointed to an official government position as an example of the practical application of Thick Black Theory. His discussion is set in the context of Imperial China, but human nature has not changed since then, and the same principles apply today.

1. Emptiness

The first requirement is to empty your mind of everything that does not pertain to your appointment to the position you seek. You must have no other goals, no other thoughts. You must concentrate on the desired appointment and meditate on it daily.

Your time must also be empty. You must have the ability to wait however long it takes. You must see yourself in the post you desire and nowhere else. You are not going to take another job. If the appointment does not come today, you will wait until tomorrow. If you don't get the position this year, you will wait until next year.

2. Boring In

You must seize every little opportunity to advance your prospects. When you find such an opportunity, you must try to enlarge it. If there are no opportunities, you must focus your thoughts on creating an opportunity. The image Lee uses is of some hard object pushing, probing, and boring away relentlessly.

3. Self-Praise

You must constantly seek to bring your qualifications and importance to the attention of those who are in a position to help you.

4. Flattery

You must ingratiate yourself with those who can help you. Flatter them to their faces. Praise them to others who will carry your words back to them.

5. Threats

You must be very subtle with your threats, because you may unknowingly threaten people with a great ability to do you harm. The threats should develop naturally out of your self-praise.

Let your listener draw the conclusion that if you are so talented, it would be unfortunate if you were to end up in a rival ministry or even be appointed to a position of authority over him. If you are so well connected to important people, you might have the ability to make trouble for him if you are not accommodated.

6. Bribery

There are two kinds of bribery. The first involves small gifts, meals, drinks. Often these small gifts create a sense of obligation far exceeding their cost. They should be given not only to the man who has the power to appoint you, but also to his relatives and friends.

Large bribes are used to seal the appointment. They should also be given to those who have great influence with the official who has the power to appoint you.

SIX WAYS TO KEEP AN OFFICIAL POSITION

If your objective is to be a government official, then you need to act virtuously (according to the standards of your time). You should smear yourself with a layer of false benevolence and pretend to be a religious, moral man. You should walk around with a pious book under your arm that exhibits your lily-white inner state—a book such as *The Thin White Theory*.

Lee also discusses the six ways to keep your position and profit from it.

1. Emptiness

You should say and do nothing. Talk about everything, but say nothing. Make an appearance of being very active, but do nothing. You should never take a definite position, because it might turn out to be wrong or might offend some powerful person. Never do anything for which you could be held accountable. Hold yourself apart from action, but in a posi-

tion where you can claim credit for anything that might go
well and disown responsibility for anything that might go
wrong.

2. Be Obsequious

You must bow and scrape before your superiors. The word
that Lee uses means to be loose-jointed, a reference to all the
bending, bowing, and nodding you must do. You must seek
every opportunity to ingratiate yourself, not only with your
superiors but with their relatives and friends. Lee notes
especially that if your boss has a mistress, or "second wife,"
you must take great care that she likes you because she will
have the greatest influence over your boss.

3. Be Imperious

You must cultivate a haughty and disdainful attitude
toward your inferiors. You must seem unapproachable. This
attitude is also manifested in two ways. The first is the outer
appearance. You must carry yourself with self-importance,
discouraging anyone from offending you. The second is to
show off your learning in your speech and writing.

4. Be Ruthless

You must be ruthless in pursuing your objectives. But in
order to make others more vulnerable to your will, you must
maintain a virtuous image. The words of Confucius must
always be on your lips. You must join organizations that have
virtuous purposes so that people will not believe you capable
of ruthless actions.

5. Be Deaf and Blind

You must not hear criticism. You must not see the disapproving looks of others. Reproaches should pass by you like "the spring wind blowing across a mule's ear." The mule does not care about the spring wind. He is a stubborn, self-centered creature who is concerned only with his own interests.

6. Harvest

The dragon undertakes a journey of a thousand miles only to make his nest right here.

— CHINESE PROVERB

Now you have come to the last step. Everything that has gone before has been just to help you attain a worthy position. The purpose of getting your post in the first place was to put you into a situation where others would pay for your favors, just as you previously paid for the favors of others. You did not expend all this effort simply to acquire a job; you did it to enable yourself to sell your influence.

In discussing Emptiness, the first step toward keeping your post, Lee briefly touched on the importance of avoiding accountability for your actions and making your actions seem much more important than they really are. Lee later elaborated on this and illustrated his point with two stories. The first concerned avoiding responsibility for your actions; the second was about making your actions seem more impressive than they actually are.

TWO METHODS OF
TAKING CARE OF BUSINESS

Sawing Off the Arrow

Chinese medicine is divided into two domains: Outer
Practice and Inner Practice. They roughly correspond to the
divisions between surgery and internal medicine in the West.

A man who had been hit by an arrow was brought to a
doctor of Outer Practice. The doctor sawed off the arrow's
shaft but did not remove the arrowhead. Nevertheless, he told
the patient that he was done. The startled patient asked the
doctor, "Why don't you remove the arrowhead inside my
body?" The doctor replied, "Because that is a job for a doctor of Inner Practice."

Many people defer accountability by sawing off the arrow.
They do as little as possible and always try to leave someone
else to finish the job. They do not care if something goes
wrong so long as the blame can be laid on whoever gave the
final approval or finished the job.

Patching Up the Wok

When a housewife discovered that her wok had developed
a crack, she summoned a repairman. The repairman asked the
woman to go build a fire so that he could burn off the soot
and examine the wok more closely. After she had left the
room, the repairman took his hammer and tapped the wok
lightly until the crack had enlarged almost to the point where
it could not be repaired. When the soot had been burned off,
the woman said, "The crack is much worse than I thought."
The repairman agreed, "It will be a difficult job. You're lucky
that I am such an excellent craftsman."

"You are right," she said. "It probably would be impossible to repair if it got any worse."

Oftentimes it is necessary to make the situation a little worse than it actually is in order to ensure the proper level of appreciation for your efforts. But you must be very careful not to make the problem so bad that you cannot remedy it.

Hitting the wok is an art. If it is hit too softly, the crack will not increase. It is hit too hard, the crack will become too large for repair. It the wok is made of clay, the whole thing might break into pieces.

TWO TYPES OF FOREIGN POLICY: THE THUG AND THE PROSTITUTE

Lee discussed the two guises under which nations conduct their foreign policy: the thug and the prostitute. The prostitute has a thick face. The thug has a black heart.

In the Orient, when a man is with a prostitute, she flatters him. She tells him how handsome he is and what a great lover he is. She swears before the moon and the stars that her love for him will endure to eternity. Of course, she does not mean any of it.

Lee said that Japanese foreign policy prior to World War II was based on the principles of Thick Face, Black Heart. Japanese diplomats took on the role of the prostitute in their negotiations with other countries. They flattered the leaders. They extolled the friendship that existed between them. They rhapsodized about how powerful a force the two nations could be as allies. They did not necessarily mean what they said, any more than the prostitute does. Whenever it became expedient for them to do so, they would break their treaties and make the same promises to another country.

The thug is a brute without a conscience who will use

whatever weapons are available to him in order to beat his victims into submission. The Japanese Imperial Army behaved as a common thug, beating and robbing its neighbors after their suspicions were disarmed by the sweet lies of the prostitute.

Lee Zhong Wu died in 1943, with the Japanese army still in control of much of his homeland. Lee's theory of foreign policy still rings true today.

A more recent example is George Bush's visit to Japan in January 1992. In the eyes of the Japanese, George Bush and his team were behaving like thugs in demanding that Japan open its market. In reality, the Japanese were practicing prostitute foreign policy with the Americans as a counterstrategy. Meanwhile, the Japanese government keeps on restating the bond of friendship between the United States and Japan, even stating that Japan is indebted to the United States because of its generous aid after World War II. However, the words *friendship* and *compassion* expressed by the Japanese bear a strong resemblance to the prostitute's oath of eternal love to her paying clients.

In a less dramatic, subtler manner, all nations utilize a combination of strategies—both as prostitute and thug—during their sophisticated international negotiations.

WIFE FEARING

A husband's fear of his wife is as natural as the heavens and the earth. It is the Universal Truth.

—*LEE ZHONG WU*

In Korea, Japan, and many other Asian countries, it is the woman's fate to be subservient to her husband. Among the Chinese peasants, it is also true that a woman is treated as an inferior being. But among the educated classes in China, it has always been understood that men of real worth respect and fear their wives. It is also true that the higher you go in the social order, the more prevalent this attitude is.

Lee maintains that this no accident. He says that a man rises in the world exactly to the same degree that he fears his wife. The peasant treats his wife like a dog or a horse. As a consequence, he is little more than a beast himself. A man who fears his wife will conduct his life properly in order to please her. By conducting his life properly, he will rise in the world. To such a man, his wife becomes a source of strength and a refuge from the misfortunes of the world.

Lee attaches an almost mystical significance to wife fearing. A man's wife is the person to whom he entrusts his whole life. Out of love for her and fear of her, he goes out into the world to make a name for himself. Lee maintains that fear of one's wife is the greatest virtue. He believed that if everyone were afraid of his wife, a truly beneficent social order would once more come about and the virtue of the Chinese nation would be restored.

AUTHOR'S NOTE

Lee was a man with unique insight into human nature. He possessed the ability to totally disregard others' criticism, and therefore he was able to proclaim Thick Black Theory a religion and himself as the pope of this religion.

As the founder of a new religion, he claimed that he was equal to the Catholic Pope in Rome. This assertion alone brought strong opposition, especially in religious circles, from many Chinese at the turn of the twentieth century. I am not quite sure how serious Lee was about his Popeship. However, he was deadly serious about his Thick Black Theory. Against all odds, he dedicated his life to promoting this theory. I salute Lee for his courage and willingness to march to the beat of a different drum in a time and a place when nothing was valued higher than conformity.

Bibliography

Gandhi, M. K. *Mohan Mala*. Compiled by R.K. Prabhu. Ahmedabad, India: Navajan Publishing, 1949

Holmes, E. *The Life of Mozart*. London: Chapman and Hall, 1845

Jnaneshvar. *Bhagavadgita,* vol. 2. Translated by V.G. Pradhan. Edited by H.M. Lambert. Bombay, India: Blackie & Son Publishers, 1969

Muktananda, P. *I Am That*. South Fallsburg, N.Y.: SYDA Foundation, 1980

Muktananda, P. *Reflections of the Self*. South Fallsburg, N.Y.: SYDA Foundation, 1980

Pickens, T.B. *Boone*. Boston: Houghton Mifflin, 1987.

Radhakrishnan, S. *The Bhagavadgita*. Translated by S. Radhakrishnan India, Blackie & Son Publishers, 1948

Singh, J. *Vijnanabhairava*. Delhi, India: Motilal Banarsidass Publishing, 1979

Tagore, R. *Fireflies*. New York: Collier Books, 1928

THICK FACE, BLACK HEART

Chin-Ning Chu gives workshops and lectures throughout the country in the areas of personal development, peak performance strategy, Asian negotiation tactics, leadership, cross-cultural training, and spirituality. For information, or to receive a complimentary copy of Chin-Ning Chu's newsletter, *The RIM Master Network*, please send your name, title, organization, address, phone, and fax number to:

> *Chin-Ning Chu*
> P.O. Box 2986
> Antioch, CA 94531
> (510) 777-1888
> Fax: (510) 777-1238
> e-mail: cap@crl.com

Warner Books is not responsible for the delivery or content of the information or materials provided by the author. The reader should address any questions to the author at the above address.